UNDERSTANDING LIBERAL DEMOCRACY

Second Edition

BARRY HOLDEN

HARVESTER WHEATSHEAF

New York   London   Toronto   Sydney   Tokyo   Singapore

First published 1993 by
Harvester Wheatsheaf
Campus 400, Maylands Avenue
Hemel Hempstead
Hertfordshire, HP2 7EZ

A division of
Simon & Schuster International Group

Typeset in 10/12 Ehrhardt
by Keyboard Services, Luton

Printed and bound in Great Britain by
Biddles Ltd, Guildford and King's Lynn

British Library Cataloguing in Publication Data

A catalogue record for this book is available
from the British Library

ISBN 0 7450 1385 6 (pbk)

1 2 3 4 5   97 96 95 94 93

To Barbara;
and to the
Memory of my Father

Contents

Preface to the second edition

Since the publication of *Understanding Liberal Democracy* in 1988 there have been hugely important changes in the world – changes which have dramatically affected liberal democracy. The original book was written in a different era, and a new text is now required.

1988 was still the era of the Cold War. But now, since the 'democratic revolution' of 1989, Western liberal democracy has 'beaten' its adversary, Leninist communism. As a noted student of Marxism-Leninism puts it, liberal democracy 'has now become the preponderant idea of the modern world and has done so by vanquishing its only substantial opponent. Communism is dead! Long live democracy!' (Harding, 1992). This is, indeed, a victory of global significance. But changes of political system have not been confined to former communist regimes. The 'triumph' of liberal democracy has been such that it has also spread widely in the Third World, another area where it was notable by its relative absence in 1988. This is not to say that all non-democratic regimes in the world are about to change: clearly this is not so. But it does support the view that the liberal democratic *idea* is now unchallenged. Whether or not this view amounts to a naive 'triumphalism' is something that is discussed in Chapter 4; but whatever judgement is made about this, it is at least clear that there has been a dramatic change in the status of liberal democracy.

Besides – and partly because of – this change, academic interest in the subject has increased. Over the last few years there has been a proliferation of books about, and relevant to, liberalism and democracy. An additional reason, then, for a new text is the need to take notice of this new literature.

This new edition has been largely rewritten and incorporates a good deal of new material. There has also been some rearrangement of sections which affect Chapters 2 and 4 (and the latter now contains the conclusions).

Acknowledgements

I should like give thanks again to Dr Christine Howell for updating the index. I should also like to thank my son, Robert, for the inclusion of the photographs and for his work in searching them out; and Mrs Ann Cade for her invaluable help on the word processor. Finally, once again my thanks to my wife, Barbara, for putting up with the disruption and lost holidays.

Photographs are reproduced courtesy of the Associated Press Ltd.

Preface to the first edition

Liberal democracy and its associated ideas are central to thought about politics, at least in the West. Up to a point these ideas are reasonably clear and we operate with them readily enough. However, difficulties lurk only just beneath the surface and they frequently cause trouble for the unwary. This may happen under the pressure of criticism, but even without it trouble is bound to be encountered at some point. It is hoped this book will be of help in such cases. It is written with the conviction that liberal democracy is insufficiently understood and its importance not widely enough realised. Indeed, the two are related; a prime reason for the failure to appreciate properly the importance of liberal democracy is a lack of understanding of its nature.

Insufficient understanding can be harmful in several ways. It can lead to lack of concern with liberal democracy because it is taken for granted by those who benefit from it. Conversely, attempts to understand it might breed confusion and withdrawal of interest. Inadequate understanding of liberal democracy can also foster or allow attacks upon it by those who mistake its nature.

One of the most potent sources of confusion is the matter of definition. What *does* 'liberal democracy' mean? This is the subject of the first chapter, where it is argued, among other things, that although there are some complexities, finding an answer to this question is not nearly as difficult as is often supposed.

More substantial as a source of confusion has been the existence of different interpretations, ideas and principles connected with the general notion of liberal democracy. There are differing traditional theories, and there are modern theories. There are theories which may or may not be counted as being about liberal democracy; and there are allegedly democratic theories which clearly challenge it. We hope to bring some order and clarity to these matters in Chapter 2.

In Chapter 3 we turn to the 'radical critique' of liberal democracy. It is important to grasp what this is about not least because understanding it further enhances our understanding of liberal democracy itself. Basic conceptions of liberal democratic theory are sometimes attacked in this sort of critique. But an important theme – even, to a considerable extent, in Marxist criticism – is one that involves acceptance of some of these ideas. What is then attacked is the failure of systems that claim to be liberal democracies to embody them. We shall be concerned to appraise this sort of attack critically, in both Chapters 3 and 4.

In Chapter 4 we focus on the justification of liberal democracy. Is it a good – indeed, the best – system of government; and, if so, why? We look at the main sorts of argument advanced on its behalf and ask whether they are applicable generally, or only to the 'developed' world.

In the Conclusions we shall again highlight the importance of our subject. And it is, indeed, hoped that this book contributes to the understanding necessary for a proper appreciation of the importance of liberal democracy and a commitment to it.

I should like to thank those without whom this book would not have been possible. Mrs Pam Tyler first put some draft chapters on the word processor for me. Mrs Margaret Bensley coped incredibly with processing the whole book – typing, re-typing and checking – under very great pressure; I am profoundly grateful. I am also extremely grateful to Dr Christine Howell for preparing the indexes. Finally, I should like to thank my wife, Barbara, who had to put up with the disruption of our normal life whilst this book was being written.

On another note I should like to honour the memory of my sister, Mrs Jean Merriton, who was notable in the practice of liberal democracy and to whom I owe a great deal.

I

☐

What is liberal democracy?

This chapter discusses the general nature of liberal democracy. We begin with the question of definition, first of 'democracy' and then of 'liberal democracy'. This paves the way for an analysis of the relationships among the three central ideas of democracy, liberty and equality. There follows an appendix on 'majority rule'. This is a subject involving matters of some complexity, taking us beyond the scope of this book; but it is of considerable importance, and the appendix highlights the main issues and gives guidance on further reading.

1.1
Defining 'democracy'

It is usually helpful to begin an analysis by defining that which is to be analysed. However, in the case of democracy (and, indeed, of liberal democracy), definition presents key difficulties, and these we shall consider first. A definition will then be offered, which will be followed by a discussion of some problems arising out of it.

The definition of 'democracy' is frequently held to be controversial. We shall argue in a moment that the problems are not as great as is supposed; but some undoubtedly do exist. To begin with, it is difficult to define any word used, often casually, in widely varying circumstances. This is particularly true of words, such as 'democracy', that are applied to political systems – entities that are themselves complex and about which thinking is often vague and confused.

There are also problems specific to 'democracy'. Let us begin with one that can be disposed of quickly. It arises from a historical change of meaning. At least until the end of the eighteenth century the use of the term 'democracy' was restricted to forms that would now be called 'direct democracy'. Today, however, both direct and indirect representative forms are clearly included in the meaning (direct and indirect democracy are considered in the next chapter).

Another difficulty arises from the fact that democracy is now approved of almost universally. This was not so prior to the end of the First World War, but today few people would admit to thinking that democracy is a bad thing. There is thus a tendency to call a system 'democratic' simply because we approve of it. When we do this, however, we convey information only about our views, not about the system itself. When this happens, it has been said that 'democracy' becomes merely a 'hurrah! word' (meaning 'hurrah! for this political system'), emptied of all descriptive meaning. Now, it can be maintained that this happens less than is often supposed, and that when it does, the word 'democracy' is being misused – it will be argued below that 'democracy' does have a correct use and an identifiable meaning. In this way, such difficulties are not with the meaning of the word itself but with its misuses. Misuse, though, can breed confusion. Moreover, this kind of confusion is associated with another, to which we shall now turn.

It is fairly commonly held that 'democracy' is a term applied so widely that it has become vague to the point of meaninglessness. Nearly every form of organisation in the political (and not only the political) sphere has been called 'a democracy' or 'democratic'. Most notoriously, political systems as different as those of the United Kingdom and the United States on the one hand, and erstwhile communist systems such as the former Soviet Union on the other, were spoken of as democracies.

Now, some of the issues raised here constitute genuine difficulties. Nonetheless the difficulties do not have the character or seriousness that is often supposed, and there is a good deal of misunderstanding of them. The fundamental point is that the disagreement involved in – and the difference in meaning implied by – the 'indiscriminate use' of the word 'democracy' is far less than at first appears. One reason for this is that disagreement about the *application* of the word reflects differing assessments of the things to which it is applied rather than disagreement about its *meaning*: for instance, during the Cold War it was applied to both the USA and the USSR, but this was done by people who were making differing judgements about the nature of their respective political systems. To put the point another way, an American critic of the Soviet system and a Russian could both agree that 'democracy' meant, say, 'government by the people', but disagree about whether government by the people actually existed in the Soviet Union. In fact, Western liberal democrats would vehemently disagree with anyone who called the USSR a democracy precisely because they knew what such a person meant. They knew he was asserting that in the USSR there was government by the people – and they maintained that this assertion was false. If the word 'democracy' were meaningless they would not have known what the assertion was and therefore could not have held that it was false.

Such differing assessments of the nature of the political systems was partly a matter of disputes about the facts, but it was also a matter of differing interpretations of the facts. And this brings us to a second reason why the meaning of 'democracy' does not vary in the way its varied use suggests. What look like differences in meaning often turn out to consist in differing ideas concerning how rule by the people – the *agreed* meaning – can be achieved. Such ideas involve varying accounts of the necessary conditions for the existence of rule by the people (see below), though these can be interlinked with differing notions of the nature of 'rule' and of 'the people'. In other words, there can be different ideas about how a political system can embody rule by the people. One such idea was that of 'people's democracy' (see Chapter 3 below), according to which rule by the people existed in the former Soviet Union when it was a communist system. (As we shall see in Chapter 4, there has recently been something of a victory for liberal democratic ideas, and this has involved the discrediting of the idea of 'people's democracy'. Nonetheless, while competing ideas of how rule by the people occurs may not be so widespread as before, they do still exist in such places as Libya, Cuba, China and Vietnam.)

We can conveniently refer to the agreed meaning – rule by the people – as the *concept* of democracy, and the differing ideas about how such rule is to be achieved we can call *conceptions*. Graham (1986) makes a similar point when he says that 'in the terminology adopted by some theorists, we might say there is one overarching *concept* of democracy but several different and rival *conceptions* of it' (he refers to Rawls, 1972 and Dworkin, 1978a). This distinction between a settled conception and rival conceptions is an illuminating one. And it throws light on another claim that is often made – that democracy is an 'essentially contested concept' (Gallie, 1955; Connolly, 1983). The key notion here is that of a shared concept about which there is both a measure of agreement and disagreement, with the disagreement perhaps involving ideological dispute of a kind that cannot be settled. Such concepts, then – and democracy is said to be a prime example – 'essentially involve endless disputes about their proper uses on the part of their users' (Gallie, 1955). However, it would seem more accurate to say that there is in fact agreement on the concept but seemingly endless disputes about the merits of rival conceptions. Moreover, regarded in this way such disputes may not necessarily be endless: it may not be in principle impossible to settle them. It is possible, for example, rationally to assess competing accounts of necessary conditions. This is, indeed, a welcome modification of the idea of *essential* contestability, for the assertion that:

> political concepts (like democracy or freedom) are essentially contestable [implies that] we have no way of resolving the respective merits of competing arguments. . . . Yet this argument is curiously defeatist and relativistic in implication. For what is the point of declaring political concepts 'contestable' if we have no way of identifying winners and losers in the 'contest'? (Hoffman, 1988)

Sources of confusion

The meaning of 'democracy', then, is much less vague than is often supposed. As was suggested just now, the failure to realise this is usually due to a failure to recognise the distinction between 'defining characterisitcs' and 'necessary conditions'. In a noteworthy article on the definition of 'democracy' May (1978) makes essentially the same point when he says that his definition 'exemplifies an effort to distinguish the nature of democracy from the nature of democracy's prerequisites' (a difficulty with May's actual definition is commented on below). A defining characteristic of an object, we can say, is one by virtue of which a word is correctly applied to that object; a necessary condition, or prerequisite, on the other hand, is something that must be present in order for the object to exist or to continue to exist.

For example, the presence of wings is a defining characteristic of butterflies – the meaning of the word 'butterfly' is such that it could not be correctly applied to a creature without wings. The presence of a certain degree of warmth, however, is a necessary condition for the existence of butterflies. The difference here is clear; and disagreement about necessary conditions (alleged observations of butterflies in polar regions or the possible evolution of a new cold-climate species might be cited) implies no disagreement about the definition of the term 'butterfly'.

In the case of 'democracy', however, confusion can become rife. Once the true nature of disputes which are about the necessary conditions of democracy become clear no disagreement about definition need remain; the trouble is that contrasting views about necessary conditions may *seem* to amount to contrasting definitions. This is the case with the different conceptions of democracy already referred to, crucial elements of which are in fact differing accounts of necessary conditions. Similarly, the identification of democracy with particular organisational forms – forms of election and legislative and executive institutions, for example – can be disputed without disagreeing on definition: such identification really boils down to the specification of those forms as necessary conditions of democracy.[1] Another example of this type of confusion concerns some of the disagreements about whether democracy requires a degree of popular participation over and above merely voting in elections. These can appear to be disagreements about defining characteristics, when in fact there is agreement about what, in a general sense, democracy *is* and the disagreement is about the possibility of its existence – or continued existence – in the absence of such participation.[2]

This is a fruitful point at which to say something about procedural definitions of 'democracy', for here, too, necessary conditions are mistaken for defining characteristics. In such definitions the concern is with the existence of procedures for the making of basic political decisions rather than, directly, with the decisions themselves and the allegedly woolly notion of their being made by the people (we shall actually define 'democracy' in terms of decision making by the people in a moment).

A key contention is that the mark of a democracy is the observable existence of certain procedures for authorising decision makers, rather than the alleged existence of some hazy 'decision', or 'will', of the people which is said to emerge from the use of those procedures. Bobbio, for example, sees democracy as 'characterised by a set of rules (primary or basic) which establish *who* is authorised to take collective decisions and which *procedures* are to be applied' (italics in the original); or, more graphically: 'What is democracy other than a set of rules (the so-called rules of the game) for the solution of conflicts without bloodshed?' (Bobbio, 1987). Schumpeter's well-known definition, quoted in the next chapter (p. 108 below), is another example. However, the use of such definitions must involve the absurdity of implying that certain political systems, widely recognised as democracies, could not in fact be such: ancient Athens, for example, the archetypal democracy (see below), could not be a democracy for here the decisions were not made by a small group authorised by certain procedures but directly by the people themselves.

Now, it might well be held that – in modern conditions at least – certain procedures are necessary for there to be decisions by the people; but this is precisely to say that such procedures are necessary conditions for, rather than the defining characteristics of, democracy. It may also be that such procedures are desirable in themselves, as is suggested by Bobbio's reference to rules for the solution of conflicts without bloodshed. And, clearly, they do not have to be defining (or, come to that, any kind of) features of democracy for this to be so: there is a distinction between desirable characteristics and defining features of democracy, just as there is a distinction between necessary conditions and defining features.

Many so-called disputes about the definition of 'democracy' turn out, then, to be disputes about something else. There is in fact almost universal agreement about the definition – and hence the meaning – of the term, although there is a great deal of disagreement about many other things to do with democracy.

Finally, one last potent source of confusion should be highlighted. This is what can be called the 'definitional fallacy'. In essence it is the fallacy of believing that the meaning of 'democracy' is to be found simply by examining the systems usually called democracies. A common example of this is the idea that if you want to know what democracy is, you simply have a look at the political systems of Britain and America. There are some deep-rooted misconceptions involved here (Holden, 1974). Apart from anything else, though, such an idea involves the absurdity of being unable to ask whether Britain and America *are* democracies: if 'democracy' actually means, say, like the British political system, we cannot ask if Britain is a democracy. (It is one thing to answer a firm 'yes' to such a question, but it is quite another to imply that such a question does not even make sense.) Unfortunately, this definitional fallacy occurs fairly widely, and breeds further confusion about the meaning of 'democracy'. Besides being an example of sloppy thinking it misleads people into thinking that the definition of 'democracy' requires little reflection, at the same time as providing the wrong answer to the question.

One way of avoiding the definitional fallacy is to view the definition of 'democracy' as the specification of an ideal system. The relationship between this ideal and actual political systems can then be assessed. Such an assessment might be a matter of 'neutral' or disinterested

Dahl

analysis. Or it might amount to a moral judgement on the extent to which an ideal has been achieved: 'the achievement of democracy, conceived as a narrowing of the gap between "the democratic ideal" and its practical realization' as Hanson (1985) – disparagingly – puts it. Dahl coined the term 'polyarchy' to mean a political system which was democratic to a relatively high degree. No systems could be expected to meet the ideal perfectly, so only polyarchies – and not democracies – exist in the real world (Dahl, 1956). Arguably, though, it is only some *conceptions* that view democracy simply as an ideal. According to the *general concept*, as defined below, there is no special reason to believe that democracy cannot exist: whether, or where, it can or does exist is a matter for separate analysis. And, as a matter of fact, the meaning of Dahl's 'polyarchy' has subtly changed over time, so that in his later writings there ceases to be this kind of contrast between the ideal – democracy – and what actually exists – polyarchy. The meanings of the two terms have become intertwined at the level of the real world (see, for example, Dahl, 1989, pp. 221–2). Indeed, it has been said that in Dahl's account of polyarchy 'a simple operationally practical model of democracy, now accepted by many academics, exists' (Bealey, 1990).

There are, then, various difficulties in the way of defining 'democracy'. Nonetheless, once the nature of these difficulties is properly appreciated they can be avoided and definition becomes relatively straightforward. Despite appearances to the contrary, 'democracy' does have one settled primary meaning (although there are also secondary meanings, as will be seen below). Evidence for this is provided, for example, by an exhaustive semantic survey (Christophersen, 1966). There is broad agreement about the general area of meaning covered by the term and it can be fairly readily summed up in a definition.

The definition

The word 'democracy' was first used in the fifth century BC by the Greek historian Herodotus; it combined the Greek words *demos*, meaning 'the people', and *kratein*, meaning 'to rule'. Abraham Lincoln's famous definition of 'democracy' was 'government of the people, by the people, for the people'. Phrases such as 'government by the people' and 'rule by the people' occur very commonly as definitions of 'democracy'. The definition can be made more precise – or more illuminating – by elaborating on the relevant notion of government or rule and assuming that a crucial element in such a notion is the idea of making and implementing decisions. One can also 'cover' certain ambiguities and difficulties by 'escape clauses'. In this way the following definition can be proposed: a democracy is a political system in which the whole people, positively or negatively, make, and are entitled to make, the basic determining decisions on important matters of public policy. We shall end this section by commenting on this definition and on some of the issues it raises (for a fuller discussion of some of the issues see Holden (1974)).

The first comment concerns the specification of 'entitlement' ('the people . . . make, *and are entitled to make*, the basic . . . decisions'). It is this entitlement to, as well as the actuality of, decision making by the people that distinguishes a democracy from, say, a weak or ailing dictatorship. A system in which the ruler gives way to the people's wishes, because of the threat of riot, insurrection or whatever, is one in which the people are making the basic determining decisions. But such a system is not a democracy because the people are not *entitled* to make these decisions. The entitlement referred to comes from a constitution, or other system of basic norms, which *authorises* the making of the basic determining decision by the people. It may not always be obvious what the constitution lays down. It might be argued that in Britain the constitution – if such it can be called – does not of itself authorise decision making by the people. Nonetheless such authorisation is given by widely and strongly held beliefs about the proper functioning of the political system, and these are sustained by, and reflected in, key conventions of the constitution – such as the convention that a government resigns if its party is beaten at a general election.

The converse is equally important. Entitlement alone is not enough: in order to qualify as a democracy the people must actually make, as well as being entitled to make, the basic political decisions. It must be recognised that it is possible to ask whether the people *actually* do make the basic decisions in political systems, such as the British and American, in which there is no doubt that they are entitled to do so; and hence whether they really are democracies. Systems with the forms of democracy are not necessarily democracies.

A second comment concerns the notion of 'basic determining decisions on important matters of public policy'. The phrase 'basic determining decisions' is more or less self-explanatory. The reference is to basic decisions which actually determine courses of events and from which subsidiary decisions and actions flow. To take an example from personal life, a decision to go on holiday which results in a holiday – that is, which results in the actual occurrence of the complex of decisions, actions and events that make up a holiday – could be referred to as a basic determining decision.

Basic determining decisions on important matters of public policy are basic political decisions; the significance of the term 'important' will be taken up in a moment. A body which makes such decisions holds supreme political power. Such bodies are often referred to as being sovereign, or as possessing sovereignty. Democracy, indeed, is often characterised as a political system in which the people are sovereign, or in which there is popular sovereignty. There are difficulties with the concept of sovereignty.[3] Not the least of these are the distinctions and overlaps between the ideas of supreme *power* and supreme *authority*[4] which concern the relationship, just discussed, between actually making, and being entitled to make, basic political decisions. Because of these difficulties some have suggested doing away with the concept of sovereignty. But its use is surely too widespread for this to be feasible; certainly the notion of popular sovereignty is very deeply embedded in democratic thought.

The third comment to be made about the proposed definition of 'democracy' relates to the escape clauses used to cover variations of meaning. Thus the phrase 'decisions on *important* matters of public policy' covers a gradation of views about the proper role of popular decision making. At one extreme are conceptions of democracy in which the people make the basic determining decisions on a few salient matters only – essentially on the appointment of governors and the broadest, and only the broadest, of outlines of the policies they are to follow. At the other extreme are conceptions in which – with the aid, perhaps, of devices such as referendums – the people make the basic decisions on all but the most routine of matters. Similarly the phrase 'whether positively or negatively' is used to cover differing notions about the origination of policy. On the one hand there is the 'positive' conception that policy should originate with the people: the notion that the people initiate policy proposals. On the other hand the 'negative' conception sees the people merely responding to policy proposals. Here the idea is that they choose among proposals that are put to them by those who would be their governors: the people then do not initiate policy, they consent to policies that are initiated elsewhere.

The meaning of 'the people'
The final comments to be made about our proposed definition of

'democracy' concerns 'the people'. This is, of course, a crucial concept. But it is also one which incorporates notions that coexist only uneasily and which sometimes are in opposition to one another. This gives rise to differing ideas, loosely, though significantly, related together within the concept of the people. Later we shall look at important contrasts between individualist and corporate conceptions of the people. But there is also another issue which gives rise to differing conceptions, based on divergent interpretations; and these cut across the individualist–corporate distinction. This divergence concerns the proportion of a relevant society that is held to be included within the meaning of 'the people'.

First, though, we must ask what a 'relevant society' is. In one sense the answer is 'the society which is subject to, and delimited by, the state whose democratic nature is being assessed'. And this is the answer usually given. Or, rather, it is the one presumed: 'democratic theorists almost invariably take the territorial unit as given' (Pennock, 1983). But, in fact, this begs troublesome questions concerning the proper boundaries of democratic states. On the one hand there is the issue of what size a democratic state should be; and we shall be concerned with aspects of this later – for example, when we consider direct and indirect democracy and participatory theories (see also Dahl and Tufte (1973)). On the other hand there is the cross-cutting issue of what 'divisions' of humanity should constitute self-governing units. Some might argue that humanity as a whole should be the unit of democratic government: Heater (1990) remarks that 'as Archbishop Temple pointed out, "The abstract logic of democracy may tend towards cosmopolitanism", for "the people" have no theoretical interest in the boundaries of states which dynastic jealousies had caused to be so bloodily defended and extended over the centuries' (see also the reference to ideas about democracy within the global system in note 5 below).

However, the general view of democracy is such that 'the people' clearly refers to a subdivision of humanity. The difficulty, then, is that 'while individuals, and humanity as a whole, are entities that are naturally given, groups of people sharing characteristics that obviously destine them for collective self-government are not' (Whelan, 1983). It is true that nationalism became very important and that for many ' "the sovereign people" came to be identified with the nation' (Heater, 1990). And 'until recently, at least, defenders of liberal democracy have accepted as given a world divided into nation-states, and liberal democratic theory is directed towards the nation-state as being the fundamental unit of politics and government' (Ware, 1992). But, as

Ware's statement suggests, this identification of the nation-state as the fundamental unit is not universally accepted; and, in any case, as Whelan for example shows, it can be very problematic. The matter of the appropriate territorial unit thus remains a troublesome issue. Democratic theorists, though, tend to ignore it, and take the unit as given. And where they 'take the territorial unit as given' democratic theorists discuss 'neither how it ought to be established in the first place nor under what conditions, if any, democratic principles would justify part of a democracy [or, indeed, of a non-democracy] seceding from the whole' (Pennock, 1983). Moreover, this issue is becoming increasingly important. From Northern Ireland to Quebec, from the Basque country to the former Soviet Union and the Balkans, the issue has become especially salient and troublesome – with nationalism causing trouble as much as providing answers. And it may also be that related issues are being generated from the different direction of 'globalisation' and what some see as the undermining of the notion of the sovereign state (Held, 1991b; and see note 5 below).

The problem of the appropriate territorial unit is clearly of very great importance. However, short of accepting the 'cosmopolitan logic of democracy' it is arguably 'insoluble within the framework of democratic theory' (Whelan, 1983). True, the 'all-affected principle' is an answer generated within the framework. Whelan points out that this principle has frequently been supported by recent democratic theorists. And May actually incorporates it into his definition of 'democracy': the relevant population is delimited by use of the notion of correspondence between governmental acts and the wishes of 'the persons who are affected' by them (May, 1978). However, there are crucial difficulties with this idea (see, for example, Spitz (1979) and Kimber (1989)) which in essence exemplify the point that the theory and practice of democracy assume and require 'a people' independently identified – which can, as it were, then be given the necessary precision of legal definition through territorial delimitation by a state.[5] (There is a connection here with the communitarian critique of liberalism – which is referred to later – since it can be argued 'a people' is a *community* in a sense not comprehended within liberal individualism; and this essential idea of community 'must ultimately come from a source different from liberalism itself' (Fukuyama, 1992).)

We remain, then, with the contention that the problem is not one for democratic theory *per se*; and it will not be considered further here (see Whelan (1983) for a useful and perceptive analysis).

Let us now return to the question of the proportion of a 'relevant society' – however that might be determined – that is to be included in 'the people'. It might be assumed that all the current members of the relevant society must be included. But straight away the qualification 'all adult members' would usually be agreed (this illustrates how the questions of determining the relevant society, and the proportion of it to be included, overlap: a highly dubious implication of the 'all-affected principle' is the inclusion of children in 'the people' (May, 1978; Spitz, 1979)). In fact the meaning of 'the people' has varied quite widely in this respect, and has not always included all adult members. In ancient Athens, often regarded as the original and archetypal democracy, only a minority of the society was included: aliens, slaves and women were excluded. Women – constituting a good 50 per cent of any relevant society – were given the vote only relatively recently in modern democracies: in 1920 in America, in 1918 (but only in 1928 with the same age qualification as men) in Britain, and as recently as 1971 in Swiss national elections.

Again, from Aristotle onwards the term 'the people' has had a sense in which it means 'the poor' or 'the poor people' (in Aristotle's case 'those of the poor who are not aliens, slaves or women'!). This meaning is echoed in those Marxist–Leninist notions where democracy is equated with the dictatorship of the proletariat (see Chapter 3 below). It is also reflected in anti-democratic thought, where the people have often been characterised as the mob. By way of contrast, 'the people' sometimes meant the middle classes rather than the poor: in this case the term was used to refer to those who had a stake in, and were thereby properly members of, society – that is, property owners.[6]

What is the upshot of this variation in meaning? Are political systems with widely differing proportions of society having a share in political power all to be counted as democracies, because different meanings are given to 'the people'? According to Schumpeter, for example, it would seem that more or less any kind of political system in which governmental power depends on winning competitive elections could be counted as a democracy (Schumpeter, 1976). Even where there is clearly rule by a minority Schumpeter maintains this is a democracy provided those who hold political power consider themselves to constitute 'the people': even South Africa in the heyday of apartheid could have counted as a democracy! This sort of view is surely unacceptable. And yet it would appear difficult to deny that the meaning of 'the people' is an arbitrary matter if one accepts any exclusions. We have already mentioned that the exclusion of non-adults is very commonly accepted. Is this not as arbitrary as counting out any other category, be it women, the rich, the poor, slaves, those with a certain colour of skin, or whatever? The answer to this, it can be argued, is provided by three considerations.

First, there has been a historical change of meaning. The development of democratic theory was tied in with the growth of the demand for universal suffrage. Whatever used to be the case, in democratic thought today 'the people' almost invariably means virtually the whole adult population (and even the democratic status of ancient Athens itself tends to be queried because of its 'undemocratic' conception of 'the people'). It is worth noting that there has been a parallel change in the meaning of 'citizenship' so that today the implication is that all adult persons should be citizens, whereas formerly this was not the case (see note 25, Chapter 2 below; and see section 3, Chapter 2, generally for a discussion of citizenship and democracy).

Second, there are good reasons for this change – for this enlargement – of meaning. They are reasons which overlap with the arguments for democracy itself. In essence they are the grounds for the view that as large a proportion as possible of the members of a society should take part in the making of basic political decisions. Essentially, democrats hold that all those who are not obviously unfit to do so should take part in political decision making. Now although Schumpeter (1976), for example, argues that such fitness 'is a matter of opinion and degree', the point is that democrats can and do reach some kind of objectively based agreement on this matter. This is reflected in the criteria for those limits to membership of the people that democrats *do* commonly accept: it is generally accepted that there are compelling reasons for not giving the vote to children, the insane and – less certainly – criminals. There are two points to note. The first is that these exclusions reflect very general agreement about what makes some people unfit for political decision making: that they are incapable of the relevant thought processes (criminals are sometimes held to have excluded themselves from the community, but here the agreement is less widespread). Moreover – and this is the crucial point – although there might be some individuals whom all would agree are unfit for political decision making, children and the insane (and possibly criminals) are the only *categories* of individuals about which there is this type of agreement. The second point to note is that a dispute about the precise location of the boundary of a category does not imply dispute about it as a category of individuals to be excluded. Disagreement about how much irrationality constitutes insanity, and what age marks the beginning of adulthood – 18, 21 or whatever – does not call into question agreement about the exclusion of the insane and children from political decision making. No one would give the vote to 3-year-olds.[7] The third consideration behind the view that the democratic conception of 'the people' is non-arbitrary and legitimate is more complex. But let us put the matter as simply as possible. In liberal democratic theory conceptions of 'the people' are to a crucial extent 'individualist'. We shall be discussing this later, but the key point here is the extent to which such conceptions imply that 'the people' is simply a collection of individuals. The question then arises: which individuals? And some are excluded, as we have just seen. However, corporate conceptions of the people also exist. Here the people is a corporate entity equivalent to, having the same boundaries as, the relevant society. As such the people is a body consisting not only of the individual members of a society at a particular moment in time, but also of the past and future members; as well as the institutions, structures and culture within which such individuals find themselves. Just as, say, a regiment consists of more than the individuals who happen to be serving in it at any particular time: its past and future membership and its history, traditions, customs and so on are crucial features of its existence. Indeed, how else could you distinguish it as a regiment or as a particular regiment? Such corporate conceptions of the people are, then, all-encompassing, being equivalent to a whole society so capaciously conceived as even to include an extended time dimension. All individuals happening to find themselves in a society at any particular time are naturally included.

Now, such conceptions occur outside liberal democratic theory – in non-liberal democratic theory (discussed later) and also within non- or anti-democratic theory. But the point is that they can be combined with the idea that supreme authority resides in the people. In contrast to the liberal democratic idea, however, it need not then be held that this supreme authority entitles the people to make policy decisions, but simply that it confers legitimacy on others who do make decisions. Decision-makers may symbolically represent[8] the people as in some medieval conceptions of kingship. And where there is no question of decisions being made by the people, the question of fitness for decision making does not arise; therefore the inclusion of all individuals within the conception of 'the people' is unproblematic. Here, then, is a concept of 'the people' as possessing supreme authority and quite clearly including all individuals within its meaning. True, this concept is not part of democratic or, at any rate, liberal democratic theory. But, the shared idea of supreme authority does influence concepts within democratic theory, thereby tending to legitimise the most inclusive notions of the proportion of individuals that are to be counted as an integral part of 'the people'.

The dominant meaning of 'the people', then, in the definition of 'democracy' includes all, or virtually all, the adult population. But we should recognise that there is also a secondary meaning. The notion of 'the people' meaning 'the poor people' has been referred to already. It has been so persistent, however, that this idea of 'the common people' must be regarded as a meaning (albeit a subsidiary one) in its own right – as in the expression 'a man of the people'.

The subsidiary meaning of 'democracy'

We should note that the term 'democracy' itself also has a subsidiary meaning, as well as the dominant meaning with which we have so far been concerned. We shall see shortly that there are close connections between democracy, in the dominant sense, and equality. But we shall also see that there is a subsidiary meaning of 'democracy' according to which a democracy simply is a society in which there is equality. Whereas in the dominant sense there is, arguably, the *implication* that equality will exist in a democracy, in the subsidiary sense the word 'democracy' actually *means* a system in which equality exists. And this may include social and economic, and not just political, equality.

1.2
Defining 'liberal democracy'

We have now looked at the definition of 'democracy' and it is time to return to our original concern with the definition of '*liberal* democracy'. We shall be looking at the relationships between liberty, democracy and equality shortly, and the contrasts between liberal and non-liberal forms of democracy will be discussed in Chapter 3, so only a brief word is necessary here. We shall focus on two main points.

The first is that defining 'liberal democracy' is complicated by the effects of differing political viewpoints. This is over and above any analogous difficulties affecting the definition of 'democracy' itself. Thus liberal democrats – those who think liberal democracy to be the best kind of political system – tend to the view that a liberal democracy is the only kind of democracy possible. Other types of political system that might claim to be democracies are viewed as bogus, the contention being that they are not democracies at all. For the liberal democrats' critics, on the other hand, it is liberal democracy that is bogus: liberal democratic regimes are dismissed as shams which disguise the existence of undemocratic social and political forms. Aspects of the important issues raised here will be discussed later, but it can already be seen how the existence of these differing viewpoints complicates the relationship between the meanings of 'democracy' and 'liberal democracy'.

This brings us to the second point. The term 'liberal democracy', for reasons we shall discuss shortly, is best understood as referring to democracy of a limited kind. This, however, is frequently obscured: precisely because of the tendency to rule out the possibility of democracy of any other form, liberal democracy tends to be treated as the same thing as democracy. Such confusions are, perhaps, more prevalent in America where 'modern . . . folklore . . . has come to assume that "liberty" (i.e. liberalism) and democracy are identical' (Hoffman (1988), referring to Hofstader (1967)). However, this is a modern development and inspection of 'the American political tradition reveals that . . . there is also . . . "tension as well as harmony"' between liberty and democracy (Hoffman (1988), quoting Crick (1982)).[9] And, indeed, in their more reflective moments, or when issues arise involving individual liberties and the need to limit the power of government, most liberal democrats will acknowledge that there are two concepts involved in the notion of liberal democracy, and that there may be tensions between them. In short, 'the conjunction "liberal democracy" is paradoxical, because the relationship between liberalism and democracy has been a deeply ambiguous one' (Beetham, 1992).

The nub of this point about there being two distinct concepts is that the adjective 'liberal', as applied to systems of government, classically implies a concern with individual freedoms that centres on the need to limit the power and authority of government. Liberals,[10] from this classical viewpoint, are those who think it desirable that the power and authority of the government should be limited, typically by subjecting the government to regulation by such devices as a written constitution and/or a bill of rights. Viewed in this way, a liberal democrat is therefore one who holds democracy to be the best form of government but believes that even a democratic government should be limited. In a democracy the government expresses the will of the people; but even so, says the liberal democrat, the power of the government should be limited. (It is true, as we shall see, that there is also another way of viewing the idea of liberal democracy, where democracy is regarded as necessary for the realisation of liberal ideals. Even here, though, government in liberal democracy is seen as limited in some important sense – but now such limitation is seen as a consequence of, rather than a restriction placed upon, democracy. This paradox, or ambivalence, is discussed in the next section of this chapter.)

'Democracy', then, refers to the *location* of a state's power,[11] that is, in the hands of people, whereas 'liberal' refers to the *limitation* of a state's power. From this viewpoint, a liberal democracy is a political system in which the people make the basic political decisions, but in which there are limitations on what decisions they can make. More precisely, and referring back to our previous definition of 'democracy', this conception would be that a liberal democracy is a political system in which (a) the whole people positively or negatively, make, and are entitled to make, the basic determining decisions on important matters of public policy; but (b) they make, and are only entitled to make, such decisions in a restricted sphere since the legitimate sphere of public authority is limited. This definition captures the classical notion of liberal democracy but it will be subject to some elaboration later when we look more fully at the relationships between liberty and democracy.

The central idea within liberal political thought concerning why public authority should be limited is that it is necessary to ensure individual freedom or liberty. (The reference here is to 'negative liberty', which is the dominant conception in the kind of liberalism we are talking about. We consider liberty – and its negative and positive conceptions – below.) Different theories contribute to and express this central idea. Historically, the two most important have been theories about individual rights and John Stuart Mill's defence of individual liberty (see also Chapter 4 below). Theories of individual rights maintain that individuals have basic rights or entitlements: it is contended that every individual has a fundamental moral right to be able to do as he or she wishes in certain areas of life. The grounds or basis for these rights, following John Locke (1632–1704), were originally seen as being provided by natural law – a universal moral code binding on all men, perhaps ultimately ordained by God (see, for example, D'Entrèves (1967), Sigmund (1971) and Finnis (1980)). Individuals' rights were therefore called 'natural rights'. This idea has recently had something of a revival, but the term 'human rights' now tends to be used because of doubts about the validity of the idea of natural law. There is, though, still the insistence that *all* individuals, whatever their social or cultural differences, have essential basic human qualities in common by virtue of which they have certain basic rights. This normally corresponds with the central liberal idea because, classically, it is held that the state – typically seen as the key constraint on individuals being able to do as they wish – must be limited if such rights are to be secured. It is true that there are those who invoke more 'positive' conceptions and argue that state action, rather than inaction, is necessary to secure rights (Gould (1988) and Plant (1991) take this latter view, but also include useful surveys of some of the considerable recent literature on rights generally). However, 'classical' rights theories involve the traditional liberal notion of an area of individuals' lives that should be protected from public authority. Despite some variations we can say that the area delimited is roughly the same as that outlined by John Stuart Mill (1806–73) who, in his famous essay *On Liberty* (Mill, 1982), proposed – allegedly from a different theoretical stance[12] – a principle whereby the individual should be left free to do as he wishes in those areas where he does no harm to others (on Mill's principle of liberty see, for example, Ten (1980) and Gray (1983)). In modern times John Rawls has based a defence of a similar area of protected individual liberty on a theory of justice (Rawls, 1972); and Thomas Spragens, in his important recent book, has provided 'somewhat different – and [he thinks] more secure – philosophical foundations' for Mill's argument (Spragens, 1990; see also Chapter 4 below).

Within liberal democratic theory and practice there are different accounts of the ways in which the sphere of public policy should be limited, and of the linkage between these and the types of entitlement by the people to public policy decision making. We cannot go into these here but, harking back to our definition, the key points to note are that, classically, in a properly functioning liberal democracy (a) the people do not make decisions in certain areas, and (b) this is because they are not entitled to make such decisions. Another important point is that this restriction of entitlement can be manifested in different forms. Restrictions in the form of a written constitution and of a bill of rights have already been mentioned. These are important in the United States, but such mechanisms reflect basic underlying ideas which can be effective in themselves if they are widely held. This is arguably the case in the United Kingdom. Here there is no written constitution or bill of rights, but there are strong currents of opinion – mobilised by 'Charter 88' – which see restriction as less effective in the United Kingdom precisely because of this. On the other hand, it may be that the American system is effective only because the constitutional mechanisms reflect widely held underlying ideas. These are matters of continuing controversy.

We have now outlined what the notion of liberal democracy amounts to. However, in order to understand its nature and significance more fully we need to look further at some conceptual issues that are generated, as it were, by the idea of liberal democracy. They concern the concepts of democracy, liberty and equality; and they can be quite troublesome.

1.3
Three key concepts

Consideration, or use, of the notion of liberal democracy soon reveals the need to answer tricky and important questions. We have already remarked that the notion has component parts which may not be fully compatible; and it is from a consideration of this that some of the key questions arise. These, and related issues, will be discussed in the next three sections.

Our discussion will be limited to the most important of these questions and issues – those that concern the relationships among the three key concepts of democracy, liberty and equality. By definition, of course, the concepts of democracy and liberty have a key role in the notion of liberal democracy; and we have already said something about their relationships. Less clear is the part played by equality. Nonetheless it, too, is of central importance, not least because of its role in the tensions between the other two concepts. Equality is closely associated with democracy; and tensions discerned between liberty and democracy may be viewed as tensions between liberty and equality. Let us now look at these matters a little more closely.

Democracy and equality

First, how is equality associated with democracy? Determining the meaning of 'equality' raises difficulties in itself, and we shall comment on some of these shortly (on equality see, for example, Tawney (1964); Rees (1971); Rae (1981); Nielsen (1985)). For the moment, however, we can say that equality has to do with 'sameness' and its proper recognition. Persons are equal if they are the same in important respects. Of course, there are key issues concerning the important respects in which people might be the same, but a familiar answer refers to the fact of our common humanity. True, as Graham puts it, this claim 'suffers from a kind of nebulousness'; but, as he also points out, Bernard Williams in an influential article (Williams, 1962) 'translates this relatively vague idea into more accessible and concrete terms' (Graham, 1986). However, questions and controversies remain.

Again, the principle with which the idea of equality is linked gives rise to further, similar, questions. The principle of equality demands that all persons should to be treated equally, that is, they ought to be treated in the same way in relation to those important respects in which they are the same; or, as Rees (1971) puts it, a common conception of the principle of equality is 'that men should all be treated in the same way save where there is sufficient reason for treating them differently'. But of course, what 'sufficient reason' or 'treating in the same way' might involve is inherently controversial. There are other sources, too, for differing interpretations and accounts of equality; indeed, Rae, in one of the most illuminating analyses of the idea, speaks of it yielding 'a vast array of meanings' (Rae, 1981). This is not the place to go into such issues, although, as indicated, some of their aspects will be included in our discussion of democracy and equality.

The principle of equality has played a central role in the democratic credo. That all men are created equal was the first of the 'self-evident' truths of the American Declaration of Independence. There is in fact a 'double strength' to democrats' typical belief in equality. First, most democrats hold that the principle of equality is intrinsically valid. They also hold that the principle is best maintained or promoted in a democracy. A commitment to equality is therefore closely linked with a commitment to democracy; and some argue that 'political equality [is] the real spirit of democracy' (Green, 1985). Indeed, it may be that this spirit is the root of democracy's appeal: 'no theory of democracy that failed to give the egalitarian idea a central place could possibly yield a faithful representation of the extraordinary grip of democracy on the modern political imagination' (Beitz, 1989). (See also Chapter 4 below.)

This link is usually connected with the second element of the bond between the ideas of equality and democracy, which is the notion that the ideas are in some sense logically tied together. This logical tie is found in the assumption or contention that equality is implied by the notion of a decision by the people.[13] This flows from liberal democratic theory's individualist conception of the people, already mentioned and further discussed in Chapter 3 below. To a crucial extent in this conception the people consist of a certain number of individuals. Now, if the people – the whole people (i.e. all the people rather than just some of them) – are to make decisions then all the constituent individuals must be involved. This means that each individual must in some significant sense have an equal say. Anything else would mean, in effect, that decisions were made by a group within – that is, smaller than – the whole people, namely those individuals with a disproportionately large say. The idea of one person one vote, widely accepted as a distinctive feature of democracy, is a direct reflection of this. (There are two important issues associated with this idea of political equality which will not be taken up for the moment. First, there are the questions that arise from the fact that in liberal democracies there are almost always differences in the way people vote. In what sense, for example, does a person voting with the minority – that is, voting against the decision that prevails – have an equal say? Aspects of the key issues here are discussed in the appendix to this chapter. Second, apart from these issues there are questions concerning the degree and genuineness of political equality understood in this way. For example, does the possession merely of equal voting rights imply or guarantee full equality of political power in any meaningful sense? Should we not also pay attention to the formation of the agenda of issues to be voted upon, and the processes and power distributions which affect this? Questions of this sort are taken up particularly in Chapter 3.)

There is, then, a very strong connection between democracy and equality. So strong is this connection that 'democracy' is sometimes actually defined in terms of political equality. However, 'nothing is to be gained by claiming that equality is part of the definition of democracy' (Beitz, 1989): it is surely more accurate, and certainly less confusing, to regard political equality as a feature – a desirable feature – that is associated with democracy but one which does not form part of the very definition. Indeed, the existence of political equality may often be regarded as necessary if a system is to qualify as a democracy; but this is to see equality as a 'logically necessary condition' (Holden, 1974), rather than as a defining feature, of democracy. In other words 'democracy' should be defined as, say, 'government by the people' – or the elaboration of this that has already been suggested – while leaving as a separate issue the question of whether, or to what extent, political equality must exist before it can be said that government by the people exists.

Having said this, however, it must be acknowledged (as we have already seen) that there are some instances where equality really does feature in the very definition of 'democracy'. Such cases, though, involve secondary meanings: there are certain usages of 'democracy' persistent and consistent enough for us to say that they give different, subsidiary, meanings – connected though they are with the dominant meaning. There is a sense, then, in which 'democracy' means a system in which there is political and/or other kinds of equality: Tocqueville, for example, often used it in this way.[14] There are also meanings in which these other kinds of equality are central. These are sometimes indicated by the terms 'economic democracy' and 'social democracy'. Although sometimes hard to pin down, they mean, roughly speaking, systems or states of affairs in which there is economic and/or social equality. Often, however, a distinction is not drawn between these forms of equality and the two meanings tend to merge.

A matter of considerable importance is the existence of a certain kind of view about the relationship between political and these other kinds of equality. It is quite often held that political equality without economic and/or social equality is a façade, and hence that democracy in the sense defined by or associated with political equality is also a façade. It is contended that claims of political equality in the absence of economic and/or social equality are bogus, and that it cannot exist in these circumstances. Views of this kind, and the issues raised by them, will be discussed in Chapter 3, and different kinds of equality are further discussed below in this chapter.

The use of the term 'social democracy' – where it is distinguishable from 'economic democracy' – implies the existence of social equality: roughly speaking a classless society, or something approaching it, in which there are few differences in status and/or social advantages. 'Social democracy' can also be used in conjunction with, or as a synonym for, 'democratic socialism'. Here there can be additional elements in its meaning: besides social equality as the desired state of affairs, the term may also refer to ideas concerning the proper means for bringing this about – that is to say, by democratic means rather than by revolution or by imposition from above.

'Economic democracy' is sometimes used to refer to the economic aspects of social equality, that is, where social equality is held to imply an equality of economic resources. However, it is also frequently used in another sense; a sense in which there are additional connections with the primary meaning of 'democracy'. Used in this way economic equality is taken to imply equality of control over the economy; or at least over those aspects of the economy that most directly affect an individual, such as the conditions of work and the running of the workplace. Such 'equality of control' can be held to imply anything from social mechanisms not affecting the general framework of the state – primarily increased worker participation, or 'industrial democracy' – to anarcho-syndicalism, in which the state is superseded by autonomous units of production under the control of the workers. Indeed, 'economic democracy' may here be viewed as a special case of the primary meaning of 'democracy': in this case the 'basic determining decisions' are those concerning the running of the economy, and 'the people' are the workers (here we see again the secondary meaning of 'the people'). Economic democracy of this kind might operate within the state, which would itself be democratic; or it might supersede the state and its activities, as in anarcho-syndicalism. These and related ideas will recur when the Marxist critique of liberal democracy is discussed in Chapter 3.

Democracy and liberty

Let us now turn to the concept of liberty. The notion of liberal democracy seeks to lock together the two concepts of liberty and democracy. In fact, they do fit together and reinforce each other to a considerable extent. This is brought home by Miller's remark that had the demonstrators in Peking's Tiananmen Square in May 1989 'been asked whether their goal was liberty or democracy, they would no doubt have replied that these two aims were indissolubly linked' (Miller, 1991, Introduction). Nonetheless, we have already seen that liberty and democracy can conflict and it is right to talk of there being a 'troubled relationship between liberalism and democracy' (Hoffman, 1988). We need, then, to look at this relationship in a little more detail. This will also clear the ground for a look at some questions raised by the further, although often overlapping, relationship between liberty and equality.

The matter of definition again raises important issues and controversies. There will be no attempt to cover these here,[15] though some key points will come up in the discussion that follows. To simplify the matter we can say that 'liberty' means freedom in a social context. The term 'individual liberty' then refers to the freedom of individuals with respect to their social, and particularly their political, environment. 'Freedom' we can say means self-determination: the free individual is the one who determines his or her own actions. Differing accounts of freedom arise from differing accounts of the nature of self-determination, the environment of the individual and the ways in which this environment does or does not interfere with individual self-determination.

As just indicated, the liberty we shall focus upon is that of the individual. This ties in with the fact that the notion of liberal democracy involves an 'individualist' conception of the people; and, indeed, in considerations of the issue of the relationship between liberty and democracy the reference is almost always to individual liberty. Were the focus to be on the idea of the 'liberty of the people' as some kind of collective entity there would in fact be no issue: liberty and democracy would simply overlap since the self-determination of the people (the liberty of the people) must consist in its making its own determining decisions (democracy). And this is, from a liberal individualist viewpoint, quite different from the matter of the relationship between the liberty of the individual and democracy (about which there *is* an issue).

We should, though, notice a different viewpoint where there is no separation between the liberty of the individual and of the people; thus according to the 'ancient' conception of liberty 'to be a free person is to be a citizen of a free political community. A free political community, in turn, is one that is self-governing' (Miller, 1991, Introduction). But since it is the modern idea of liberal democracy with which we are primarily concerned the basis for our discussion will be the liberal individualist conception and the assumption that there is, indeed, an issue concerning the relationship between liberty and democracy. It is true that the 'republican', or 'civic republican', tradition has an important role in some thinking about liberal democracy.[16] And this involves a 'republican' conception of liberty which is in some respects similar to the 'ancient' conception (Miller, 1991, Introduction). Nonetheless, this republican conception does also have links with the liberal individualist conceptions (Skinner, 1986); and the latter will remain our prime focus.

It should be noted that initially we make the key assumption that there is a very close connection between individual liberty and limited government. This assumption will come under fire at various points later on, but for many liberal democrats it appears self-evident. We shall go along with this for the moment and assume that the problematic threats to individual liberty come only or mainly from government (that is, from the governments of states), and hence that individual liberty exists, or is most likely to exist, where, and to the extent that, the power of government is limited. Looked at in this way the relationship between individual liberty and democracy is the same as the relationship between limited government and democracy.

Let us turn first to the affinities between liberty and democracy. It is clear that they do intermesh in some – important – ways, some of which we shall now look at. What is not so clear is when, and the extent to which, this is essentially a matter of the necessary, conceptual links between the two ideas.

One of the most important of these links is central to the distinction, discussed in Chapter 3, between liberal and non-liberal ideas of democracy. It concerns fundamental ideas about the way in which the people can make a decision. The central point is that a liberal democrat can make sense of the notion of the people making a decision only where there is freedom to present different viewpoints to the people and where the people are free to make whatever decision they wish. In this way, freedom of speech, organisation and assembly, and so on, are seen as essential if democracy is to exist at all. In other words key individual liberties must necessarily be present in a democracy. For a recent argument to the effect that the democratic process itself provides protection for fundamental rights rights, see Dahl (1989). Whether or not wider individual liberty is safeguarded in a democracy will be discussed below.

Another link between liberty and democracy – though not *conceptually* one of the tightest – arises from a tendency to view 'the people' and 'the government' as separate and potentially hostile bodies. This tendency is particularly marked in Anglo-American, as distinct from 'Continental', democratic theory (see Chapter 2 for the nature of this distinction). It can be best understood by contrasting it with the view, more common in Continental democratic theory, which sees the government as the agent of the people.[17] In this second view the government is simply the agency through which the people act. It is therefore an integral part of the people; rather as, for example, a pianist's hands are an integral part of the pianist. According to the first view, however, the government is a body separate from the people and one which governs – 'governs over' – them. Despite the greater importance of one or the other in any particular form of democratic theory, these different views tend to co-exist – somewhat uneasily – and there is a tendency to shift back and forth between them, often without the realisation that this is being done.

The idea of separateness is illustrated when conceiving the people as being able to act independently of the government, as when a government is overthrown by the people. This is an idea which is important in the political philosophy of John Locke (see Chapter 2), who holds that the power of the people lies in their right to revolt against the government if and when it acts improperly by attacking individuals' fundamental, or natural, rights. This idea of the power of the people is reflected in later, more properly democratic, theory in the key notion of the people being able to remove the government at an election.

Where the government is viewed in this way as a body separate from, and potentially hostile to, the people, there is a close connection between liberty and democracy. If the government is 'above' the people and rules over them, the people themselves have power only insofar as they limit this other power exerted over them. In the last resort the people have more power than the government: they are able to make the basic determining decisions. Here the ideas of limiting the power of government, and of the people making the basic decisions, coalesce; and limited government exists by virtue of popular power. Democratic government is limited government and liberty is necessarily maintained by democracy. It should be realised, though, that this view rests upon two, related, questionable assumptions both of which have already been briefly mentioned.

The first assumption is our initial one, that the only really significant threat to liberty comes from the government. A key idea in classical liberal theory is that although government is necessary – to protect individuals from invading each other's liberty – it is also itself a dangerous threat to individual liberty; it is a necessary evil. It is set up to protect individual liberty; and this it does, so long as it sticks to its proper limited function. But once set up it has tremendous hostile potential; the potential to use – to abuse – its power in ways that invade individual liberty.

The second assumption is that the liberty of the people and of the individual are the same thing. Threats to the liberty of the people are necessarily also threats, and are the only threats, to the liberty of the individual. But this is an assumption incompatible with an individualist conception of the people, and what it overlooks is that the individual can also be oppressed by the people. This point will be taken up in a moment.

What of the other view of the relationship between the government and the people? This notion of the government as the agent of, rather than as governing over, the people involves a different conception of the connections between liberty and democracy. This conception, although more typical of Continental theory, is nonetheless of some importance in Anglo-American ideas about democracy. The 'agency' notion is involved to an important extent in the very ideas of state and government and as such is one that everyone tends to use at some time, although they often slip in and out of using it without always realising it.

When this idea is used in democratic theory a republican conception of liberty is involved and there is a link between liberty and democracy through the connection between self-government and self-determination: the self-determined – the free – individual is the self-governing individual. Here individual liberty is seen to involve participation in, rather than the absence of, government activity. Individuals are free not just when they are unsubjected to the processes of government but also when they participate in, and thereby help to take charge of, those processes. This idea can also link up with other conceptions of the way in which self-government enhances liberty, which we shall consider when we come to look at liberty and equality.

As noted, 'the self-determination view' can be found in Anglo-American democratic theory, although it is more characteristic of participatory (Chapter 3), than orthodox liberal, democratic theory. It also shades off into ideas centring on Continental theory's positive conception of liberty which are largely alien to Anglo-American theory. (Again, though, there is something of a bridge in civic republicanism with its notion of freedom linking the 'self-determination' and orthodox liberal individualist views.) We shall look at this positive conception in a moment, but we should note here the role it has in coming to grips with an issue that tends to baffle Anglo-American theory in this context.

When the 'self-determination view' surfaces in Anglo-American theory a paradox emerges. The view implies that individuals participating in a self-governing people are necessarily free. Yet, in an individualist conception 'the people' are a collection of separate individuals so that particular individuals are separate and distinct from the people. This means that the self-determination of an individual is different from the 'self'-determination of the people; and, indeed, that in a very real sense the individual, rather then being free, is governed by the people. In Anglo-American theory, then, where a link is postulated between liberty and democracy via the notion of self-government, there is an issue (often improperly understood) which is problematic. With the positive conception of liberty, though, the issue can be transcended by ideas which merge the will of the individual with that of the people. The matter of whether it is a strength or a weakness of liberal democratic theory that it resists such 'transcendence' raises questions that will be taken up at various points later on.

Within liberal democratic theory, then, there are significant tensions as well as close connections between liberty and democracy. We have just seen that one of the bases for such tensions lies in the relationship between the individual and the people. And we shall come back to this in a moment.

There is, however, another source of tension. This lies in the liberal conception of the opposition between state power and individual liberty: liberty is seen to consist in the silence of the law and to exist to the extent that governmental power is limited. As we saw just now, the thought is that whilst state power is necessary to protect individuals from one another, it should be limited to this protective function: any extension beyond this amounts to an unwarranted violation of individual liberty. Individual liberty, then, consists in the absence of state power and exists only in those areas of life in which the individual is not subject to the power of government. But – and this is the key point – democracy is a form of state; so the basic tension which the liberal sees between individual liberty and the state becomes incorporated into the very notion of democracy. To put the point another way, the definition of 'democracy', as we remarked earlier, refers to the location of power within the state, namely in the hands of the people, but says nothing about the limitation of the state's power. (Indeed, as we saw, it is necessary to *add* the element of limitation to arrive at a definition of '*liberal* democracy'.)

Now, it may be assumed that the people would wish to limit the power of government; and if so they would necessarily have the power in a democracy to translate that wish into reality. Such an assumption would, indeed, seem to be inherent in the link between liberty and democracy associated with the first conception of government and people, that we discussed just now. Here the government was seen as separate from and potentially hostile to the people. It is in fact very probable that the people will have a wish to limit the power of government; but it is a mistake to assume that they will not also, or at other times, have other and incompatible wishes. For example, much of the modern welfare function of government derives from the wish of the people for governments to do things to help them, to provide social security, combat unemployment, and so on, rather than to refrain from doing things.

Let us not go too fast, though. Might it not be mistaken to assume that the wish for the government to do things implies a decrease in individual liberty or that the people wish for such a decrease? Might not the idea of a government as a separate and potentially hostile body, rather than as an agent, be a mistake? Might it not be, in fact, that the classical liberal view of the antithesis between liberty and state power is flawed? If the government is viewed as the agency through which the people act – and if, in the way already indicated, individual liberty is seen in terms of participation in the governmental process – then positive, interventionist, governmental activity can be seen in a different light. Action by government to do what the people wish can be seen as a component of, not a threat to, liberty.

The individual and the people

There is, indeed, much in this argument. However, we have already seen the complexities that arise here for liberal democratic theory, to do with the relationship between the individual and the people. It is true that action by the government to secure benefits desired by the people may be seen as enlarging rather than as restricting their liberty. This, though, is the liberty of *the people*, and it might still involve interfering with the liberty of particular *individuals* (the owners of 'dangerous dogs' for example) whose wishes conflict with those of the people as a whole (which might be that ownership of such dogs should be prohibited). Allowance of – indeed, sometimes an insistence on – a difference between the liberty of the people and of the individual can be seen as a strength of liberal democratic theory. However, there is so often a failure to recognise this difference and to assume that an issue is simply one concerning the relationship between the individual and the government, when in fact it may be the relationship between the individual and the people that is crucial.[18]

This brings us back to the point that there are two different, but intertwined, threads in the twisting argument about the ways in which liberty can be threatened by democracy. One concerns the threat to the liberty of the individual inherent in the institution of the state. As a form of state, democracy merely incorporates – or fails to modify – what one might call this 'pre-existing' threat. There is, though, often muddle and a failure to recognise this thread because of the frequent failure to discriminate between threats to the individual and threats to the people. The existence of the former is obscured by the non-existence of the latter, which are 'by definition' prevented in a democracy. (We are talking here about the *idea* of a democratic state. This does not preclude the possibility that in practice such a state is not possible because the people cannot in fact control the state. This kind of anti-state perspective on democracy has been forcefully restated by Burnheim (1985).) The second thread, however, focuses explicitly on the difference between the individual and the people. Here the concern is actually with the way the individual may be oppressed by the mass of the people. This reveals that democracy can amount to an especial threat to individual liberty over and above that already constituted by the state.

More accurately, the threat 'already constituted by the state' is made more severe, since it is a case of the state being used by the people: that is, the people act *through* the government.

Let us look just a little more closely at this notion of the individual being subject to oppression by the people (see also the excellent discussion in Dahl (1985)). The key point is that within Anglo-American democratic theory it is not really possible to equate the 'will of the people' with the will of every individual. There are, in fact, critical difficulties here, as we shall see in the discussion of majority rule in the appendix to this chapter. Within the terms of this type of theory, as usually understood, it has to be accepted that it is usual for the wishes, and therefore the wills, of some individuals to clash with those of others. It follows that the 'will of the people' cannot, except in the unlikely case of unanimous agreement, comprehend the will of every individual. Therefore action regarded as implementing the people's will must conflict with the wills, and thereby threaten the freedom, of some individuals. This source of conflict between the individual and the people has given rise to three sorts of view of democracy as a threat, actual or potential, to liberty.

First of all there is the 'majority tyranny' argument. Here the focus is on the threat to the liberties of minorities constituted by what is seen as the existence in democracies of rule by the majority. A central feature of much democratic thought has been the idea that since unanimity does not exist the 'will of the people' is in fact the will of the majority of the people (see the appendix to this chapter). Some have held that this involves actual or potential tyranny by the majority – the minority being ruled despotically by the majority. Madison, Tocqueville and John Stuart Mill feared this; and in recent times Hayek.[19]

Second, there is the idea that the possible tyranny is by the many over single individuals, rather than over some particular minority group or groups of individuals. As John Stuart Mill put it, 'the "self-government" spoken of is not the government of each by himself, but of each by all the rest' (Mill, 1982). Although it involves conceptions that are alien to individualist liberal democratic theory, there is often a slide from this idea into one which sees the individual as being subject to the corporate people or the society or the community. This involves a move from the notion of one or a few particular individual(s) being subject to many other individuals, to the notion of *any* or, indeed, *all* individual(s) being subject to the people or the society or the community. This clearly involves a move to non-individualist ideas and, once again, it is really in Continental rather than Anglo-American democratic theory that the relevant conceptions exist. Nonetheless, there is a strand of theorising about Anglo-American democracy that worries about the individual being subject to direct pressure from the community – that is, pressure from 'the people' in addition to that which is exerted via the government. The contention is that public opinion, social convention and so on, as well as laws and other governmental actions, can restrict an individual's liberty. Both John Stuart Mill and, before him, Tocqueville were concerned about this. Tocqueville also argued that the 'atomising' of society into isolated and vulnerable individuals was characteristic of democracy and that this exposed the individuals to oppression.

The third view of how democracy is a threat to liberty arises from a consideration of the special power of popular government. A government whose function is to implement the will of the people can be extremely powerful. This is a development of the point already made about democracy posing an especial threat to individual liberty by making more severe the threat constituted by the state. The focus is on the fact that a democratic government is more threatening, because it is more powerful, than an autocratic government. An autocratic government has only its *own* power and does not also embody the power of the whole people.[20] Also, although public opinion may shelter dissidents in an autocracy, who is to shelter the dissidents from public opinion itself? An additional, and rather different, argument sometimes creeps in. This relates not so much to democracy as to systems which purport to be democracies, but where government may 'get away' with tyranny because people are lulled into a false sense of security by the thought that their government is democratic:

> Every man allows himself to be put in leading strings, because he sees that it is not a person or a class of persons, but the people at large, that holds the end of his chain. By this system the people shake off their state of dependence just long enough to select their master, and then relapse into it again. (Tocqueville, 1968)

In the face of these various arguments and ideas suggesting a hostility between liberty and democracy one cannot simply be content with the notion that there are some inherent or 'natural' connections between the two conceptions. It would, indeed, seem more satisfactory to maintain that for a democracy to be a liberal democracy there should exist at least some of the traditional liberal limitations upon government. This has in fact already been implicitly recognised in our definition of 'liberal democracy' (p. 17 above). If this is seen as a limitation of democracy – since it is a limitation of the instrument of the people's will – then so be it. This simply shows that liberal democracy is an amalgam of different, to some extent conflicting, ideas. As long as this is realised, the ideas can be allowed to modify each other in harmony rather than fundamental discord. Yet not all theorists or supporters of Western democracy would support this view. Some would emphasise only the 'inherent' connections between liberty and democracy; this would include those who focus on the ideas, to be discussed below, about democracy being necessary for the realisation of liberal ideals. It also includes Dahl who argues, in effect, that it is the democratic process itself that forms the only proper protection for fundamental liberties (Dahl, 1989, Chapter 13). Others, though, highlight illiberal tendencies by a stress on the importance of what they see as the democratic aspects at the expense, if necessary, of the traditional liberal limitations on government.[21]

If illiberal tendencies can be discerned in liberal democracy, how much more illiberal might another a type of democracy be. We shall discuss later Continental theories of democracy and theories of 'one-party democracy'. These can be seen as variants of a type of democracy, inspired by the famous French philosopher Jean-Jacques Rousseau (1712–78), in which a government implementing the single all-powerful will of the people seems to leave no room at all for a limitation on government control of minorities or individuals. The view that this kind of democracy is illiberal and totalitarian is common; and there is a well-known book entitled *The Origins of Totalitarian Democracy* (Talmon, 1952). It must be realised, however, that the Rousseauist notion of democracy is tied in with Rousseau's idea of freedom according to which individuals can be perfectly free in a democracy of this kind. Those who see it as illiberal are viewing it in terms of the liberal's negative – rather than Rousseau's positive – concept of liberty.

Negative and positive liberty

The difference between negative and positive liberty can be considered only briefly here,[22] but in outline it is as follows.

Both concepts have two key components. In the case of the negative concept – 'freedom from' – the first is a view which sees liberty in terms of the absence of constraints. Individual self-determination consists in the individual doing what he wants in the sense that he is not obstructed by other men from doing what he wishes. Secondly, there is an account of 'doing what one wishes' where it is conceived to involve simply acting to fulfil one's desires.

In the positive concept – 'freedom to' – on the other hand, the first component is the actual ability to do what one wants, even where there is no obstruction by others: a man without a car, for instance, cannot go for a drive if he wishes even where others are not obstructing him. The focus is on 'enabling conditions or positive conditions for action as distinct from the constraining conditions, the absence of which defines negative freedom' (Gould, 1988). Freedom, if you like, involves 'empowerment'.[23] The second component is an account which sees individual self-determination as rational autonomy. The individual is self-determined when his or her actions embody reasoned decisions and are more than reactions to the desire of the moment.

The difference between this and the account in the negative concept can be illustrated by an example – albeit one that over-simplifies in order to bring out the contrast. Consider the position of a person who has decided to give up smoking but who finds himself with a cigarette in front of him. The advocate of the positive concept of freedom would say that the self-determined individual is the one who would resist the desire for the cigarette and refrain from smoking it. But, such an advocate would argue, the negative concept implies that self-determination would consist in fulfilling the desire to smoke the cigarette. In terms of the positive concept, however, giving in to desires in this way is not so much freedom as slavery – being a slave to one's desires.

This example can be used to show connections between the components of the concepts. In the negative concept there is a natural connection between the idea of an individual simply fulfilling his desires and of leaving him alone to do so, whereas in the positive concept the notion of an individual resisting desires easily flows into the idea that he might be helped – enabled or empowered – to resist them.

This difference between positive and negative freedom translates itself into a political context. The negative concept implies, as we have seen, absence of governmental restraints: the absence of restraints upon individuals carrying out their various desires. A classical liberal, it might be said, is one who values individual freedom in this sense. A crucial part of the positive concept, however, is the idea that individuals should be enabled or empowered, if necessary by the state, to achieve what they want. This can involve provision by the state of the necessary material conditions. This idea, too, is characteristic of the thought of some important thinkers called 'liberal', even in the Anglo-American tradition; though they would often be called 'social' – as distinct from 'classical' – liberals.[24] But the positive concept can also involve – and this is what particularly upsets the liberal – the idea of the state 'assisting' the individual to overcome selfish desires. The individuals' pursuit of their desires might give way to the rational guidance of the state.

The state is the organisation for the promotion of the common good. The promotion of the common good is the rational objective of all individuals, and therefore the state is seen as the manifestation of all individuals' rational will. Hence the guidance of an individual by the state is, according to this view, not a limitation of freedom but a vital part of it. Rousseau's conception of the general will, which we shall look at in the next chapter, incorporates these ideas and also contains the notion that the common good is actually, even if not apparently, willed by every individual. It is not merely that the common good is what would be the objective of those who thought about it – rather it is actually willed by everyone.

Seen in its own terms, then, the Rousseauist conception of democracy contains no negation of individual liberty. Indeed the opposite is the case – in such a democracy perfect freedom exists. Individuals are free because they are acting in accordance with their own rational wills. There is, in fact, a good deal in such a conception. This can be illustrated by a down-to-earth example. Although some British motorists carp about interference with the liberty of the individual, most would not regard the drinking and driving law in this light. Many a motorist in a pub will drink less than he would have done had the law not existed, but rather than seeing this as oppression, he will feel that he has acted in accordance with his true intentions. Is this Rousseauist conception of freedom, and its relationship to democracy, acceptable then? Or perhaps it is even superior, in some sense, to the liberal democratic view? This issue will be taken up later when we come to discuss 'people's democracy'. A crucial point to mention here, though, is that a central failing in the use of the conception is its association in practice with tyrannical government. To this extent, at least, the traditional liberal democratic view of Rousseauist democracy does, after all, have much to commend it. Even so, matters are less straightforward than liberals commonly recognise; and elements of Rousseauist thought, which is in many ways the more profound, do have to be accepted.

Liberty and equality

We have looked at some of the important ways in which democracy is related to equality and to liberty. And the connection of each of the latter with democracy gives them important relationships with each other. But there are not just indirect relationships via the concept of democracy:

equality and liberty are also directly linked. Democracy, equality and liberty form, as it were, the three points or angles of a triangle. And lines of relationship go not only from equality and liberty to connect with each other at the third point, democracy, but one line also forms the final side of the triangle connecting equality directly with liberty. By the same token one could focus on democracy and talk of both direct and indirect links with the other two concepts.

Let us turn, then, to the direct relationship between liberty and equality. We do so in recognition that both are of fundamental importance in liberal democratic thought – an importance that amounts to more than the fact that each is conceptually connected with democracy.

The first thing to notice is that although they have affinities with each other, since both are important in liberal democratic thought, they are in tension as well. As J. Roland Pennock says, ' "Liberty" and "equality" comprise the basic elements of the democratic creed. Yet these twin ideals . . . are not easily reconciled. Between them, at best, a considerable tension exists' (Pennock, 1979). We shall consider some of the tensions first. These include differing social analyses as well as conceptual inconsistencies, and can be conveniently summarised as falling within two contrasting categories of arguments.

On the one hand, there is the idea that equality suffers at the hands of liberty. Here we have arguments to the effect that the existence of extensive 'formal' liberty[25] allows, creates or maintains an unacceptable degree of inequality. The essence of such arguments is that undesirable economic inequalities flourish where the state does not intervene to prevent them: where individuals are free from governmental regulation they are also free to amass wealth at the expense of, and to exploit, other individuals. As we shall see later, it is also usually held that the social structure – until and unless it is changed by state action – gives immense advantages to some individuals in the pursuit of economic interests. Under such conditions of freedom there are great inequalities in the distribution of material resources and, more generally, of the means to a good life. We shall be looking further at arguments of this sort in Chapter 3, but we should notice now some of the important viewpoints with which they are associated. The basic view is that such inequalities are undesirable. Then it is also held that economic inequality involves economic power: those with the most material resources have power over those with the least. This in turn is considered undesirable – not least because it is undemocratic. It is often further argued that economic power goes hand in hand with political power so that the existence of economic inequality means that both economic and political power is concentrated in just a few hands. This is even more clearly undemocratic.

On the other hand, there are the arguments that it is liberty that is endangered by equality. Where social equality exists and/or is pursued as an ideal, individual liberty is threatened. This was argued most notably, perhaps, by Tocqueville, and J. S. Mill was much impressed by it. It has two main elements. First, the pursuit of equality – or rather the governmental action which may be necessary to bring it about – can involve the invasion of individual liberty by the state. Second, social equality destroys the varied social structures which not only create inequalities but also check the state by providing bulwarks against governmental power. Social uniformity also involves 'atomisation', whereby society is reduced to a mass of uniform individuals bereft of the varied relationships provided by complex social structures. Such individuals are vulnerable both to government and to social pressures, including the pressure of mass opinion.

Fears about state power are deepened when attention is paid by libertarians to remedies for inequality, favoured by those who think it is equality that is endangered by liberty. Attention centres on the state intervention – and the threat to individual liberty this involves – needed to correct inequalities: 'egalitarians rely for the achievement of their objects on the coercive power of the State' (Joseph and Sumption, 1979; quoted in Norman, 1982). The importance of the idea of liberty as the protection of the individual from the state is reaffirmed. Extreme forms of the argument maintain the overriding importance of individual liberty and maintain that there should be no state action to 'remedy' inequality. An argument of this type is developed by Robert Nozick in his well-known – not to say notorious – book *Anarchy, State and Utopia* (Nozick, 1974; see also Paul, 1982 and Wolff, 1991). Nozick argues that individual rights are sacrosanct, that the state has only the minimal function of protecting these rights and that action by the state to promote welfare or remove inequalities cannot be justified.

There are other ripostes to the argument that the price of liberty is too high because it involves an undesirable degree of inequality. These tend to focus on two main themes: the extent to which economic inequality is justifiable or desirable; and the question of just what inequalities are at issue in the first place.

A key idea in the first theme is that individuals ought to be allowed the fruits of their labour and if this means that some obtain more material goods than others, then so be it. This is often supported by the argument that economic inequalities are permissible (at least up to a certain point) since it is only other kinds of equality that are crucial. What is really important is equal treatment by, and equal political participation in the control of, the state; in other words equality before the law and equal political participation. This is because the state with its immense power over us – including matters of life and death – plays so important a part in our lives that it is crucial for justice and fairness that this should be an equal part. There is, in fact, usually an amalgamation of arguments in an overall libertarian case against economic egalitarianism. In this case the contention that it is only political equality that is important is combined with the notion that individuals ought to be free to keep the fruits of their labour. Here the condemnation of coercive attempts to 'remedy' economic inequalities is buttressed by the argument that such attempts are, in any case, not required for egalitarian reasons.

The argument that economic inequality is permissible – indeed, perhaps desirable – merges into more general considerations concerning what is to count as inequality in the first place. Instead of saying (what some call) economic inequality is justifiable one might make much the same point by denying that it really is inequality. The argument here is that individuals are not in all ways the same and that equality merely demands that individuals should be treated equally with regard only to those important respects in which they are the same (see p. 20 above). This opens up two large questions. First, in what important respects are individuals the same? Second, with regard to these respects, what does 'treating them equally' amount to?

Now, some perspectives go beyond, and call in question, what can be seen as the narrow 'economic dimension' centring on material goods: the focus can move to fuller dimensions of human well-being, such as the capacity of individuals for self-development which is central to Carol Gould's argument (Gould, 1988). We shall come back to this shortly, but we should note here what such perspectives involve for answers to our questions. First, there is a recognition of – indeed, an emphasis upon – the ways in which individuals differ and a concentration, instead, only on *fundamental* human characteristics as the respects in which they are the same. Secondly, and as a corollary, there is an insistence that treating individuals equally does not mean treating them uniformly. Individuals, because of their (non-fundamental) differences, need to be treated differently to ensure that each can express his fundamental nature to the same extent. Self-development, for example, will involve something different for an athlete and a musician. And, as Gould points out, the same kind of argument is involved in Dworkin's distinction between a right to equal treatment and the right to treatment as an equal (Dworkin, 1978a). The notion that what is important is that individuals should be treated with equal concern and respect (Lukes, 1973) is similar. But let us return, for the moment, to the economic dimension. Considering our two questions we can say that the argument that economic inequality does not offend against the general principle of equality would become one or both of the following. First, that since individuals are not the same in their desire for – or, indeed, their capacity to obtain – material goods, the principle of equality does not require that they be treated equally in the distribution of these goods. This point is well made by Rae (1981) in his distinction between 'person-regarding' and 'lot-regarding' equality. Second, that even if individuals are – or to the extent that they are – the same in their desire for, and capacity to obtain, material goods, treating them equally in the distribution of goods implies something other than 'allocating' the same or the same quantity of goods to each individual. The point is that treating individuals equally does not involve arranging things so that they are all 'given' the same, or the same quantity of,[26] material goods so much as ensuring that they have a place in society from or within which they have an equal opportunity to obtain these goods. There is a more general argument lying behind this concept that brings us back to the underlying libertarian point: the idea of 'opportunity to obtain' ties in with the idea of individuals deciding what they want to obtain; and – referring back to the first contention above – individuals may not all want to obtain, or obtain the same amount of, material goods. Equality of opportunity means all individuals having an equal opportunity to live their own lives in the way they wish.

The rendering of the principle of equality as equality of opportunity is well supported but also controversial. This is not the place to discuss all the issues raised but it is worth noting that these are considerably illuminated by Rae's distinction between two forms of equality of opportunity: (i) 'prospect-regarding', where everyone has the same *prospect* of obtaining 'x', and (ii) 'means-regarding', where everyone has the same *means* to obtain 'x' (Rae, 1981). Rae points out that (ii) does not necessarily involve (i), although the principle of equality of opportunity derives considerable bogus support from the common failure to recognise this.

We shall confine ourselves to two further points regarding equality of opportunity. The first is that much of the controversy turns on differing interpretations of what equal opportunities are, and whether they can actually exist. Do individuals with differing abilities really have equal opportunities where they merely have places in society that are in some sense equal? They may, for instance, have equal means without having equal prospects. At the extreme, for example, mentally and/or physically handicapped people need to be *un*equally treated – positively helped – if they are to have anything approaching equal prospects. Other issues concern the sorts of social arrangement that are necessary for 'equal places in society' to exist – if, indeed, they can exist at all.

A key question involves the extent to which social structures such as class so shape the lives of individuals as to make equality of opportunity extremely difficult if not impossible to achieve. Another concerns the extent to which (if this is not impossible) equalising opportunities may, again, in some cases involve *un*equal treatment for some people. One example of this is 'positive discrimination' where, in its best-known exemplification, whites must be discriminated against (have their 'means' made unequal) in order to give blacks, with all the disadvantages they suffer in a white society, equal prospects. Another example is the provision of equal opportunities for all young people to obtain places at universities. This results in inequalities of prospects thereafter, most notably in respect of career opportunities, between those who get to university and those who do not. This is connected with a general argument to the effect that if equality of opportunity means '"opportunity to compete in a hierarchical system", then it is not a substantially egalitarian principle' (Norman, 1982).

The second point about the issues raised by the notion of equality of opportunity concerns the implications for the relationship between equality and liberty. In fact these implications cut both ways. On the one hand, the pursuit of equality of opportunity can be viewed as threatening to liberty. Here the focus is again on the state action that is, typically, seen as necessary to create equality of opportunity. In the more extreme cases this might involve coercion (of some individuals) in order to create equality of opportunity. An example is the argument that parents who wish to give their children a private education should be prevented from doing so in order that all children should have the equal opportunities provided by their all being educated in the same – the state – education system. On the other hand, attachment to the idea of equality in the form of equality of opportunity has clear libertarian implications. The basic point is the contrast between two ideas. On one side is the idea that society should be arranged – that is, organised by the state – so that all individuals are allocated the same. This, it is commonly held, can lead off into totalitarian directions; and it is compared unfavourably with the other idea, which is that individuals should have the equal opportunity to live their lives as they themselves choose. This brings us back from the tensions between liberty and equality to their affinities. We can point to three main types of argument suggesting that it is the affinities which are important. The first is the sort just indicated, showing the libertarian implications of equality of opportunity. There is, however, no hard and fast line between this and the second type. Here we find it argued that liberty and equality are both important, that both should be promoted and that to a considerable extent they can be harmonised despite the tensions. In one of the best-known examples of this sort of argument John Rawls in *A Theory of Justice* (1972) combines the idea of the fundamental importance of individual 'negative' liberty with a belief in the importance of equality of opportunity, and equality in the distribution of goods,[27] into a theory of justice. This theory in turn underpins a justification of liberal democracy (see Chapter 4).

Rawls does recognise that there can be conflicts between liberty and equality. And here he maintains the primary importance of basic liberties: where there is a conflict between liberty and the remedies for inequalities not justified by his 'difference principle', it is liberty that must take precedence. Nonetheless, he does not maintain that these liberties are such as always to forbid state action to promote welfare and to remedy inequalities. He is in fact subjected to a thoroughgoing criticism by Nozick (1974) for allowing that justice can require the invasion by the state of (what Nozick holds to be) the rights of individuals. Arguably, even in Rawls' theory a tension remains between liberty and equality.

However, we come now to the third type of viewpoint regarding the affinities between liberty and equality, which is that rather than being in tension, let alone hostile, these values are closely interconnected. Let us call this the 'liberal-egalitarian' viewpoint. At another level we find this in Rawls when he restates the idea, important in liberal democratic theory, that all individuals should have equal liberty: 'each person is to have an equal right to the most extensive basic liberty compatible with a similar liberty for others' (Rawls, 1972). Dworkin (1978a) is another modern theorist who sees a close connection between liberty and equality; in fact, he derives liberty rights from the right to treatment as an equal.

There are, however, some difficulties in relating this to the viewpoint according to which tensions are unavoidable because of the existence of economic inequality. True, the salience of economic inequality is diminished by invoking a perspective wider than the 'economic dimension'. But why should this perspective be given primacy? Why should equal liberty be more important than economic equality? We are still left, essentially, with the issue of economic inequality and the tensions this provokes between basic values. It makes little difference, it might be said, that these are now tensions not simply between liberty and equality, but between equal liberty and economic inequality. This point has validity where the classical liberal negative concept of liberty is involved: the argument that 'where individuals are free from governmental regulation they are also free to amass wealth at the expense of, and to exploit, other individuals' (p. 35 above) is not altered by individuals being equally free from governmental regulation. But matters are different from the viewpoint of 'fuller', more positive, conceptions of liberty. Here liberty can itself involve the provision of the material conditions (see p. 33 above) upon which 'economic egalitarians' focus – so that to seek equality is to seek liberty for all.

Now, this characterisation suggests that harmonisations of liberty and equality using positive conceptions of liberty simply focus on the economic perspective, ignoring the wider perspective in which liberty and equality essentially involve other – or more – than material goods. However, this is not the case; rather, the point is that tension between the two perspectives is now removed. It would also be thought by classical liberals that such harmonisations, because they rely on a positive rather than a negative concept of liberty, are bogus. But this, too, is misleading.

In fact, account is taken of both these 'objections'. Liberal-egalitarian conceptions *do* focus on wider perspectives – treatment of individuals with concern and respect (Lukes, 1973), human well-being (Nielsen, 1985), individuals' self-development (Gould, 1988) – which go beyond, though they include, the economic dimension. They also involve conceptions of liberty that incorporate, rather than reject, the negative concept. Thus, although lack of constraints is not seen as a sufficient condition of individual liberty, it *is* seen as a necessary condition (see, especially, Norman (1982, 1987) and Gould (1988)).

Democracy, liberty and equality

We have now looked at the direct connections between the 'three points of the triangle' (see p. 35 above) – the relationships between democracy and equality, democracy and liberty, and liberty and equality. But, as we remarked before, there are also the indirect connections. For example, the view that equality threatens liberty often involves the idea that democracy threatens liberty because democracy is linked with equality. Similarly democracy can be seen as threatening equality because of democracy's involvement with liberty.

Among theorists who focus on tensions of this sort it is those broadly sympathetic to liberal democracy who hold that it is liberty that is threatened. We have already seen how Tocqueville viewed democracy as a threat to liberty; and this was because he saw democracy as involving equality.[28] According to Tocqueville 'though democratic nations did not despise liberty, unfortunately it was not liberty but equality which was their idol. To them liberty was a secondary aim, but equality a primary one' (Bramsted and Melhuish, 1978).

On the other hand the idea that it is equality that suffers – suffers at the hands of liberty and democracy – is typically developed by theorists who are critical of liberal democracy. We have already seen that left-wing critics argue that equality will not be brought about where 'formal liberty' is given priority; but such arguments are usually part and parcel of a critique which sees such liberty as a necessary feature of liberal democracy. Not that these arguments are necessarily wedded to a full-scale critique of liberal democracy, though this is where they might be developed most coherently.

We can in fact draw a broad distinction between Marxist and non-Marxist left-wing critiques (though it should be noted that not so much is heard of the former these days). Marxists argue that equality cannot be achieved in those systems which go under the label of liberal democracy but which are in fact shams. In these systems there is formal liberty and no real democracy (see Chapter 3). Non-Marxist left-wing critics do not agree that liberal democracies are complete shams, but they do agree that liberty is promoted at the expense of equality – though there is some ambivalence about the extent to which this is purely formal liberty. But they also believe in the possibility of reform: to the extent that democracy exists there is a chance for the people to elect a government to put matters right.

There are doubts on this score, however, for two main reasons. First, even the non-Marxist left are much impressed by what they see as the difficulties in the way of a left-wing party being elected to government. Second, if such a party is elected there is a limit to what can be done: this is precisely because in a *liberal* democracy there are limits on what the state can do.

However, not everyone sees tensions. We have already looked at the liberal-egalitarian viewpoint which, instead of hostility or tensions, sees liberty and equality as interdependent or interconnected, or even fused in one basic value. And this viewpoint is of considerable importance. [29] Such a viewpoint entails that democracy, too, is freed from tensions, with all three basic concepts being in harmony. Indeed, they, and perhaps others, are seen as essential to each other. 'Equality, liberty, autonomy, democracy and justice ... come as a packaged deal' (Nielsen, 1985). In the package democracy is required because it secures the other values. In Chapter 4 we shall see that democracy is often justified as the system necessary to realise the values of liberty or equality. And from the liberal-egalitarian viewpoint the argument is that what is seen as the joint basic value can only be realised in a system in which all have an equal say in determining the conditions of their life. And – for reasons discussed later, in our assessment of non-liberal democracy – such a system is usually[30] seen as a *liberal* democracy.

Issues raised by the relationships of liberty, equality and democracy often involve, or are involved in, problems posed by the very notion of a collective decision; and we shall briefly indicate the nature of some of these problems in the appendix that follows.

Appendix: Democracy and majority rule

We have defined democracy in terms of decisions made by the people. It follows that some account is necessary of how such collective decisions can be made.

There is a central difficulty: how can many and different individual decisions be combined into a single collective decision? We shall return in Chapter 3 to the point that decision making can only be done by individuals. A collective decision must then, in some sense, be a combination of individual decisions – even though, as we shall argue, a purely individualist account is not possible.

The difficulty is usually conceived and stated in terms of preferences, although, as we shall see shortly, this involves a misconception, which in fact largely creates the difficulty in the first place. If all individuals' preferences were the same, the decision of the people would simply be a register of what all individuals preferred. But such unanimity is so rare that we must assume its non-existence. How, then, can it be said that there is *a* (collective) decision, rather than a diversity of (individual) decisions?

A very common response to this problem is to say that the will of the majority should prevail. Usually this is based on a simple line of reasoning. Where unanimity is lacking, that is, where preferences are divided, it is the greater rather than the lesser number of preferences which should prevail. This is because the greater number is nearer to being the whole number – and it is certainly nearer to being the whole number than is the minority. The decision of the majority of the people is accepted because it is *counted as* the decision of all the people. This is sometimes buttressed by another argument, found in Locke, to the effect that since the majority is the greater number it is the greater force. Apart from anything else this means it will in any case eventually get its way; so it might as well have it now and avoid conflict: 'we count heads in order to avoid breaking them'. More respectably it might be said that it is 'natural' for a body to move in the direction it is propelled by the greater force within it.[31] These responses are complemented by another, to the effect that for the democrat there is no alternative to majority decision making. Abraham Lincoln expressed this well: 'unanimity is impossible; the rule of a minority, as a permanent arrangement is wholly inadmissible; so that, rejecting the majority principle, anarchy or despotism in some form is all that is left' (First Inaugural Address, 4 March 1861).

Whatever their plausibility as arguments for majority decision making *per se*, the 'greater force' and the Lincoln arguments do not establish that a majority decision can be equated with a decision of the whole people; indeed the Lincoln argument might be said to establish the impossibility of democracy. The argument that the majority is nearer to being all rapidly loses its plausibility as soon as the majority ceases to be overwhelming: 999 people out of a group of 1,000 is indeed very nearly the whole group, but there is no sense in which 501 people can be counted as the whole.

There are a number of possible responses to the failure of these arguments for majority rule. We have not the space to go into them and we shall simply mention some. For further discussion see Kendall (1941), Dahl (1956), Berg (1965), Holden (1974, Chapter 4), and Spitz (1984). (One point to be noticed here is that the 'justification of majority rule' tends to become absorbed into the larger question of the justification of democracy. This is true, for example, of Spitz (1984). However, we are here primarily concerned with whether majority rule achieves, or is to be equated with, democracy. The question of whether democracy itself is desirable we discuss in Chapter 4. There other questions, too, which are only tangentially related to – although at times they overlap with – our concern. One of these is the desirability of majority rule as against the existence or protection of minority rights. Another is whether any decision rule short of unanimity involves an unacceptable loss of autonomy – that is, by the 'losers' (Wolff, 1970); there is a good discussion of this issue in Gould (1988, Chapter 8).)

Possible responses include arguments to the effect that majority decision making produces the greatest happiness of the greatest number (the utilitarian argument); that it is normally the fairest decision-making procedure (Rawls, 1972); that it preserves the maximum possible amount of autonomy (Gould, 1988); or that it is likely to arrive at the correct or most reasonable decision (Black, 1963). Again, though, these may be arguments for the majority decision-making rule but they do not in themselves show that it is a *democratic* decision-making rule – that is, that a majority decision can be conceived as a decision of the whole people. And it should be noticed here that there is an ambiguity in the whole discussion. There is in fact an important distinction to be drawn between (a) statements of a rule or method for making decisions: 'when a decision on policy alternatives is to be taken, that alternative which secures the greatest number of votes should be chosen'; and (b) statements about there being rule by a certain group of people, who constitute a majority. The use of the majority decision-making method only implies rule by a majority group in certain kinds of polarised society. Otherwise 'the majority' is a mathematical expression and does not imply that it is the same individuals who are in the majority on every issue.

Focusing on this distinction clarifies the issues and puts the majority principle in a better light (Holden, 1974). It opens the way for arguments about there being a logical connection between the decision-making rule and equality and popular sovereignty (Spitz, 1984). But Spitz further argues that the majority decision-making rule only achieves democracy when set in a wider context which modifies the purely individualist analysis of most discussions. In fact it would seem that the majority principle cannot itself give sense to the notion of a collective decision by the people. And it is the narrow individualism with which the majority principle is associated that is the basic problem here. But before we take this further there is a different set of problems that must be considered.

These problems show that attempts to demonstrate the possibility of collective decisions, where there are differing preferences, involve difficulties that go even deeper. Even if the idea of a majority decision were acceptable, these difficulties would still be there because, in essence, it is arguable that majority decisions cannot exist in crucial cases. There is now a large and complex literature on this wide subject. The basic argument is that the logical and mathematical problems of aggregating preferences are such that neither the majority decision-making rule, nor any computational procedure, can guarantee that what is preferred by a majority will be the outcome.

These problems become visible when the focus shifts from the notion of voters having only one preference, or account being taken of only their first preference, on each issue. Once orders of preferences (for example a voter who prefers policy (a) to policy (b) might still prefer policy (b) to policy (c), and so on) are taken into account, it can be shown that in crucial cases there is no policy which can be said to be preferred by a majority. Another aspect of, or another way of stating, the problem is to focus on the different ways of putting the issues to be decided by the majority decision-making rule – for example, in taking amendments in committee – and then to point out that these can produce contrary results. 'Cyclical majorities' and the 'the paradox of voting' are terms used to describe problems of this kind. Kenneth Arrow stated the problem generally in *Social Choice and Individual Values* (1963). And it is a problem that can be viewed as very serious: 'put crudely, what Arrow has done is to show that strict democracy is impossible' (Runciman, 1969). (Of course such a view assumes that there would be no problem in the first place in saying that a majority decision, if it could be had, was a democratic decision.)

Not everyone agrees that the position is that serious,[32] but the problem is seen as important and a whole new branch of theory – 'social choice' or 'public choice' theory – has grown up with this as one of its main subjects. (Others are the analysis of how and why, on the same individualist assumptions, governments come to provide 'public goods' in cases of 'market failure' – protection of the environment, for example – and the paradox of why individuals bother to vote when the probability of their own, particular, vote affecting the outcome is negligible.) As indicated, the literature is large, but useful surveys or discussions are: Elster and Hylland (1986), McLean (1987) and Rowley (1987); Mueller (1989) and Miller (1992) are recent and contain short analyses; McLean (1986) contains a vigorous short discussion of some of the key issues; for a more extended analysis, which concerns itself with the 'confrontation between the theory of democracy and theory of social choice', see Riker (1982).

Not surprisingly, analysts differ over many of the issues, but the predominant view did seem to be that the 'Arrow problem' is insoluble within its own terms of reference: and even recent work which might be said to solve it in some sense arguably does so only by making unsatisfactory assumptions about voters (see note 32). But are these terms of reference valid? There are two main lines of counter-argument here.

First, it has been argued that there is no need to try and rescue the majority principle since it is in any case defective, as we have already suggested. One of its faults is that it takes no account of *intensities* of preference – on the problems this raises: see Dahl (1956, Chapter 4), and Kendall and Carey (1968); see also Jones (1988). (Another fault is that it assumes that divergencies of preferences can be neatly categorised into majorities and minorities. In fact, of course, there is usually a great diversity of preferences rather than a split into just two categories. The 'bargaining approach' mentioned immediately below also brings in this very important point.) But if the assumption that preferences are *fixed* is challenged one can take on board differing intensities. Moreover, one can then build on the notion of bargaining and reconciliation, and alteration of preferences in the face of divergencies, to arrive at the idea of unanimity.[33] This avoids all the difficulties associated with trying to aggregate diverse fixed preferences. This line of argument was elaborated by Buchanan and Tullock (1962). Their argument does not succeed (see the critical analysis in Barry (1970)); but two, interrelated, ideas they utilise are important in the second type of counter-argument, which is surely the decisive one.

This moves on from the ideas of preferences being modified and of a decision emerging from a process of interaction (rather than being calculated from data about fixed preferences). If we push these ideas further we get to the crucial point of recognising that people have (sometimes complex) views rather than mere 'preferences'; and the process of interaction involves *discussion* and the bringing together of views. A crucial aspect of this is that views can emerge in the interaction process, rather than being fixed 'original' data about individuals. These ideas tie up with the kind of valid critique of the excessive individualism of much Anglo-American liberal democratic theory, recognised by the 'neo-Idealist' theory mentioned in the next chapter. In fact it is neo-Idealist theory which gives us the notion of 'decisions by the people' emerging out of a process of discussion (see Barker (1942), Lindsay (1935, 1943) and Thompson (1970); see also Berg (1965, pp. 48–57) and Holden (1974, Chapter 4)).

This kind of approach has, in effect, recently been revived in considerations of democracy (influenced by the work of Habermas) as a form of 'communal rational practice' (Spragens, 1990) and notions of 'discursive democracy' (Dryzek, 1990) or 'deliberative democracy' (Manin, 1987; Miller, 1992). There are three key features here. First, the focus on views being *formed*, in a process of discussion or deliberation, rather than on fixed, 'given', preferences. Second, the idea that what emerges from this is some kind of *collective* view,[34] rather than the notion of a mathematical calculation regarding the ineluctably differing preferences of ineluctably separate individuals (which amounts to *some* individuals' and their preferences 'winning' rather than a decision of *all* the people). Third, the focus on practical rather than theoretical reason, and the idea that the process of deliberation is concerned with rational justification and reaching agreement rather than with establishing the truth and arriving at a correct answer (Miller refers to the distinction between deliberative democracy and 'epistemic democracy').

It should be noted that an important aspect of this line of argument is that views can, more easily than 'preferences', relate to something beyond the individual. People can and should ask themselves 'the right question', as Rousseau would put it: they should ask not what is in my interest (what is my 'preference') but what is in the public interest? In fact, a focus on the public interest results from the very logic of a process of discussion on public issues (and note Manin's illuminating analysis of deficiencies in Rousseau's theory because of its exclusion of a process of discussion). This crucially modifies the problem of majority decision making since a majority's view of that which is in the public interest is very different from – and can prove crucially less difficult for a minority than – that which is in the majority's interest, that is, the 'preference of the majority'.

In conclusion, then, we can say that bargaining, compromise and discussion are central to the notion of a decision by the people. At some point a vote is necessary, when the majority view should prevail. However, this should be not the majority's preference, but its view of what is in the public interest. Moreover, this must be set – and arguments for majority decision making only make sense – in the context of the interactive and discursive process. (Spitz (1984) develops a similar viewpoint.) And, as both Barker and Manin, for example, point out, in this context the majority's view takes into account that of the minority: in a real sense it is the view of *all* the people. In short, what is a central problem in narrowly individualist liberal democratic theory is insoluble in its own terms. To make sense of the notion of a decision by the people it is necessary to move away from narrowly individualist assumptions and recognise the ways in which common views can arise which are not necessarily attributable to any particular individuals as such.

Notes

1. This also provides a corrective to Hanson's view – following Habermas – that the identification of democracy 'with particular organizational forms [eliminates] any chance of criticizing those forms and the distortions they embody' (Hanson, 1985): such 'identifications' are apparent only, and once this is realised it is quite possible to criticise – critically analyse – these specifications of the necessary conditions of democracy without criticising the idea of democracy itself. Similarly, there is a corrective here to Hanson's argument – following MacIntyre – that there cannot be a transhistorical concept of democracy existing independently of a set of (varying) ideas and practices in an unfolding tradition: the various ideas and practices amount to differing *conceptions* of democracy incorporating varying specifications of necessary conditions. More generally, arguments to the effect that the concept of democracy changes historically with the varying socio-economic and political conditions to which it is applied (Hanson, 1985; Hoffman, 1988) refer – insofar as there *are* changes of ideas – to varying conceptions rather than to changes in the concept.

2. The position is actually rather more complicated than this as there is a further important distinction between what might be called empirically and logically necessary conditions. See Holden (1974) for a discussion of this distinction (p. 4), and an analysis of the role of this distinction in discussions of participation as a necessary condition for democracy (pp. 185–6).

3. On the notion of sovereignty see, for example, Stankiewicz (1969) and Hinsley (1986).

4. See, for example, Holden (1974, pp. 10–11).

5. This statement, in fact, brushes over four further – important and complex – issues. First, some would challenge the notion that democracy is necessarily a form of state (this issue is commented upon in Chapter 3 below). Second, even if it is a form of state it might not necessarily be that 'a people' coincides with – or is delimited by – an actual existing state: in fact some of the current problems just commented upon in the text involve precisely this point. A third, and closely related, point is that it may well be that 'the people' in any particular case is 'a people' in the sense of a genuine community (perhaps a nation) with an existence of its own, rather than a collection of individuals whose membership is defined purely by the jurisdiction of a state ('corporate' and 'individualist' conceptions of the people are commented on in the main text). Fourth, although traditionally there has been – as argued – a conceptual link between the democratic idea of 'the people' and territorial social units, it may be that changes are afoot which will allow some recognition of the 'cosmopolitan logic of democracy': for a number of reasons concerning the current preoccupation with the nature of the international order the question of 'overall' democracy within

– or 'democratisation' of – the global system is beginning to be discussed: Burnheim (1986), Held (1991b).

6. See, for example, Spearman (1957).

7. See Harris (1982) for a critical discussion of the exclusion of children. He disputes the idea that children should be excluded; however, acceptance of his arguments would not really invalidate the underlying point, made in our text above, concerning the lack of disagreement about the exclusion of categories of individuals, and the compatibility of this with the existence of dispute about the boundaries of such categories: even Harris would exclude children under ten. Dahl (1979 and 1989, Chapter 9) discusses the exclusion of children and comes to conclusions similar to the present author's; Dahl's discussion is part of a useful general analysis of who is to be included in 'the people' that, *inter alia*, highlights the extent to which conceptions of 'the people' were *un*democratic in ancient Athens and in traditional democratic theory – e.g. Locke, Rousseau and J. S. Mill.

8. On 'symbolic representation' see, for example, Birch (1972). We shall be discussing 'representation' in the next chapter.

9. On the confused relationship between the meanings of 'liberal' and 'democracy' see Sartori (1987, Chapter 13). On the tensions within the American political tradition between liberty and democracy see also, for example, Hanson (1985, Prologue).

10. On the nature of liberalism see, for example, Gray (1986b).

11. It may be more accurate to refer to 'the location of the control of a state's power' since it would normally be held that the power in question is an attribute of the state: in a democracy the people control the state – and thereby have power. Some, though, would dispute this view of democracy and the state (see the references to the state and democracy in section 3, Chapter 3 below). Sartori (1987) says something very similar about the relation between the meanings of 'liberty' and 'democracy': 'liberalism is above all the technique of limiting the state's power, whereas democracy is the insertion of popular power into the state.' This formulation might be interpreted as ambivalent on the popular power/state power relationship; and Hanson's in some ways similar characterisation bypasses the issue: 'in short, democracy established the *identity* of the sovereign in society, whereas liberalism defined the *limits* on sovereign power, regardless of who exercised that power' (Hanson, 1985).

12. Mill explicitly appeals to considerations – based on utility – other than natural rights to delimit an area of individual liberty. It is arguable, though, that in fact his political theory is not consistently utilitarian, as opposed to rights based: see, for example, Ten (1980) and Ryan (1983).

13. Beitz (1989) would appear to dispute this. However, his is more an argument about equality and the decision procedures usually linked to, rather than about the very idea of, one person one vote. In effect the point made in the present text is that one person one vote can be seen as a *necessary* condition of democratic decision procedures, whilst Beitz points to a way in

which it fails to be a *sufficient* condition. In addition, Beitz is concerned with the nature of the moral case for political equality whilst, at this point, the present text is concerned merely with the logical assumptions or implications of the notion of a decision by the people.

14. Tocqueville (1805–59) is a very important theorist in the context of the relationships between democracy, equality and liberty. His most important work (Tocqueville, 1968) has been extremely influential. It is analysed in Dahl (1985).

15. There is an extensive literature but perhaps the most useful guide is Miller (1991) which contains a selection of writings which 'represent (in the editor's opinion) the most significant analyses of the idea of liberty in the last century or so'; plus a very helpful Introduction.

16. We shall be saying something about the 'civic republican' tradition in Chapter 2, section 3.

17. These conflicting views of the nature and role of the government are reflected in difficulties Anglo-American theory tends to have with the concept of the state, which (when the 'first view' is invoked) has to be seen – in a way that is at variance with its basic logic – as a body purely external, and hostile, to the people and the individual. It is noteworthy that in 'citizenship theory' – which constitutes something of bridge between individualistic Anglo-American and communitarian Continental theory – there is more subtlety (or ambivalence) concerning the citizen having rights against *and* duties towards the government and state (see Chapter 2, section 3 below).

18. In fact, of course, there are three relationships here: those between (a) the individual and the government, (b) the individual and the people, and (c) the people and the government. Liberal democratic theory tends to mix them all up. In particular it often assumes that an instance of (a) is one of (c) and thereby overlooks the possibility of its being one of (b). The converse of this, as it were, is the frequent inability to see how, in many cases, (a) involves (b): to the extent that the people act through government an action of the government *is* an action by the people. In other words, here the government versus the individual is also the people versus the individual (see also the main text below).

19. Hayek (1978); see the helpful discussion in Held (1987, Chapter 8).

20. The point is really a bit more complex than this. The notion of 'the state' carries with it the implication of action in some sense by the whole community, so that *any* – including an autocratic – government of a state in a crucial sense has more than its *own* power. Nonetheless, it is only in a democracy that the power of the whole community is actively involved; moreover, a government which becomes ever more autocratic tends increasingly to be seen as an alien body detached from the community – thus diluting the conception (and the associated authority and power) of it as a manifestation of a state.

21. See, for example, Ranney and Kendall (1956). Willmoore Kendall has even interpreted Locke in this light, in Kendall (1941). Continental views of

democracy are more likely to be of this kind than are Anglo-Saxon views – see Sartori on 'Empirical democracies and rational democracies' (Sartori, 1965 and 1986); but see also the paragraph which follows in the main text.

22. The distinction between the 'negative' and 'positive' concepts of liberty was made famous by Isaiah Berlin in his lecture on 'Two concepts of liberty', reprinted in Berlin (1969) and (abridged version) Miller (1991). Miller (1991) is also useful as a source for further analysis and criticism of this distinction, including MacCallum's well-known critique (MacCallum, 1967; see also Baldwin, 1984) and for discussion, in the Introduction, of the relationship between this distinction and those which Miller draws between three traditions of thought about liberty – the 'republican', the 'liberal' and the 'idealist'. See also the helpful discussions of liberty – including 'negative' and 'positive' liberty – in Norman (1987) and Plant (1991).

23. This sort of idea has become important on the Left; see, for example, Hattersley (1987) whose characterisation of socialism in terms of the power of the maximum number of individuals to exercise their rights is central to the argument that socialism is as much about freedom as it is about equality, since the two are intertwined (see also the discussion of the relationship between liberty and equality in the text below). The notion of 'empowerment' has also become important in varieties of feminist theory.

24. There can be significant differences between English and American terminology. In England, 'liberal', without qualification, would usually be taken to mean 'classical liberal' whereas in America it would normally signify 'New Deal' or 'social liberalism'. The position is further complicated by the recent 'reflowering' of classical liberalism (for example in the work of Hayek and Nozick), which is sometimes referred to as 'libertarianism'.

25. The use of terms such as 'formal liberty' shows how these arguments link up with different ideas regarding liberty itself. The point is that those who use such arguments reject a purely 'negative' view of liberty and embrace the more 'positive' view that liberty involves 'empowerment', something that is not realised simply by the absence of governmental restriction (see the discussion of liberty in the main text above). The mere absence of such restriction then amounts to 'formal' and not genuine liberty.

26. There is of course a further dimension of variation here. Arranging an equal distribution of material goods does not necessarily mean giving everyone the same goods since people's tastes differ. So perhaps it is the same *amount* that we should focus on. But how do you quantify amounts of, say, camping equipment as against audio goods? Monetary value provides the standard answer, so that the principle becomes one of equal distribution of money (equality of income, for example); moreover a 'monetary system . . . allows people to choose their material goods in accordance with personal preference' (Norman, 1982). See also Dworkin (1978b) who focuses on the importance of differences in individuals' conceptions of the good life rather than the more superficial 'tastes'. He also sees the free

market and representative democracy as the institutions necessary to give effect to the principle of equality of treatment (this connects up with the 'liberal-egalitarian' viewpoint discussed in the main text below).

27. According to Rawls' famous 'difference principle' inequalities are, it is true, justified. But equality is, in an important sense, the key value, since departures from an equal distribution of goods *do require* special justification. Thus inequalities are only justified insofar as they are to the benefit of the worst-off – as happens when overall prosperity is raised (in a way which improves the lot of even the worst-off) by the operation of systems of incentives to hard work and entrepreneurial activity which necessarily involve inequalities of income and wealth. See Chapter 4 for further references to Rawls.

28. Tocqueville held that a democracy (in the primary sense of the term) was a system in which equality necessarily existed to some extent, and in which further equality was vigorously pursued as an ideal. But half the time he goes further than this and treats 'democracy' and 'equality' as synonymous – that is, he moves to the secondary meaning of 'democracy' we identified earlier.

29. The notion that, for the democrat, liberty and equality are inextricably linked goes back to Aristotle. For modern analyses, besides the works already referred to, see the references given by Norman (1987, p. 131). For a critical analysis see Charvet (1981) who argues that 'the notions of freedom and equality must be taken together in the idea of the equal value of individuals as free or self-determining beings, and yet that this necessary combination of equality and freedom cannot be elaborated into a coherent system of ethical thought. The principles of freedom and equality are as much opposed to each other as they require each other.'

30. Some qualification is needed because of some ambivalence concerning the 'positive aspects' of the understanding of liberty in the liberal-egalitarian viewpoint and the meaning of 'liberal' in 'liberal democracy'. It is, for example, debatable whether the 'participatory democracy' which some see as necessary for realising their understanding of the liberal-egalitarian value(s) (e.g. Gould, 1988) is a form of, or an alternative to, liberal democracy (see Chapter 3 below). We should also note, however, that some see the liberal democratic process itself, and its requirements, as a key element in the harmonisation of liberty and equality (Dahl, 1989).

31. We have here an example of a common feature in discussions of majority rule: a shifting between individualist conceptions of the people, as simply a collection of individuals, and 'communitarian' conceptions of the people as a corporate entity – a conception implied by the notion of the people being 'a body'.

32. And there have also been new developments in public choice theory. Mueller (1989) argues that 'recent research has gone a long way toward resolving' the paradox of voting. However, he still entertains serious doubts – doubts about the extent to which votes in schemes which (arguably)

overcome the voting paradox are meaningful.
33. And it *is* unanimity that is ideally required. It is the burden of the argument in the text above that only unanimity can give sense to the notion of a decision of (all) the people. But it can be argued, as does Manin (1987), that unanimity also 'seems to derive inescapably from the fundamental principles of modern individualism' (Manin argues, too, that 'it is impossible coherently to reconcile the majority principle with the requirement for unanimity').
34. Arguably this can in a very significant sense be seen as the view of everyone. Manin, however, puts forward a different interpretation in distinguishing his account from that of Habermas, who sees the ideal process of deliberation generating a 'constraint-free consensus [which] permits only what *all* can want' (Habermas, 1976). Manin maintains only that 'the better argument is simply the one that generates more support and not the one that is able to convince all participants' (Manin, 1987). Different, again, though is the notion that the collective view – because of the process of rational discussion and give and take by which it is generated – is one which all can *accept*; this is surely the more satisfactory account.

2

□

The nature of liberal democracy

In this chapter we shall be concerned with some further dimensions of the basic ideas contained in the notion of liberal democracy. We shall attempt to clarify some of the key ideas and theories that have given it life, as well as comparing it with rival notions. We begin by looking at the central ideas in the historical tradition of thought about democracy, before turning to consider the fate of these ideas in the modern world.

2.1
Direct and indirect democracy

We saw in the last chapter that the meaning of 'democracy' was extended around the end of the eighteenth century to include 'indirect' as well as 'direct' democracy. And it is now time to consider the nature of these two ideas and the relationship between them.

Both ideas fall within our general definition of 'democracy' by virtue of the differing accounts of what are 'important matters of public policy' and differing interpretations of the notion of the people making decisions. In a direct democracy, decisions on most matters of public policy are made directly by the people; in an indirect democracy, although a few – the most important – are directly made by them, most decisions are made only indirectly by the people.

A direct democracy, then, is a political system in which the people directly make the policy decisions – 'directly' in the sense that the decisions that are implemented are not merely 'derived' from, but *are*, the decisions the people have actually made. The usual idea about how this can happen involves many of the people being, and all having the chance to be, present and participating when the decisions are made; and the proportion of matters specifically decided by the people in this way being high. Given the relevant pre-supposition about the desirability of extensive popular decision making, then if the people *can* be assembled to make decisions there is no reason why all non-routine decisions should not be made by them. By contrast, in an indirect democracy although the determining policy decisions are still made by the people, to an important extent this is done indirectly. True, the fundamental decisions are made directly – at elections; but most others are actually made by elected representatives: it is these that are made only 'indirectly' by the people. But though it may be done indirectly there is still an important sense in which it is the people who make them, by virtue of the way in which the representatives are affected by, and are ultimately subordinate to, the direct electoral decisions. Beyond, or alongside, this basic idea, different democratic theories have differing ideas about the relationship between the representatives' decisions on the one hand and the opinions and interests of the people on the other. But in all cases – besides, or in association with the effects of, the electoral decisions – the representatives are in some sense or other deciding for, or on behalf of, the people.

Direct democracy

Direct democracy is often viewed as the very archetype of democracy; and it is often held up as the ideal against which indirect democracy is to be judged. It is the most thoroughgoing form of democracy. And the original – and now highly esteemed – democracies of ancient Greece were of this type. Direct democracy therefore continues to have an important influence upon democratic thought. It is true that it is commonly considered to be totally impracticable in modern conditions of large industrialised societies and states of corresponding scale and complexity. Nevertheless it often continues to be seen as the ideal of democracy. And some do see modern forms of direct democracy – 'electronic democracy' – as being made possible by modern communications technology: televised debates with viewer interaction via computer keyboards and so on (see, for example, Margolis (1979), Barber (1984, Chapter 10), McLean (1986, 1989) and Arterton (1987)). The 'information revolution' might, indeed, 'render obsolete the idea that true democracy requires face-to-face contact of the sort possible only in small autonomous communities' (Dryzek, 1990). Ross

Perot put forward some ideas along these lines in the 1992 American presidential election campaign. However, whether such arrangements would in fact provide anything like the experience of discussion in face-to-face meetings of participants is another question (see, for example, Dagger (1982)).

Be that as it may, the ideal of direct democracy still casts its spell and it continues to affect practice. One reason is that there do exist today examples of direct democracy. True, these are not at the level of states, and they mostly involve relatively small-scale, non-state bodies – a students' union, where the general meeting has a key role, is one instance. But some examples are local government units; and although not at the level of the whole state, they are state institutions. The best known are the New England town meetings (for a fascinating and detailed empirical study of two examples of direct democracy, one of them being a New England town meeting, see Mansbridge (1980)). But arguably more significant are the five small Swiss cantons which are still governed by assemblies of the people, or *Landesgemeinden*. As Hansen (1991) puts it: these 'constitute a real – indeed the only real – parallel to Athenian democracy; for, although nowadays the cantons are only subordinate units, with limited local powers, in their day they were

Direct democracy in a Swiss canton
(women now included for the first time)

sovereign states, governed by means of direct democracy' (see Barber (1974) and Hansen (1983)).

The survival of direct democracy in its traditional form and the possibilities of 'electronic democracy' have helped to fuel a resurgence of interest in direct democracy in recent times, and this has been central in current 'participatory theories' (see Chapter 3 below). Belief in, and calls for, participatory democracy often involve a denunciation of at least orthodox representative institutions, and a corresponding demand for an increased direct involvement by the rank and file in decision making.

As already mentioned, the main inspiration and model for direct democracy has been the theory and practice of ancient Greek democracy. The all-important political unit in ancient Greece was the city-state or *polis*. This was more on the scale of a modern medium-sized town than of a modern state. Some of these city-states were direct democracies, albeit with a conception of 'the people' which modern democrats would not accept since women and slaves were excluded!

Above all it has been Athens of the fifth and fourth centuries BC that has inspired subsequent democratic thought. The Athenian *polis* contained between 30,000 and 45,000 citizens and the quorum for the Assembly was 6,000. The Assembly made decisions on matters put to it by a Council. But the Council was itself chosen by lot and was a microcosm of the people; and the matters put to the Assembly were all the important ones. The Assembly met frequently – up to forty times a year – and it engaged in genuine and decisive debates. Political decision making, therefore, was in a very real sense directly in the hands of the Assembly. Moreover, the important role and rotating membership of the Council and the very large popular courts added greatly to the extent of popular participation in government:

> The level of political activity exhibited by the citizens of Athens is unparalleled in world history . . . Most notable of all . . . is the level at which ordinary folk took part: they were not confined to choosing the decision-makers, but, in their hundreds of thousands, prepared decisions, made them, and administered them in person. (Hansen, 1991)

On Athenian democracy see, for example, Held (1987, Chapter 1), Sinclair (1988), Hansen (1991) and Hornblower (1992).

As already mentioned, it is usually held that it was the smallness and lack of modern social and technological complexities that made ancient Greek direct democracy possible. The question of the viability of something like direct democracy in the modern world will be one of the themes in our discussion of 'participatory theories' in Chapter 3.

Indirect democracy

Let us now turn to indirect democracy. And we should remember that from the French Revolution onwards this came to be regarded as the only practicable form of democracy. It should also be remembered, however, that Jean-Jacques Rousseau, whose political philosophy is often considered one of the inspirations of the French Revolution, is widely seen as being in favour of direct, rather than indirect, democracy.[1] We shall have more to say about Rousseau later in this chapter.

As we have seen, indirect democracy means representative democracy: a political system in which the people elect representatives to act for them for certain purposes. As was said just now, the great disadvantage of direct democracy on the ancient Greek pattern is held to be its impracticability on a larger scale. The idea of representation was later incorporated into democratic thought as a device for overcoming this disadvantage. The concept and practice of representation emerged during the Middle Ages to develop and be utilised in the flowering of democratic theory, beginning in the late eighteenth century, so that representation became an integral part of democratic theory. Indeed, in some instances representation was joyously seized upon as a miraculous solution to the problems of applying popular rule in large-scale societies. Tom Paine was of the view that, as the ancient 'democracies increased in population, and the territory extended, the simple democratical form became unwieldy and impracticable'; an 'original simple democracy . . . affords the true data from which government on a large scale can begin. [But] it is incapable of extension, not from its principle, but from the inconvenience of its form.' However, the system of representation is the remedy for this defect of form, and 'by ingrafting representation upon democracy we arrive at a system of government capable of embracing and confederating all the various interests and every extent and territory of population' (Paine, 1969). James Mill proclaimed that 'in the grand discovery of modern times, the system of representation, the solution of all the difficulties, both speculative and practical, will perhaps be found' (Mill, 1955). As we shall see, not all theories of representative democracy view representation as simply overcoming the problems of size, although all would give it at least, if not only, this function.

Representation: concepts and theories

The idea of representation, then, plays a central role in indirect democracy. But what does this important idea amount to? The first thing to notice is that there are several conceptions rather than a single straightforward one. Arguably these are separate, though related, ideas; but it may be that they are best seen as different variations on one basic notion.[2]

The basic notion identified by Pitkin (1967) is that of *re*-presenting, 'making present', in some sense, that which is not literally there. But this 'making present' can be thought of in different ways. Thus Birch talks of three main usages of the term 'representative': (a) to denote an agent who acts on behalf of his or her principal; (b) to indicate that a person shares some of the characteristics of a class of persons; and (c) to indicate that a person symbolises the identity or qualities of a class of persons (Birch, 1972).

A representative in the first sense is one whose duty it is to promote certain interests or wishes of another person or persons – the 'principal'. (Birch sticks to the term 'interests' here, but this begs important questions: as we shall see later, the relationship between interests and wishes, or opinions, is important to the differences between the various theories of representation.) Sales representatives and lawyers would be examples. As Birch points out, there can be a variety of types of relationship between agent and principal. In the second sense the term refers to the possession of characteristics typical of some larger group or category within which the representative is included – and of which he is 'representative'. Birch gives the example of a representative sample, as used for instance by public opinion pollsters, where a 'sample of the relevant population [is] chosen by statistical methods so that the main characteristics of the population will be mirrored in the sample' (Birch, 1972). The third sense of 'representative' is less important in democratic theory. We came across it in the last chapter in those medieval notions of kingship in which the king 'represented' the corporate people. In this sense the representative 'stands for' or 'symbolises' that which is said to be represented, as a piece of sculpture might 'represent', say, courage.

There are differing ideas about *what* – as well as the *ways* in which – persons or groups are to be represented. And there are also varying ideas about the function of representatives in the political system as a whole. This number of variables entails the possibility of many different relationships. And, in part as a reflection of this, there are different theories of representation. Here, however, we are concerned only with those theories which occur in democratic theory. (It is often assumed that theories of representation are necessarily democratic. But this is not so: the groups being represented need not comprise the whole people.

Even where it is the whole people who are represented this need not involve them in making decisions: for example, in the medieval notion according to which the king represented the people it was the king who made the political decisions. As already indicated, the concept and practice of representation in fact pre-date theories of representative democracy – see for example Pitkin (1967).)

In democratic theories of representation the whole people are represented; and the whole people decide who are to be their representatives and, roughly at least, what they are to do. It is, of course, essentially through the electoral process that this is achieved: through the process of electing representatives the people decide how and by whom they are to be represented. It should be noted, however, that the democratic selection of personnel need not be by elections – though without them an indirect democracy would need some alternative mechanisms, such as the use of referendums, for the actual making of (at least the basic) decisions by the people. Selection by lot was used in ancient Greek democracy, but it would usually be held that this method had grave disadvantages in modern indirect democracies. For a useful discussion see Dahl (1990); for an interesting recent – but only ambiguously democratic – argument in favour of selection by lot see Burnheim (1985).

Different theories of representation arise through (amongst other things) differing accounts of the relationship between electors and their representatives. But in all of these a key idea is that the fact of being elected ensures that those elected do actually behave as representatives. The important arguments here are that the members of an assembly, *because* they are elected by their constituents, will actually (a) behave as agents of, and/or (b) have the same characteristics as, those constituents. (In fact (b) is much less likely to obtain than (a) – a point which is developed in Burnheim's (1985) important book.) 'Symbolic representation' is of only minor importance here.

There are four main ideas about the manner in which election is supposed to ensure representation in these ways. First, there is one of the ideas behind argument (a), that only those persons will be chosen who say that they will advance the opinions or interests of the electors. Second, there is the idea in argument (b) that election will help to ensure that those chosen as representatives will have characteristics typical of their electors. With each of these first two ideas the assumption is that the electors will vote only for such candidates as will be representative. The third conception, which relates to argument (a), is that electors will make sure that the representative will behave in the appropriate way after election. The idea here is that members of the assembly who in fact fail to do what they were elected to do will not be re-elected by their constituents. This has the double effect of helping to ensure that most members will remain representative, and of removing any that do not. These ideas concerning the continued representativeness of the elected members rely on the notion that the members will wish to be re-elected. Hence, by anticipating the reactions of their electors, they will see to it that they do nothing to prevent this happening. This conception is sometimes expressed in terms of the 'rule of anticipated reactions'. A fourth idea, again relating to argument (a), concerns the insecurity of tenure implied by election. Representatives will, it is argued, refrain from promoting legislation that could later affect them adversely as ordinary members of the public.

It is, then, the system of election that provides for the people to decide, at least in broad outline, the policy to be pursued by their elected representatives. And it is because, or to the extent that, this is so that a system of representative government is a democracy. Again it is 'agent representation' that most directly fits the argument. 'Sample representation' – insofar as it is separated from agent representation – fits it indirectly. There is the idea of legislators being elected because they have characteristics similar to their electors, and this relies on the expectation that similar characteristics will imply similarity of interests and policy views.

Election of representatives is, then, crucial. But representation as such is also important in its own right; indeed, in a representative democracy there is a double form of responsiveness to the people. The people make the basic decisions through elections. But, over and above this, the representatives have the inherent function, and therefore duty, of promoting the people's interests and/or views. This function exists even apart from elections, although elections are extremely important in ensuring that the function is actually performed, and necessary for ensuring it is performed in a way the people approve.

The different theories of representation in democratic theory centre on differing ideas regarding (a) the degree of autonomy of the representative in relation to his electors; (b) whether there is a difference between the representation of constituents' interests and representation of their opinions, and, if so, how they relate to each other; and (c) the extent to which it is the function of the representative to promote the national interest rather than – if there is a difference – the interest(s) or views of particular constituents. The issues here are interrelated and the ways in which they are treated in different theories of representation are interconnected.

We shall now turn to these theories and look at them as key elements in traditional liberal democratic theory. We should note, though, that conceptions of representation were modified by the development of mass political parties and ideas about their functions in a democracy. As we shall see, these conceptions became grafted on to traditional democratic theory. But let us look first at the original democratic theory that pre-dated these developments.

2.2
Traditional democratic theory[3]

A theory of democracy, or democratic theory, is a body of thought that provides, analyses and justifies a conception – a model – of democracy; and explains the actualisation of the model in the world. There is also another use of the term 'democratic theory', meaning something like a scientific theory, where the reference is to a body of theory concerning the workings of actual political systems that are presumed to be democracies. We are not primarily concerned with this sense of the term here.

There are, of course, different models of democracy that can fit within the general idea of liberal democracy; and, indeed, there are different democratic theories. Broadly speaking these theories may be divided into 'traditional' and 'modern', though some twentieth-century theorising consists, essentially, in restatements or refinements of traditional democratic theory. In this section we shall be concerned with traditional democratic theory, sometimes called 'classical democratic theory'.

We should really talk of traditional democratic theor*ies*, since there are different types of theory that fall under this heading. The differences are in fact important, though often overlooked. Nonetheless, the different theories do also have certain common features. Perhaps the chief reason for grouping them together under the same label is historical: they were all formulated in the same general period, over a century ago. Traditional democratic theory, then, consists of theories of democracy formulated in the period roughly between the middle of the eighteenth and the middle of the nineteenth centuries. Theories relating to ancient Greek democracy were often influential in their formulation, but the term 'traditional democratic theory' is usually taken as referring to the theories of indirect[4] democracy relating to this later epoch.

Traditional democratic theory, then, did not really emerge until the second half of the eighteenth century, as part of the Enlightenment. There had, though, been anticipations of it in the thought of the Levellers of the mid-seventeenth century (Gooch, 1954; Wootton, 1992). And we must also recognise the importance of the political philosophy of John Locke.

According to the usual perception Locke is not really a democratic theorist (but see note 5); yet his political theory has been extremely influential in democratic thought, especially in the United States. Indeed, he is often regarded as the founding father of liberal democratic theory. This paradox arises because, on the one hand, Locke is an important thinker whose influential political philosophy has important democratic features; whilst, on the other hand, these features – although developed by later theorists into a full-scale theory of democracy – are but aspects of a theory that ultimately is not democratic. The democratic elements of Locke's political philosophy are his theories of popular consent and of majority rule. But these are set within an overall theory which does not properly give the people constitutional power. Although the whole people have power in the sense of having an ultimate right to revolt if they find that the governors have abused their trust, there is no constitutional mechanism for exercising this right. Nor, it is usually said, does Locke believe that all the people, the masses, should have the vote.[5]

Whatever the democratic status of Locke's own political philosophy, it fathered what can be regarded as the two main streams of Anglo-American traditional democratic theory (we shall discuss later the relationship between Anglo-American and Continental democratic theory). We can characterise these streams as follows.

Types of traditional theory

On the one hand there is what we might call 'conventional democratic theory'. This inherits Locke's view of the government as an entity separate from, and 'above', the people and sees this entity as having a positive and independent function. The people have a negative and passive – although in the end decisive – role. The term 'conventional' is used principally because of the extent to which the theory became part of the conventional view of the British political system. Historically the British system was the chief object of theorists' attention, although the American political system has a somewhat similar status here. In a dialectical relationship the theory's model of democracy was perceived to fit, but also inspired and legitimised, the conventional view of the nature of the British political system. The term 'liberal democratic theory' is sometimes used to refer to what I here call conventional democratic theory. There are some good reasons for this, but there is the risk of confusion since 'liberal democratic theory' also has the generic sense in which it means *all* theories about liberal democracy.

In conventional democratic theory an important notion, connected with the people's negative role, is the idea of government by consent – that is, government with the consent of those, the people, who are being governed. Where consent is required for the performance of some action(s), those who give or withhold that consent can be seen as playing a decisive but negative role – 'decisive' because their decision is necessary before the action(s) can be performed; 'negative' because they merely respond to initiatives put to them by someone else. One can also stress the 'negative aspect' of consent by distinguishing between a 'self-assumed obligation' as the 'free creation of a relationship' (as in making a promise); and consent to something already in existence (as in agreeing to abide by the rules of an institution) (Pateman , 1985). In the idea of 'government by consent', then, the people can be seen as performing a decisive but negative role. They are viewed as giving consent to – or withholding consent from – the government; and this can incorporate the idea of the people having negative power over the government.

It is not, however, always realised just how complex and vague is this notion of government by consent. Indeed, in some renderings the idea is not even necessarily connected with democracy. For example, consent by the people simply to the existence of a regime – rather than to the policies pursued by its government – does not amount to the people making the basic policy decisions: in fact it might be that the people consent to a non-democratic form of government. To further indicate some aspects of this vagueness and complexity, we can say that the meaning of 'government by consent' varies principally along two main dimensions. One dimension concerns that to which the people consent. At one end of the scale it is consent to the existence of government as such. This varies through consent to particular forms of government and particular governments to, at the other end of the scale, consent to the policies pursued by the government or even to particular legislative or administrative acts. The other dimension concerns that which constitutes consent. This varies from acquiescence under duress, through various kinds of manipulated, habitual and traditional acquiescence – and also the process of 'socialisation' – to freely and deliberately choosing to give assent, which may involve the giving of permission. For further discussion of government by consent see, for example, Partridge (1971) and also Pateman's (1985) important book, which explores what she regards as the manner in which the ambivalences of consent theory have been 'exploited' to mask the non-voluntarist character of the modern liberal democratic state.

The other stream of traditional democratic theory fathered by Locke contains theories we can label as 'radical democratic theory'. In effect Locke's right of revolt is here developed into a positive, initiating role for the people. Rather than the people merely responding to initiatives put to them by the governors (actual or potential), as in conventional democratic theory, it is the governors who respond to initiatives from the people. We shall look further at conventional and radical democratic theory in a moment. Before that, though, there are a couple of important points to note.

First, the division of traditional democratic theory into just two types in this way is something of an over-simplification – although, arguably, a permissible and helpful one. The point is, of course, that there is more than one way of grouping and distinguishing the various different theories that go to make up traditional democratic theory.

In particular we should note another significant category of distinctions that cuts right across that between 'conventional' and 'radical' democratic theory. These are distinctions reflecting the differing basic philosophies or underlying theories with which thinkers have linked the democratic idea (further discussed in Chapter 4). Broadly speaking we can, perhaps, discern three main types of theory when we look at it in this way.

First, there are theories in which the idea of a democratic form of government derives from, or is intermeshed with, a basic theoretical or philosophical analysis in which fundamental moral principles are seen as having a central role. Such theories have often been centred on conceptions of natural law and natural rights: Tom Paine's *Rights of Man* (1969) is a leading example. But bases for theories which see democracy as necessary for the realisation of fundamental moral principles have also been found in Christian philosophy and the philosophy of Kant (1724–1804). An important modern example of something like a Kantian basis for democratic theory is to be found in John Rawls' *A Theory of Justice* (1972).

In theories of a second type the idea of democratic government flows from an analysis of how interests are best protected. These are utilitarian theories of democracy, the classic exponents of which are Jeremy Bentham (1748–1832) and James Mill (1773–1836).

In a third category are theories which see democracy as necessary for the proper development of the individual. To what extent this is properly a category of traditional liberal democratic theories is debatable. Such 'developmental theories' tend to have roots in Rousseau rather than in Locke; and some central ideas are considered when we discuss 'participatory theory' generally in Chapter 3. Anglo-American examples have mainly been twentieth-century products: 'neo-Idealist' democratic theory and 'citizenship theory' are referred to later in this chapter. But, having said this, it must also be pointed out that one of the central figures in traditional liberal democratic theory, John Stuart Mill (1806–73) – James Mill's son – does appear in this category. In fact John Stuart Mill is something of an eclectic theorist of democracy. He considered himself to be a utilitarian,[6] and important aspects of his theory focus on democracy as a means of protecting people's interests. But at least as important in his theory is a 'developmental' view of democracy: democracy being seen, and valued, as promoting the proper development of the individual.[7]

The second important point to note before looking further at conventional and radical democratic theory is that, as implied just now, there is a very important theorist of democracy whose thought we are not counting, for the moment, as part of traditional democratic theory, namely Rousseau. There are two, interconnected, reasons for leaving him aside at this point. First, Rousseau differs importantly from the other thinkers we are here concerned with in being a theorist of direct democracy: he is, indeed, widely understood as being against representative government (but see note 1). Second, as will be remembered, our concern is in fact with traditional *liberal* democratic theory. And Rousseau's political philosophy and the sort of democratic theory he inspired is arguably not liberal democratic theory. We shall in fact be discussing this matter in a later section when we compare Anglo-American and Continental democratic theory. But we must acknowledge right away that despite not counting him at this point as a traditional liberal democratic theorist, Rousseau's political philosophy has been extremely important here. Continental democratic theory, stemming from Rousseau, is itself very important; but the immediate point is that Rousseau's thought – striking and profound as it is – has directly influenced traditional Anglo-American democratic theory by virtue of its similarities with, and the inspiration it has given to, aspects of radical democratic theory.

But let us return to traditional liberal democratic theory. We have seen that there are differences among the theories within this general category. But there is, of course, also an important common element in the theories. This can be summed up as a form of 'individualism'. All liberal democratic theory is individualist to an extent; but what characterises traditional liberal democratic theory is the prominence of a form of individualism. This is in contradistinction to 'modern' democratic theory, which ascribes an important role to groups rather than (or as well as) to individuals. True, some traditional theories contain contrary tendencies. For instance John Stuart Mill was very conscious of the general influence of society and of majority groups; and some American theories – such as those of Madison and Calhoun – which historically, and on the whole conceptually, are part of the mainstream of traditional democratic theory, focus on the role of groups. But it is still a predominant individualism that is typical of traditional democratic theory.

What is this form of individualism? We shall be discussing individualism in more detail in the next chapter, but for the moment we can say that in a general sense individualism has two main aspects.

First, 'moral individualism': this term indicates viewpoints which give great moral importance to the individual. They are typically expressed by statements such as 'the individual ought always to be treated as an end in himself and never only as means'. Moral individualism is central in some varieties of traditional democratic theory – in John Stuart Mill, for example. But it is not (or, at least, it is crucially qualified) in others: utilitarian theory notoriously yields interpretations which give greater moral importance to general happiness than to the just treatment of an individual.[8]

Second, there is what we might call 'ontological individualism' – 'ontological' meaning having to do with the nature of being or reality, in this case the nature of social reality. Individualism in this sense involves seeing society as composed only of individuals and having its character determined by the characteristics of its constituent individuals. Groups, institutions, processes, structures, cultures, communities and so on are viewed merely as collections of individuals and the patterns they set up in their relationships. The nature, validity and significance of ontological individualism will be discussed in the next chapter; but here we should note that ontological individualism is especially important in traditional democratic theory. We are not just talking of the theory's individualist views of social reality generally. Rather, we are saying that there is a typical view of the political system itself in which the behaviour of individuals is central. The functioning of institutions and the political process generally is seen primarily in terms of the decisions and interactions of individuals. In 'modern' democratic theory, by contrast, even though there is an underlying ontological individualism, the functioning of the political system is seen primarily in terms of group interaction. (We shall see later, though, that traditional theory was itself subsequently modified by the 'grafting on' to it of theories about key groups in the democratic process – political parties.)

Conventional and radical democratic theory

Let us now go back to 'conventional' and 'radical' democratic theory. We have already seen that the basic difference between them concerns the difference in roles ascribed to the people, and we shall now say a little more about this.

In conventional democratic theory the people have the negative role of choosing, at elections, among options presented to them. The options involve personnel and policies – different candidates and their various plans – and the choice of personnel is important as well as the choice of policies. Indeed, the policy choices by the electorate are seen as being only general and broad rather than detailed and specific. This is associated with the expectation that the representatives will be wiser and more knowledgeable than the people who elect them. There is considerable autonomy for such representatives in the making of political decisions, although they act within the general control of their constituents.

In radical democratic theory, on the other hand, the positive, initiating role of the people involves the idea of elected representatives being closely controlled by their electors, so that they act as little more than messengers conveying the policy decisions of their constituents. In a word they are 'delegates'. In this well-known sense of the word a delegate is contrasted with the idea of a representative as a 'trustee' – one who exercises personal judgement on behalf of his electors, rather than simply conveying their views. (Somewhat confusingly, though, the term 'representative' is itself sometimes used in contradistinction to 'delegate' to convey this idea; this specific, narrower, sense of 'representative' must then be distinguished from the generic or general sense which also includes delegate within its meaning.) The electors' decisions not only initiate the policies the delegates are to follow, but these policy decisions are fairly detailed and specific. Indeed there is a sense in which the ideal system for radical democratic theorists remains a direct democracy, with a system of representation being favoured merely as an unfortunate necessity for dealing with the problem of scale.

By contrast, in conventional democratic theory representation is seen as having virtues of its own: as a means to 'refine and enlarge the public views, by passing them through the medium of a chosen body of citizens whose wisdom may best discern the true interests of their country' (Madison, 1961). With some radical democratic theorists – for example Thomas Jefferson (1743–1826) and Richard Price (1723–91)[9] – active popular 'participation', other than just voting at elections, is seen as an important part of the positive role of the people. (As we have seen, the conventional theorist John Stuart Mill also sees participation as very important. It may be that there is an inconsistency in his thought here as Pateman (1970) argues, but since Mill focuses on participation in local government this, arguably, does not clash with his conventional view of the role of representatives at the national level.) Here there is a notable parallel with democratic theory stemming from Rousseau. Indeed, this important theme of popular participation has at least as much to do with Rousseau as with traditional liberal democratic theory and is not a feature of all varieties of radical democratic theory. It has in fact been much discussed in recent times in the context of critiques of liberal democracy, and we shall postpone further consideration until the next chapter.

The models of democracy in both conventional and radical democratic theory consist, then, of political systems in which the people make decisions by electing representatives to govern them. In the radical model these elections also constitute specific decisions, or sets of decisions, on the policies to be followed by the representatives. In the conventional model, on the other hand, elections, although they also decide policy to an important extent, are decisions of a far looser and broader kind; and as such, representatives are left room for considerable autonomy in decision making.

In order to highlight some other important aspects of traditional democratic theory we can now expand our remarks on the role of representatives. This will bring in other important aspects of, and differences among, the various conventional and radical models of the democratic process.

Traditional models of the democratic process

The democratic process here essentially consists in the making of decisions by numerous individuals and the combining of these into decisions by the people. This involves more than, but includes, the process by which those decisions are transmitted into government action. (The issues are different from those that were indicated in the discussion of majority decision making in the appendix to the previous chapter, although they also overlap with them.) The ideas involved relate to what it is that decisions by individual electors express; and also the relationship between these decisions and the functions and activities of the electors' representatives.

Opinions and interests

First, then, let us look at the individual electors' decisions. Ideas within different democratic theories reflect differing responses to a key question: whether it is interests or opinions that are expressed by these decisions. (A decision which expresses an interest links a conception of what the interest is with a decision to advocate its promotion. Similarly, one which expresses an opinion links an indication of what the opinion is with a decision to advocate promotion of action in accordance with it.) It is true that electors' decisions do not necessarily always fall neatly into this interest–opinion dichotomy. And the relationships between interests and opinions can become quite complex and the distinction very blurred in the thought of some theorists. Nonetheless, in a rough-and-ready way key differences are highlighted by drawing such a distinction.

We can say that the individual's interest(s) – or that which is in the individual's interest(s) – is that which benefits him or her.[10] A significant and complicating point is that an interest can be said to exist independently of the individual supposed to have it. An opinion, on the other hand, is simply what its holder conceives it to be (the question of its validity is another matter). This difference can have far-reaching implications.

Within traditional democratic theory it is above all utilitarian democratic theory that focuses on individuals expressing interests.[11] Utilitarianism became an influential moral and political theory in nineteenth-century Britain.[12] It was most widely known, and was incorporated most clearly into traditional democratic theory, in the work of Jeremy Bentham and James Mill. (John Stuart Mill was a more profound thinker, but despite his claimed or modified utilitarianism his was a crucially different theory of democracy, as we shall see further below.) We may characterise utilitarianism as asserting that happiness is pleasure, and the absence of pain; that pleasure is good; and that the equal pleasures of any two or more people are equally good. From this was derived the famous criterion of moral action: that which is right is that which produces the greatest happiness of the greatest number.

Utilitarianism also asserts that individuals do in fact seek pleasure and avoid pain; that they obtain pleasure by fulfilling their desires (doing that which is pleasant); and that doing that which is pleasant is what benefits them. In other words the promotion of individuals' interests consists in fulfilling their desires. Now, since only the individual concerned knows what desires he or she has, and knows best how to fulfil them, it follows that each individual is the best judge of his personal interest. And this implies that individuals should themselves decide how their interests are to be promoted. And it is from this that utilitarian democratic theory springs: the idea of people themselves deciding how their interests are to be pursued leads naturally (despite some difficulties and inconsistencies that are touched on below) to the idea that the people should govern themselves.

It is in fact a species of radical democratic theory that is generated in this way, since it follows from the notion that people are the best judges of their own interest that they should have full and detailed control over how their representatives pursue those interests. One of the most succinct statements of utilitarian democratic theory is to be found in James Mill's *Essay on Government* (1955) (see also Lively and Rees, 1978). Mill had some rather odd ideas on the extent of the franchise and C. B. Macpherson, for example, sees them as fatal to the view that James Mill is properly a democratic theorist (Macpherson, 1977a). However, they need not be seen as integral to his theory, the central logic of which is radically democratic.

In conventional democratic theory, individuals' decisions are not typically seen as expressing interests. This is not because the concept of interest plays no part in conventional theory. Rather it is because central to such theory is the view that ordinary people do not properly, or clearly, know their own best interests. One reason for this is that interests are not viewed simply in terms of the fulfilling of desire (even Bentham is pushed in this direction at times). Wise representatives can best know their electors' interests; but only if they are aware of those electors' opinions. Hence it is opinions that are seen as being expressed in voting decisions; and it is the representatives who, taking account of these expressions, decide what the interests of the electors are. Conventional democratic theory here echoes the famous words of Edmund Burke (1729–97) – although he was not himself a democratic theorist – when he said that a representative owed his constituents a 'devotion to their interests *rather than* to their opinions' and should if necessary go as far as maintaining their 'interest even against [their] opinions' (Burke, 1949). Such conceptions are incorporated into democratic theory by John Stuart Mill, the most influential British conventional democratic theorist. His ideas are in many ways different from those of Burke, but with respect to the nature and role of voters' decisions as expressions of opinion, there are key similarities.

In conventional democratic theory, then, individuals' decisions are typically seen as expressing opinions; whilst in one of the main forms of radical democratic theory – utilitarian – such decisions are seen as expressing interests. But there is not always this kind of line up.

On the one hand there are important varieties of radical theory in which the electors are, implicitly, seen as expressing opinions rather than interests. Jefferson and Tom Paine, for instance, focus primarily on the will of the people; the views of individuals are then seen as but constituent elements of this popular will. And, since the popular will has as its object the benefit of the (whole) people, this too must be the object of the constituent individual wills. Individuals, then, are expressing opinions about the good of the community, the whole people, rather than concentrating on their own particular interests. (It is true that the second part of Tom Paine's famous book, *Rights of Man* (1969), is essentially utilitarian in character, but this is not true of the more widely read Part One.)

On the other hand the expression of interests does in fact play some part in conventional democratic theory. For example, the notion of class interests has a place in John Stuart Mill's thought, where an important element is the notion of the more enlightened representatives holding the balance of power between the opposed class interests that find expression in the legislature. But, more than this, there is one important figure, James Madison (1751–1836), who should be counted as a conventional democratic theorist and in whose thought the expression of interests plays a central role. Madison has the conventional democratic theorist's typical view of the role of a representative, and his thought as expressed in his contribution to the *Federalist Papers* (Madison, 1961) has a standing in the American tradition of democratic thought not unlike that of John Stuart Mill's *Representative Government* (1912) in the British tradition.

Madison, however, is untypical of traditional democratic theory in that he concentrates on the role of groups rather than on individuals. (In some ways his thinking has more in common with modern, group-orientated, pluralist democratic theory than with individualist, traditional democratic theory. Unlike pluralist democratic theorists, however, Madison is worried about the power of groups: he accepts their presence as inevitable but seeks to 'tame' them – to deal with the 'evils of faction'.) For Madison it is group interests that are at the heart of the democratic process. Like the utilitarians he conceives of individuals as themselves knowing their own interests. However, in contrast to utilitarianism, these are not the interests of each particular individual but the interests of the group or 'faction', to which the individual belongs. An individual who is a farmer knows his own interests, but these are his interests as a farmer.

Also in contrast to utilitarian democratic theory, the idea that individuals know their own interests does not lead to a delegate view of representation. This is because utilitarian theory fails to come properly to grips with the problem of the relationship between individual interests and the general interest, and it sees representation simply as a means of translating individuals' interests into legislative action. In Madisonian theory, however, to protect the general interest, groups' interests and their expression are to be tamed by the actions of representatives in the legislature. This brings us to the issue of the relationship between the electors' decisions and the behaviour and functions of their representatives.

The functions of representatives

There are, in fact, two important and different, but overlapping, issues here: the first concerning the representative's proper role with respect to his or her own particular constituents, and the second concerning the relationship between this and the representative's role with respect to the nation as a whole.

The first issue gives us the line of divide between conventional and radical democratic theory that we have already noted. Radical theory views representatives as delegates only, while conventional theory emphasises the relative autonomy of representatives. Conventional democratic theory, indeed, sees representation as something more than simply a device to deal with the problems of scale. The 'something more' is provided by the special wisdom and expertise of the representatives as compared with the ordinary person. In fact, in conventional democratic theory representative institutions are viewed as a way of combining the merits of democracy with the merits of rule by an educated and informed elite. John Stuart Mill is in favour of 'Parliament containing the very elite of the country' (Mill, 1912). And Madison sees the public's views as being not so much directly expressed as refined and enlarged 'by passing them through the medium of a chosen body of citizens, whose wisdom may best discern the true interest of their country', and 'it may well happen that the public voice pronounced by the representatives of the people, will be more consonant to the public good than if pronounced by the people themselves' (Madison, 1961). In short, in conventional theory the people choose representatives to govern for them. But, if this is so, can it really be said that it is *democratic* theory? The answer is a qualified, but nonetheless definite, yes. Both Madison and Mill have their undemocratic aspects, but when it comes to the point the people are the masters. 'The meaning of representative government is that ... the people ... exercise through deputies periodically elected by themselves, the ultimate controlling power. ... This ultimate power they must possess in all its completeness' (Mill, 1912). For Mill 'the people ought to be *masters*, but they are masters who must employ servants more skilful than themselves' (italics added) (Mill, 1859). The people may choose representatives to govern for them, but in doing so the people make the ultimate, the basic, decisions on important matters of public policy.

Conventional democratic theory's view of representation is best summed up by Hanna Pitkin:

> The wonderful theoretical advantage of representation as Liberalism sees it, then, is this: representation makes it possible for each to participate in government as the final judge of whether his particular shoe pinches; yet it allows the rulers to use their wisdom and information to further people's true interests, where direct action would be misguided by short-range, hasty decisions. And, at the same time, representation makes it to the interest of the ruler to act in the interest of the subjects – not to give in to their passing whims, but to act in their true interest. For if he gives in to their passing whims, they will not really be pleased; the shoe that looked so attractive in the store will turn out to pinch. Only if he uses his wisdom to promote their true, long-range interests will they be truly pleased, and support him at the polls. (Pitkin, 1967)

In contrast to conventional democratic theory, the delegates of radical democratic theory are elected to the representative assembly simply to convey the wishes of their constituents: to act as messengers, or to act as their constituents would have done had they been there. This is clear in Paine if less clear in Jefferson. (Jefferson recognises a need for above-average intelligence in representatives. But he nonetheless thinks they should be very frequently accountable to the people; and he is, moreover, in favour of direct popular participation wherever possible.) The logic of utilitarian theory – despite some qualifications by Bentham – leads clearly to a delegate view of representation: if people are the best judges of their own interests it follows that those interests can be properly pursued only by representatives who are guided by the express directions of the people. This argument is complemented by another, succinctly expressed by James Mill:[13]

> There can be no doubt, that if power is granted to a body of men, called Representatives, they, like any other men, will use their power, not for the advantage of the community, but for their own advantage, if they can. The only question is, therefore, how can they be prevented; in other words, how are the interests of the Representatives to be identified with those of the community?
>
> Each Representative may be considered in two capacities; in his capacity of Representative, in which he has the exercise of power over others, and in his capacity of Member of the Community, in which others have the exercise of power over him.
>
> If things were so arranged, that, in his capacity of Representative, it would be impossible for him to do himself so much good by misgovernment, as he would do himself harm in his capacity of member of the community, the object would be accomplished. (Mill, 1955)

And the way to achieve this is to have frequent elections. It is then always apparent to the representatives (a) that they may at any time revert to being members of the community, and (b) that in order to remain in office they must promote their electors', and not their own, interests. Tom Paine expresses a very similar view (Paine, 1976).

We might note here that utilitarian democratic theory, which focuses on individuals and their interests, is paralleled by a group theory – rather as the more individualist strand in conventional theory is paralleled by Madisonian theory. This is the theory, important at least in America, put forward by John C. Calhoun in his 'A disquisition on government' (Calhoun, 1851). Like Madison, Calhoun accepts the idea of the representation of sectional interests. But, unlike Madison, he thinks that representatives should merely reflect these interests and act primarily as spokesmen for their constituents. Control by elections would make 'those elected the true and faithful representatives of those who elected them instead of irresponsible rulers as they would be without it; and thus by converting it into an agency and the rulers into agents, to divest government of all claims to sovereignty and to retain it unimpaired to the community' (Calhoun, 1851).

Let us now turn to the second of the issues involved in ideas about the relationship between representatives and their constituents. This concerned the local constituency and the national interest: is the representative merely to promote the opinions and/or interests of his particular constituents, or primarily to identify and promote the *national* interest, the interest of the whole community? Is there, indeed, a conflict here at all? The answers to these questions are enmeshed with the accounts of electors' decisions and representatives' functions that we have just been discussing.

In conventional democratic theory there are a number of factors at work. To begin with there is the central idea that the representative is wiser than his constituents and should exercise his own judgement. This becomes closely associated with the idea that the representative is best able to discern the national interest and that he has an overriding duty to pursue it: the representative's judgement here is likely to be superior to his constituents' opinions.

Where electors are regarded merely as expressing opinions this settles the issue. Where, however, as is sometimes the case in conventional theory, it is electors' interests that are focused upon, the matter is a little more complicated, but two basic ideas intermingle.

First, there is the idea that the national interest ought to prevail over the interests of particular constituencies. Again, it is the enlightened representative who has the capacity and the duty to discern and promote the national interest. And in doing so he or she is acting as something other than simply an agent for constituents' interests. And, again, it is Burke who is often echoed in conventional democratic theory. In his famous words, speaking to the electors of Bristol:

> Parliament is not a congress of ambassadors from different and hostile interests, which interests each must maintain, as an agent and advocate, against other agents and advocates; but Parliament is a deliberative assembly of one nation, with one interest, that of the whole – where not local prejudices ought to guide, but the general goal, resulting from the general reason of the whole. You choose a member, indeed; but when you have chosen him he is not a member of Bristol, but he is a member of Parliament. (Burke, 1949)

John Stuart Mill focuses primarily on opinion. But he does also recognise that interests will find expression; and insofar as this is the case the national interest should prevail over local or sectional interests. This should in part be achieved by the wise action of representatives: or, at least, by the wise action of the most enlightened representatives, who should hold the balance of power in the legislature. But Mill also seeks to discourage the expression of local interests by advocating a system of proportional representation that plays down local constituencies and allows voters to choose from among candidates throughout the country. Madison, too, values the pursuit of the general interest above sectional interests. In his case, however, there is not the confidence that representatives will always be capable of rising above sectional interests.[14] He is therefore in favour of sectional interests gaining expression in the legislature so that they can be balanced against one another and thereby neutralised. In this way representation is 'a way of bringing dangerous social conflict into a single central forum, where it can be controlled by balancing and stalemating' (Pitkin, 1967).

The second idea denies that there is, essentially, any conflict between the national and particular constituency interests – even where there appears to be. What might appear as particular interests, in conflict with the general interest, are in fact not so; they are not the genuine, long-term interests of those involved. It is an important aspect of the representative's superior wisdom that he can see this even when his constituents cannot. (The electors do have the last word – conventional theory *is* democratic – but by that time they will probably have seen, and approved, the wisdom of their representatives' decisions.)

Particular interests and the general interest
In radical democratic theory there is, typically, no particular issue regarding a representative's respective duties to his constituents and to the national interest. This is because, as we have already seen, the sole duty of a representative (delegate) is to convey his electors' opinions and/or their own conception of their interests. Now, this means that the problem of the particular versus the general does not get discussed at this point, and remains as an issue unrelated to the specific question of the role of representatives. In the case of those radical democrats who think in terms mainly of opinions and their representation, the problem tends simply to be ignored. It is assumed that what individuals decide in favour of will constitute the national interest. This is part of a general failure to perceive that the whole people are not the same as a single individual 'writ large', and that there are fundamental problems regarding the relationship between particular individuals and the sum total of individuals. (As we saw in the last chapter, there is a tendency in these theories to assume that the only important issues regarding the relationship of the individual to the state are those that concern the individual's relationship with the government – which ignores the relationship with the people as a whole.)

In the utilitarian variety of radical democratic theory we can see how the problem is, in part, obscured by the delegate view of representation. The delegate view does not push to the fore the question of differing, possibly conflicting, functions of representation. Unlike the representative of conventional theory the utilitarian delegate's only duty is to pursue constituents' own conceptions of their interests, since this is what those constituents' interests *are*. The delegate has no duty to focus on any other objective; and therefore other, and possibly conflicting, objectives – such as a national interest – do not really come into the picture.

But there are deeper reasons than this. There are in fact crucial difficulties in utilitarian theory regarding the relationship between particular interests and the general interest. The particular interests focused upon by the original utilitarian theorists were those of individuals, and the constituency/general interest problem in effect becomes submerged in the individual/general interest problem.[15] At one level, utilitarian theory really implies that there is no such thing as a general or national interest that could be in conflict with anything. The only interests that exist are those of individuals, and the 'general interest' can mean nothing other than the interests of all the individuals somehow added together. But this view is not consistently held to; indeed it cannot be, since it becomes incoherent.

In fact there is also in utilitarianism another, typically liberal individualist, account of the general interest. Here there is the postulate of some kind of harmony among, rather than a simple addition of, the individual interests. In this way, in fact, the general interest consists in the *harmony* among particular interests, and not in the interests themselves – not even the alleged 'sum total' of interests. The assumption that there will be harmony among particular interests, plus the assumption – fundamental in utilitarianism – that each individual is the best judge of personal interests, supports the idea that harmony results from leaving each individual unfettered in the pursuit of his or her interest. This is a central conception in classical liberalism and reached its most famous expression in the classical economists' notion of *laissez-faire*, in particular in Adam Smith's conception of the 'invisible hand' which ensures that the pursuit of private gain results in the promotion of the interests of society as a whole. Here the focus moves from the fact of harmony to its beneficial results. According to such views as these, there seemed little need for government of any kind – even democratic government.

However, utilitarianism did also recognise that government was necessary. As Hobbes had earlier argued, life without government would be insecure. Individuals would be in mutually destructive competition for limited resources. In other words, individual interests are not naturally harmonious and need to be artificially made so.[16] This is the task of government. 'Government . . . is to make that distribution of the scanty materials of happiness, which would insure the greatest sum of it in the members of the community, taken altogether, preventing every individual or combination of individuals, from interfering with the distribution, or making any man to have less than his share' (Mill, 1955). But there is a problem: the government will be composed of persons who, like all individuals, will have to pursue their own private interest. We saw earlier how this problem is solved: the representative system was conceived to get over this difficulty and ensure that the interests of the representatives are made to coincide with those of the community as a whole. The idea is that if the people control their rulers, then the interests of the people rather than those of the rulers will be promoted.

There is, of course, a crucial difficulty in this argument. Government is necessary to control the clash of particular interests among the people at large. How, then, can the people at large have *an* interest, and control of the rulers to ensure its promotion? (The 'harmony of interests' idea cannot be invoked here since it is this idea's deficiencies that make government necessary in the first place.) James Mill seems unaware of this difficulty. 'Sometimes the Utilitarians simply ignore this difficulty, speaking of the people only as a unified whole with one interest [thereby contravening the individualist basis of utilitarianism]. That is James Mill's solution, and one sometimes used by Bentham' (Pitkin, 1967). Bentham, though, does have a more sophisticated side to his theory. This involves a recognition of individuals having shared public interests as well as ethically inferior selfish and private ones. It also involves a contradiction of the original axiom that each individual is the best judge of their own personal interest, and a departure from the delegate view of representation.[17] It is, however, the simple – and inconsistent – theory exemplified by James Mill that has been regarded as the typical utilitarian legacy.

Finally, on this question of the general and particular interests in radical democratic theory, we should note that Calhoun's 'group theory' tends to get into the same sort of muddles as the utilitarian democratic theory that it parallels – with the particular interests in this case being those of groups rather than of individuals. However, there is also in Calhoun a 'weak' theory of the general interest, that later was to become important in modern democratic theory in the notion of 'consociational democracy'. It is a negative conception of the general interest as consisting in not harming any particular interests. That which is in the general interest is that which offends no group's interests. According to Calhoun, the political institutions should be such that it is 'impossible for any one interest or combination of interests or class, or order, or portion of the community, to obtain exclusive control', thus preventing 'any one of them from oppressing the other'. This forces the different interests 'to unite in such measures only as would promote the prosperity of all, [since this is] the only means to prevent the suspension [by mutual veto] of the action of the government; – and thereby, to avoid anarchy, the greatest of all evils' (Calhoun, 1851).

Traditional democratic theory: Modifications and assumptions

Before we leave Anglo-American traditional democratic theory there are two more points we should notice.

The first of these concerns the relationship of ideas about political parties to traditional democratic theory. The essential point is that the relationship is ambivalent: political parties and their role are seen both as being discordant with, and as important complements to, traditional theory.

The discordance is partly a matter of the relative unimportance of political parties at the time when traditional democratic theory was being formulated. There is very little in traditional theory about parties; and what there is, is largely hostile. Essentially, the hostility has two, interrelated, sources.

First, there is the tension with individualism: political parties and their operations do not accord with the individualist view of the polity typical of traditional democratic theory. With parties playing an important role, the electoral decision becomes a highly structured and limited mass choice among a relatively small number of parties rather than the aggregation of unfettered decisions by separately acting individuals. Moreover, the elected legislature becomes a forum for group entities – political parties – rather than for individual representatives. And the relationship between parties and the electorate subverts that between individual representatives and their constituents.

The second basis for hostility to political parties comes back to the question of the general interest again. Despite traditional theories' own difficulties with analysing the general interest and the popular will, when it comes to political parties it tends to be assumed that these conceptions are clear and that they are subverted by political parties. Parties are then seen as groups with particular interests that interfere with the people willing what is in their – that is, the general – interest. This view of parties as factions with partial or particular interests is to some extent an echo of Rousseau's hostility to partial groups because they interfere with the people seeing and willing the common good of the overall community (the general will). But within Anglo-American theory there is a classic discussion, to which we have already referred, of the dangers of faction and how to cope with them: Madison's famous 'Paper 10', of *The Federalist Papers* (Madison, 1961).

The view of political parties and their role has changed, though. It is true that echoes of the traditional hostility can still be found in arguments in favour of multi-party systems, and against 'restrictive' two-party systems with their limitations on electoral choice and legislative behaviour. Moreover, the work of Weber and Michels (see section 2.4 below) gave rise to a renewed current of concern about the anti-democratic implications of the role of political parties. This work emphasised the way in which the electoral – and indeed the whole political – process was being organised by 'mass' political parties which were, in fact, under the control of bureaucratic leaderships. Indeed, this kind of analysis became part of a hostile critique in which traditional democratic theory had to give way to modern elitist democratic theory (see section 2.4 below).

Nonetheless, the predominantly hostile view of parties was modified to a considerable extent; and another current of thought became influential in which hostility to political parties gave way to a view which saw them as essential components of democracy. Hostility to the pursuit of particular interests was transferred to pressure groups, and Burke's conception of a political party became widely accepted: 'a body of men united, for promoting by their joint endeavours the national interest, upon some particular principle in which they are all agreed' (Burke, 1861). Concern about restrictions on individual choice and behaviour was overlaid by a perception of the ways in which political parties made electoral decision making and control more effective. Parties came to be seen as mechanisms invaluable for organising millions of separate individual votes into unified policy decisions: and for keeping those in government in touch with, and accountable to, the electorate. Indeed, appreciations of the democratic functions of political parties virtually became incorporated into traditional democratic theory – grafted on, as it were.

In combination with conventional democratic theory we get a view of parties as providing, on the one hand, the leadership and organisation necessary for firm and wise government, and on the other hand, structures through which governmental organisations can be held ultimately responsible to the electorate. In the case of radical democratic theory, the doctrine of the mandate emerges: parties and their programmes are viewed as instruments of the popular will, so that a (party) government must, and must only, pursue such policies as it was elected to carry out.[18]

The second point to notice here about traditional democratic theory concerns the assumption of rationality that is said to underlie it. It is commonly held that traditional democratic theory assumes that people are rational and, in particular, that electors vote rationally. (It is important to notice that from some viewpoints – but not those of traditional democratic theory, apart from what might be implicit in utilitarian theory – it may not be rational for an individual to 'vote rationally'. In terms of cost-benefit analysis it can be argued that the 'costs' involved in, for example, an individual acquiring the information necessary to vote rationally, far outweigh the benefits obtainable from rational voting. Indeed, looked at in this way it can be shown that the 'costs' to any one individual of simply voting – for example, in terms of the effort needed to get to the polling station – outweigh the benefits that can be obtained from that vote, virtually unnoticeable as it is among the thousands or millions of others. In fact, quite a literature has grown up around this subject, really starting with Downs (1957).[19] The assumptions on which such arguments are based are strongly disputed by participatory theorists of democracy, who argue that any political participation, including voting, far from being a 'cost' has inherent virtue.)

Rationality is a complex notion but the focus here is primarily on 'instrumental rationality' and the idea that the rational individual is the one who uses reason in seeking to obtain objectives and has sufficient relevant knowledge to do so. What, and what degree of, knowledge is relevant and sufficient can obviously be a controversial matter. But in the case of traditional democratic theory and voting the criteria are essentially given by the theories. To be rational is to use reason based on knowledge in a way that enables one's voting to express the sorts of decision which a theory postulates as being taken by the people. Thus, according to radical theories of democracy, in order to be rational, voters need sufficient knowledge to express detailed policy views.

We shall see when we look at the 'academic challenge' that traditional democratic theory has often been criticised for its unrealistic assumptions about the rationality of the people. We shall comment on this later, but it should be pointed out here that such criticism properly applies only to radical democratic theory. One of the features of conventional theories of democracy is their idea of the limited nature of popular decision making: the electors are neither expected nor presumed to have the substantial degree of rationality necessary for the kind of detailed decision making postulated in radical theories.

'Anglo-American' and 'Continental' democratic theory

Let us now return, for a moment, to the question of the general and particular interests. As already indicated, our analysis so far has really been concerned with Anglo-American traditional democratic theory, including the discussion of the issue of the general and particular interests. But it is very important to realise that this issue does not arise – or, at least, that it is treated entirely differently – in another tradition of democratic theory which we can call 'Continental'. It is time now to have a brief look at this and to compare it with Anglo-American traditional democratic theory.

In fact the term 'traditional democratic theory' is to some extent ambiguous here; or, at least, it is in an Anglo-Saxon context. Sometimes, as has been the practice in this chapter so far, traditional democratic theory is used only to refer to Anglo-American democratic theory. Such restricted reference sometimes reflects hostility to Continental democratic theory and the wish to distance it; and it certainly points to some crucial differences between Anglo-American and Continental theory. At other times traditional democratic theory is used in a way that includes both types of theory.

Continental democratic theory

What is meant by Continental democratic theory? What is the sort of democratic theory that is sometimes called 'Continental' – or, perhaps, 'French'? We shall attempt to characterise it by briefly sketching in its main features, comparing it with Anglo-American theory and asking whether, or in what sense, it is a species of liberal democratic theory.

Frequently in talk about democracy, distinctions are not drawn between different types of Western democratic theory. However, in more thoughtful discussion it is not uncommon for an important distinction to be pointed up by the use of a term such as 'Continental democratic theory'. It refers to that kind of democratic theory characteristic of Continental Europe and especially of France. There is a special connection with France because of the origins of this type of thought in the political theory of the French philosopher Rousseau, and in the happenings and understandings of the French Revolution. Indeed, as Sabine shows so lucidly, the contrast between the Anglo-American and Continental democratic traditions stems essentially from the contrasts between Locke and the English Revolution on the one hand, and Rousseau and the French Revolution on the other (Sabine, 1952).

Continental theory's model of democracy has a distinctive account of the nature of the people and the way in which they wield power. One of the key features of this account is that the people are – indeed it is perhaps more accurate to say the people 'is' – a corporate entity with a single will. This is partly a matter of a tendency to employ a juristic notion according to which 'the people' refers to a legal category rather than directly to an actual group or set of persons – rather as there is a crucial difference between, say, a parish legally defined and an actual assembly of its inhabitants in a parish meeting. But this is only part of the story since Continental theory contains important propositions about how the people act.

Anglo-American theory – with its focus on an empirical rather than a juristic notion – sees the people as a collection of individuals, with the 'will of the people' being some kind of aggregate of separate individual wills; indeed, it gets into great difficulties here. Continental theory, on the other hand, conceives the people as being, in a significant sense, a single entity with its own, single, will. In a similar way one talks about organisations of people such as, say, ICI as single corporate entities being possessed of wills – they plan, they act and so on. (It is important to note that the idea of the people as a corporate entity is, somewhat paradoxically, combined with a radical individualism. The constituent parts of the entity are of only one kind – individuals. There is here an important contrast with that appreciation of the importance of groups and sections of society which so often modifies Anglo-American individualism. Indeed, in Continental theory there is a positive hostility to any partial groups which would divert attention from the overall community and the common good.)

The other key feature of Continental theory's account of the people and their power is a very strong notion of popular sovereignty, which stresses the idea that there is no proper limit to the people's authority. The will of the people is supreme: there is nothing they are not entitled to do. By contrast Anglo-American democratic theory is much preoccupied with the limits to state action, even – or, in some cases, especially – when such action is the embodiment of the will of the people.

These differences between Anglo-American and Continental theory largely reflect those between Locke and Rousseau. We have already said something about Locke and we should here focus on a key feature of Rousseau's political theory:[20] his notion of the general will. As already remarked, in Anglo-American democratic theory the 'will of the people' is viewed as some kind of aggregate of the *separate* wills of the individuals, the collection of whom makes up the people. According to Rousseau, however, there is an important sense in which all individuals can have the *same* will by willing the same thing; in fact this possession of a single will is a key aspect of the way in which individuals constitute a single corporate entity. This is the 'general will', which consists in every individual willing the common good (or the 'general good' or 'general interest').

There are three important points to note here about the idea of the general will. First, it assumes that there is no disagreement in principle about what is for the general good. It is true that conflict can arise between apparent, short-term particular interests and the general interest; and this may blind people to the common good and cause dispute about what to do. But this does not mean disagreement about what genuinely is for the common good. Secondly, it does recognise that individuals are indeed sometimes distracted in this way from focusing on the common good, by apparently willing what is in their own particular interests. This could happen, say, if every individual were offered relief from jury service. But everyone opting for this could constitute what Rousseau would call the 'will of all'; the general will of citizens might well be for the maintenance of the jury system. In fact, when distracted in this way individuals are only apparently willing what they see as their particular interests.[21] They are responding to a question about their particular interests rather than to one concerning what they see as being in the general interest. They are being asked the wrong question, as Rousseau would say; they still really will the common good (note the connection with the notion of 'positive freedom'). The third point follows on from this: all individuals can be said to be willing the same thing – the common good – even when, apparently, they are not. Indeed, that it is the will of every person is a defining characteristic of the general will: the subject of the will is general as well as its object (the general good).

This idea of the existence of a single will, even where there is an apparent diversity of wills, cuts through the difficulties Anglo-American theory experiences in trying to give an account of a will of the people. It also cuts through the difficulties concerning the relationship between – and the proper roles for participants in pursuing – the general and particular interests. It is clear that the general interest is distinct from (narrowly conceived) particular interests, that it is morally superior to them and that democracy requires that it motivate everyone's political behaviour.

Besides the difference between Locke and Rousseau, the contrast between Anglo-American and Continental theory has much to do with the historical contrasts between the English and French Revolutions, and between English and French historical experience generally. There are many facets to this (Sabine, 1952), but their main effect is to emphasise, on the one hand, the pragmatic nature of Anglo-American theory together with its focus on the limitation of state power and on the importance of non-state groups and structures; and on the other hand, the rationalistic character of Continental theory and its pre-occupation with the unlimited power of that overall abstract entity, the sovereign people. Sartori has similar things to say about the differences between 'empirical' (Anglo-American) and 'rational' (French or Continental) democracies (Sartori, 1965, 1987).

Is Continental theory a form of liberal democratic theory?

Let us now turn to the question that has so far been left hanging in the air. Is Continental theory a form of liberal democratic theory? Should Continental theory's model of democracy be counted as a liberal democracy? The answer is a little complicated, and is best arrived at by looking at the cases for and against.

First, what is the case against counting Continental theory as a form of liberal traditional democratic theory? To begin with, it can be said that Continental theory gives more importance to equality than to liberty (Sabine, 1952). But this is an assertion hard to pin down and assess. More important here is the view of the Continental model as being an 'absolute' rather than a 'liberal' or a 'limited' democracy. There are two aspects to this: the Rousseauist theory itself and the practice with which the theory became associated. In the theory we have seen that the will of the people is sovereign and that it should be subject to no limits. Indeed, as the general will is the true, moral will of each individual it would make no sense to try and limit it. There should not, then, be any limits to the democratic state's activity : its power should be absolute. This is obviously in stark contrast to the idea, central to the notion of liberal democracy, that the power of the state – even a democratic state – should be limited.

Even more clearly illiberal is the practice which was to an important extent inspired, and/or explained and justified, by Rousseauist theory. To put the matter bluntly, Rousseauist theory was to be called in aid of such grossly illiberal regimes as the Napoleonic dictatorships and the twentieth-century totalitarian systems. Indeed, as we have already noted, it is not uncommon for Rousseau to be regarded as the origin for the theory and practice of totalitarian democracy (Talmon, 1952).

What, then, of the opposing case – the case for counting Continental theory as a form of traditional liberal democratic theory? First, despite what the Anglo-American liberal would say, Continental theory *is*, in its own terms, concerned with democracy as the way to promote freedom. But it is a different conception of freedom. We saw in the last chapter that Rousseau has a 'positive' conception of freedom. Now, in a properly constituted democratic state, laws are expressions of the general will – which means that such laws ensure that people do what they really want to do. In other words laws, the manifestations of state power, assist people to act freely so that the unlimited democratic state, far from threatening or extinguishing freedom, is a necessary condition for it. However, the Anglo-American liberal does not, typically, accept this account of freedom and persists in seeing unlimited democracy as a threat to freedom as properly understood. In any case, even if the Rousseauist theory is given some credence, the practice of certain of the alleged democracies that were inspired by the theory very clearly threatened and diminished individual freedom on any understanding of the concept.

But now we come to another argument. This starts from the point that, although they might claim otherwise, those regimes which are illiberal and totalitarian may in fact owe their nature to something other than Rousseauist theory. Indeed, their nature may be crucially different from that theory's model of democracy. It may be that it is *mis*interpretations of Rousseau that contributed to the non-Western, non-liberal theories of democracy, as in the former 'people's democracies' of Eastern Europe. Moreover, there are other, Western, democracies which also see Rousseau as their inspiration and which are not illiberal and totalitarian – most notably in France. The practices of French democracy, indeed, have much in common with those of Anglo-American democracy: free competitive elections and so on. This is partly because both democratic traditions have in fact been called on in France. But so, conversely, have Britain and America called upon the

Continental tradition to some extent: 'the evolution of democratic government throughout the nineteenth century continually drew upon both [traditions]' (Sabine, 1952). The traditions have important similarities with each other as well as differences; and both have common origins in Western political theory and experience (Talmon, 1952, Introduction). 'The two traditions have remained persistently linked, both in the sense that they were felt to express only different aspects of a single ideal and also in the sense that practical democratic politics made drafts as occasion dictated almost indifferently upon both traditions' (Sabine, 1952).

Continental traditional democratic theory, then, can certainly be seen as a variety of Western democratic theory; although whether it is properly described as 'liberal' is less certain. Be that as it may, it remains important in understanding liberal democracy. This is because of the influence it has had not only on the practice but also on the theory of the archetypal liberal democracies,[22] where it has especially been reflected in radical democratic theory.

2.3
Neo-Idealist and citizenship theory

Our discussion of Continental theory highlights the point that within the conspectus of traditional democratic theory there are counter-influences to the individualism of the kind of traditional Anglo-American theory that we have so far considered. And we shall now look at two important varieties of liberal democratic theory which, whilst remaining distinct from Continental theory, are in important ways reactions against this sort of individualism.

Neo-Idealist theory

First, there was an intermixing of Continental with Anglo-American theory which in effect became a central feature of a kind of 'hybrid' form of democratic theory which was important in the earlier part of this century. Some of its ideas have come to the fore again in contemporary radical critiques of mainstream liberal democracy; and it does, indeed, provide something of a bridge between traditional and some contemporary theorising about democracy.

This type of theory is much influenced by Rousseau and collectivism but also contains distinctively Anglo-American ingredients; indeed, its authors were English and American. We can perhaps refer to it as 'neo-Idealist' democratic theory since some of its most important exponents were influenced by the philosophical Idealism[23] of the German philosopher Hegel (1770–1831) through the medium of the English philosophical Idealists T. H. Green (1836–82), F. H. Bradley (1846–1924) and B. Bosanquet (1848–1923).

The best-known neo-Idealist democratic theorists are A. D. Lindsay and Ernest Barker (see especially Lindsay (1935, 1943), and Barker (1942)). The key feature of their theories of democracy is a variant of Rousseau's idea of the general will – called by Lindsay 'the spirit of the common life' – which emerges from the democratic processes of discussion (as already noted in the appendix to the previous chapter, there is in fact a significant difference, or development, here since Rousseau himself excludes a process of discussion (Manin, 1987)). Here we have elements of Continental theory – the general will – developed by Englishmen with typical Anglo-American democratic ideas: the process of discussion, after all, requires those (negative) liberties of the individual that are central in Anglo-American liberal democratic theory. Indeed, in this sort of synthesis we have the most convincing kind of liberal democratic theory. As we have already seen, in the emphasis on the generation of views about the common interest, through a process of discussion, the difficulties of liberal democratic theory which focuses only on individuals and their preferences are greatly diminished.

We also saw, in the appendix to Chapter 1, that there has recently been a revival of interest in conceptions of democracy that focus on the process of discussion, and similar and overlapping ideas. One of the inspirations for this has been the work of the very important social theorist, Jurgen Habermas and his theory of communicative action (see, especially, Habermas (1989); for a useful introduction to Habermas see Williams and Fearon-Jones (1992)). In this kind of approach there is a focus on the process of rational communication and the way which it integrates individuals. This has two overlapping and mutually reinforcing aspects of particular interest here. First, because of this process there is an interactive texture connecting individuals: they are not, therefore, separated, isolated entities in the way mainstream traditional Anglo-American democratic theory supposes. Second, the logic of the process centres on the generation of *common* views; and 'raw' preferences – the particularity and fixity of which prevent aggregation into a meaningful collective decision – are discounted.

Citizenship theory

The second variety of, or contribution to, liberal democratic theory which modifies mainstream liberal individualism is citizenship theory. Neo-Idealist democratic theory shares some central ideas with a stream of Anglo-American democratic theory which has been called 'citizenship theory' (Thompson, 1970), a category which includes the work of theorists such as G. D. H. Cole and John Dewey.[24] Like Lindsay and Barker these are twentieth-century thinkers. However, they are very different from the modern democratic theorists that are discussed in the next section; indeed, Thompson contrasts citizenship theory with modern elitist democratic theory. And in fact, to an extent the concerns of citizenship theorists overlap with those of traditional radical democratic theory, since they are concerned with an informed and motivated citizenry.

As portrayed by Thompson, such citizenship theory focuses on activities and standards proper for citizens – participation, discussion, rational voting and equality. More recently, however, there has been a concern with the very nature of the concept of citizenship, which refocuses attention on the fundamentals of citizenship theory.

What citizenship and neo-Idealist theory share is a sense of the importance of the relationship of the individual to the community and a rejection or modification of the kind of individualism that can be seen as typical of Anglo-American liberal democratic theory. In fact, as we shall remark in a moment, this ties in with the increasingly discussed theme of the 'communitarian critique' of liberal individualism. (Indeed, as we shall see in the next chapter, neo-Idealist and citizenship theory constitute something of a bridge between Anglo-American liberal democratic theory and its radical critics for whom the communitarian critique is often central.) In the case of neo-Idealist theory the emphasis is on the processes – most importantly the process of discussion – involved in a focus on the common good and which link individuals into a genuine community. In the case of citizenship theory the emphasis is on the generation of the outlook and motivation individuals need for a successful linkage of this kind, and the role of the idea of citizenship in this. The key notion is in fact that liberal democracy requires something other than the interaction of individuals *per se* – that it requires individuals to *become* (to perform the role of) citizens. It is necessary, then, to understand what the role of 'citizen' is – to understand the idea of citizenship.

As already indicated this idea of citizenship has, in fact, lately received considerable attention. 'Politicians, in Britain at least, are currently searching with a certain air of desperation for a viable conception of what is called "active citizenship"' (Oldfield, 1990). In part this is because of a dimly perceived notion by some on the 'new right', that in their thinking about democracy there is a need for something of an antidote to their thoroughgoing individualism. But this interest is not confined to the right. 'All the major British parties have . . . been hard at work rediscovering citizenship' (Heater, 1990). There is in fact now a widespread concern with identifying the idea of citizenship as a necessary condition for developing and enhancing the practice of citizenship; so much so that in 1988 a Speaker's Commission on Citizenship was set up, which reported in 1990.

As the phrase 'rediscovering citizenship' implies, a tradition of thought is being tapped. In fact the tradition originates in ancient Greece and is encapsulated in Aristotle's famous statement (Aristotle, 1981) that 'man is by nature a political animal' (see also p. 132 below). 'Citizenship was temporarily almost lost as a political concept' (Heater, 1990) following the collapse of the Roman Empire. However, it was revived in the medieval city-states of northern and central Italy, most famously in Florence. Indeed, Machiavelli (1469–1527) is a key figure in the origination of 'civic republicanism' or 'civic humanism' which is important in transmitting citizenship theory to the modern world (Oldfield, 1990; Pocock, 1975). Rousseau and Hegel are other crucial theorists. Tocqueville also is important. In *Democracy in America* (Toqueville, 1968), first published in 1835 and 1840 he suggests civic republicanism is of key significance in the American political tradition. This perhaps remains true, despite the fact that it has subsequently been obscured by the predominance of liberal individualism (Oldfield, 1990). Modern citizenship theory also draws inspiration from the work of Arendt (1959), Wolin (1960) and Oakeshott (1975).

There are differences between the various forms of theory, but they 'share the interpretation that classical political thought created a qualitative difference between life as lived in the political realm and life as lived in the nonpolitical realm, and that citizenship, the name for public life, remains a valuable ideal in the modern age' (Schwartz, 1988). And, as we have already indicated, the significance of this for a theory of liberal democracy lies in the way it overcomes key defects in mainstream liberal individualism. In doing so it gives an analysis of the relationship between the citizen and the community which is more fruitful than liberal individualism's troubled account of the relationship between the individual and the people. And this not only throws light on the notion of a collective decision but also provides an account of what is necessary to maintain the existence of a liberal democratic polity.

Let us now turn, then, to the central question of what is meant by 'citizenship'. It is a complex notion; and it is this complexity that, in part at least, accounts for the uncertainty that dogs the current interest in the concept. Everyone seems to be interested in it, but few appear to have a clear idea about what it is; the Report of the Speaker's Commission, for example, comments on the difficulties resulting from the absence of a definition of the concept of citizenship. Moreover, insofar as ideas are specified they quite often conflict in important respects. Nonetheless, there is a solid core to the concept in the idea – already indicated in the statement by Shwartz just quoted – that 'one of the forms of collective life is the political community' (Oldfield, 1990). This is a form of life appropriate to, and constitutive of, the realm of politics and it is the form of life proper for all of the people in a political system.[25] We are apt to think of forms of life, in this sense, in the context of particular institutions or settings – the 'monastic form of life', say, or 'college life' or 'business life'. But in the idea of citizenship it is the *general* setting of the political system or the state that is involved.

Many liberal democrats have trouble at this point; and this is symptomatic of the contrasts between the liberal individualist and the civic republican traditions. The difficulty for such liberal democrats is that they view this general setting as one within which persons interact purely as unmodified individuals, each pursuing their own particular interests (a change of focus from individuals, to groups pursuing their own particular interests, makes no essential difference). By contrast, from the civic republican perspective this view fails to see that the setting provides a form of life and activity in which persons are engaged as practitioners – rather as, say, cricket provides a set of structures for the special activity of those who are engaged in playing it. Indeed it is just such a 'blindness' that can be seen as a failing of standard liberal democratic theory and which has been a factor in the revival of the idea of citizenship.

In fact the very notion of a 'setting' is itself misleading – and involves a liberal individualist perspective. A crucial aspect of the form of life in question is that it is communal: being a member of a community is central to engaging in this form of life. The community is not just the setting within which the activity takes place; rather the activity *constitutes*, but is itself also *constituted by*, the community. As already remarked, the communitarian critique of liberal individualism is currently a focus of discussion, and, as Oldfield (1990) points out, the recent revival of interest in the idea of community has been one of the reasons for the current concern with the idea of citizenship.[26] The civic republican tradition can, in fact, be seen as a link between the general communitarian and the individualist traditions of political thought.

The 'setting', then, is the political community – the community that is coterminous with the state. Imprecise statement is necessary here to avoid begging questions that arise about the nature of the state, not the least of which precisely concern the extent to which the state *does* take the form of a community rather than simply being an organisation, a framework of rules. Be that as it may, a key notion in citizenship ideas is that membership of the state involves being a member of a community.

This is a special sort of community. To an extent it is special because it is associated with, and partially defined by, the state. That is to say, distinctive features of the state constitute distinctive features of this community. Thus it is all-embracing. This does not mean, necessarily, that the whole life of individuals is communal. That is another issue; and although the Aristotelian tradition stresses the priority of communal life, in modern liberal thought – that which recognises citizenship and community at all – communal life is held at arm's length from the separate and all-important private life of individuals. What it does mean, though, is that where there are limits on communal life these are not set by reference to types of activity: the community is not functionally delimited. Unlike communities which are delineated by a defining activity – an amateur dramatic society, say – the political or state community has no such boundaries: the communal parts of individuals lives are not limited by virtue of the nature of the community to any particular aspects of life.[27] This is, indeed, one of the reasons for a tension between citizenship theory and mainstream liberal individualism. Liberal individualists do see a conceptually clear boundary to the public realm: the moral importance of this boundary is tied in with its conceptual clarity.

The state community is also usually seen as special in respect of the manner in which people come to be its members. The key factor is that, typically, one is simply born into a state – and hence the associated community – so that membership is to a crucial extent non-voluntary and automatic. Apart from the point considered in the next paragraph, the statement is made in this qualified way to take account of the fact that some people (naturalised citizens) *do* straightforwardly choose to become members of a state community; and that within liberal theory there is an ongoing issue concerning the extent to which membership of a state should properly be seen as a matter of individual consent.[28]

Nonetheless, there is a clear and significant difference between the ways in which people come to be members of the state community and members of other, 'private', communities. And this difference is typically, and understandably, summed up as the contrast between membership which is automatic and non-voluntary, and that which is chosen and voluntary.

There is, however, another feature of the civic republican view of the state community that to some extent contrasts with this. And here there is an emphasis upon the difference between the concepts of the state and of the community with which it is associated. This point is brought out, for example, by Oldfield who highlights the contrast between demographically defined communities and a political community. The latter is to an important extent a matter of *will* and *choice*:

> In a political community what is shared is identity, born in part from self-determination, and in part from a common history or language, or continued occupancy of the same territory Political solidarity and cohesion result from the equality of a shared identity, which is at least in part self-determined and chosen. In other words, political solidarity and cohesion do not follow from the sharing of a history or a language, and so on. Political identity involves [a commitment that is] self-consciously recognised, acknowledged and taken on. It is this choosing of a political identity that gives rise to the solidarity and cohesion of a political community. (Oldfield, 1990)

People are born into a state: this is not – subject to the qualifications in the previous paragraph – a matter of choice. But a state or political community exists (only) where, or to the extent that, people choose to relate to the situation in which they find themselves in a certain way and engage themselves in the kind of commitment Oldfield describes. There are three respects in which this understanding of a political community incorporates central ideas of liberal democratic theory.

First, the existence of the community is bound up with choice. This is in part individual: the individual 'choosing . . . political identity' and commiting himself to the community. But it is also a matter of collective choice – the collective formulation of an entity *as* a political community. Oldfield comments on the importance of collective acts of will, such as revolutions, in establishing political communities; and we can see many – perhaps too many – contemporary examples of these collective acts of will, such as in the splitting of Yugoslavia into separate political communities. This emphasis on choice involves an emphasis on autonomy and liberty. We have, in fact, already noted an important linkage between ideas of citizenship and liberty (Chapter 1). But a key point is highlighted for us again here by Oldfield when he talks of 'the spirit of autonomous beings making judgements in concord. It is this which constitutes citizenship' (Oldfield, 1990).

The second point is that we are talking about a community of equals ('the equality of a shared identity'), so there is also an important connection between the ideas of citizenship and equality (the connection between equality and citizenship is stressed in Marshall's (1973) classic discussion of citizenship and social class). Citizenship necessarily comes in equal shares (see also note 25). A key part of the very concept of 'a citizen' is that even if individuals are not equal in other capacities, *as citizens* they are.

The third point is that an aspect of the community being willed or chosen is that the ties between its members, between citizens, are akin to those of friendship. Oldfield points to the salience of Aristotle's discussion of friendship or 'concord' (and we have already noted the 'making [of] judgements in concord'). Friends are *chosen*; and relationships that are akin to friendship are to be contrasted with bonds that are provided simply by being *subject to*, or moulded by the same set of conditions – the same culture, the same historical experience and so on. In a different idiom, this is to stress the third in the democratic triumvirate of values, after liberty and equality: 'fraternity'.

We can see, then, that citizenship theory can be regarded as a variety – or component – of liberal democratic theory. But we have also seen that it is something of a bridge between mainstream liberal individualism and the opposing communitarian tradition of thought; and as such it is able to overcome some of the most damaging communitarian criticisms of mainstream forms of liberal democratic theory.

This bridging character of citizenship theory accounts for a significant ambivalence in the concept of citizenship between a more individualist and a more communitarian understanding. On the one hand citizenship is a role relating to individuals: it is individuals who are – who play the role of – citizens. Moreover, the role is one that stresses the importance (the equal importance) of the individual actors. Accordingly there is a stress on safeguarding the position of these individuals, which ties in with the liberal democratic value of protecting individuals from government. On the other hand, as we have seen, the concept is one that relates to, and stresses the importance of, a conception of community: the political community. And the role of citizen is one that links the individual to the community. Now, to the extent that the individual is the focus of attention there is a tendency to see citizenship in terms of the rights and privileges of individuals: the rights and privileges that citizens have against (or in relation to) the state. This is the dominant tendency, for example, in the current British concern with citizenship: the notion of a 'citizens charter' is primarily one of a charter of rights for individuals. In contrast, the logic of the other aspect of the concept is to emphasise duties and responsibilities that individuals have to the political community: a citizen is one whose status is *defined as* someone who is a member of that community. But not simply a passive member so much as one whose membership consists in the contribution that person makes: a political community is precisely characterised in terms of the active engagement of its members.

This implication of duties and responsibilities as well as rights and privileges is not always properly recognised or understood. When it is half perceived there is a tendency for the understanding of citizenship to oscillate confusingly between the rights and duties 'poles'. But properly understood there is not opposition here so much as complementarity. Citizenship theory *does* bring together individualist and communitarian perspectives. And the idea of citizenship incorporates, and balances, both the rights and the duties of individuals who are associated together in a democratic polity.

Citizenship theory has further implications for, and contributions to make to, liberal democratic theory. Leading on from the bridging function just noted, citizenship theory is of importance in understanding, and helping to provide for, the integration of the individual into the community. This is desirable not only for constituting the right kind of community (and individual lives within it) but also for providing for its continued existence. There is always a need to sustain and maintain a political community. A major concern, in fact, of empirical democratic theory and analysis is with understanding the conditions necessary to sustain a democratic system. A principal focus of such analysis is the crucial role of political culture in maintaining democratic polities; and, as Oldfield points out, civic republicanism is significant in stressing the importance of, and in providing, a certain kind of political culture (Oldfield, 1990). The practice of citizenship thus not only helps constitute, but is also crucial in maintaining, the desirable form of political community, and citizenship theory is valuable in explaining and encouraging this.

More generally – and connected with both the preceding points – citizenship theory is important in directing attention away from individual and group self-interest and towards the common good. The point is that in the concept and experience of citizenship there is a central focus on the common good. This is not only desirable in itself; it also brings coherence and sense to ideas of individuals acting together as a people which must be central to any democratic theory and with which the liberal individualism of mainstream democratic theory has such difficulties.

To sum up, citizenship theory by centring on the idea of the citizen rather than that of the elementary individual – by focusing on the individual in his role as citizen rather than simply on the individual as such – provides for a much richer and arguably more coherent account of the process of liberal democracy. In short, citizenship theory, and the tradition of civic republicanism on which it is based, together with neo-Idealist theory and the focus on the process of deliberation, have an immense contribution to make to liberal democratic theory.

2.4
The academic challenge to traditional democratic theory

The topics just discussed in section 3 above show that there is a renewed interest in theorising about issues central to traditional democratic theory. And this kind of renewal can only be spurred on by the dramatic rise in interest in liberal democratic theory associated with the remarkable changes in the status of liberal democracy that are discussed in Chapter 4. In a sense this amounts to a re-engagement with traditional theories of liberal democracy. However, before this very recent development, traditional democratic theory had been brought under attack by an academic challenge in which the findings of the modern academic study of politics are used to demonstrate that traditional theory is outmoded and unrealistic. And, despite the recently changed situation, this academic challenge is still very much on the table. Any re-engagement with traditional theory must be conducted in the light of – and include a response to – this challenge; and we shall now turn to an assessment of it.

Traditional democratic theory was historically important, providing the theory that accompanied and inspired the development of democracy in the nineteenth century. But it also remains important today (even apart from the recent 're-engagement'), for it continues to provide for most people their account of what democracy is, and why it is desirable. For most citizens of Western democracies, traditional theory is the lens through which they see their systems *as* democracies; and so for them the traditional models of democracy remain fairly accurate as pictures of what those systems are like. However, important though it continues to be, traditional democratic theory has been subject to a strong academic challenge in modern times. Traditional ideas have been measured against contemporary reality and then found wanting: empirical studies of the workings of Western democratic systems have seemed to show traditional democratic theory to be hopelessly unrealistic.

What precisely is meant by 'unrealistic' here, and why it should be taken as a fault, are matters we can leave aside for the moment. It is sufficient at this point to say that in the mid-twentieth century it became very widely held in politically knowledgeable circles that traditional democratic theory was deficient because its models of democracy were seriously out of accord with reality. The nature and functioning of actual democracies were revealed as being crucially different from what was portrayed in the model.

To be more accurate, it was the discrepancy between reality and *radical* democratic theory's model that was focused upon. The critics, though, did not always realise this: those who criticised it for being unrealistic seldom specified clearly what they meant by 'traditional democratic theory'; indeed, they often seemed not to appreciate how different the various theories are that cluster under the 'traditional' label. In fact, as we have seen, there are even significant differences in the theories under the 'radical' label. These latter theories do, though, have even more significant features in common, centring on the positive role of the people. And it is clear that it is democratic theories with these features that were being primarily challenged. Moreover, since it is from radical theory that the public tend to obtain their picture of democracy, it is theories with these features that constitute the operational form of traditional democratic theory amongst the general public. *Conventional* traditional theory – which tends to be operative amongst political leaders – is in fact in certain key respects more like the modern theories which were supposed to replace traditional theory (see the section on modern democratic theory, p. 106).

But why did this widely accepted form of traditional democratic theory, radical theory, come to be seen as unrealistic? In summary, it was due to a changing perception in informed circles of the reality of the political systems, known as 'Western democracies', to which the theory was applied, so that the theory could no longer be regarded as being in accord with the reality. This changing perception resulted essentially from insights brought by developments in the academic study of politics, although it is hard to separate these from developments in the reality being studied. At all events, it was such things as the growth in the scale, scope and complexity of governmental activity, and an increased awareness of the nature of pressure groups, elites and the facts of voting behaviour, that led to the dismissal of radical democratic theory as unrealistic.

The argument from scale and complexity focuses on matters such as the sheer size of modern states, the development of science and technology, the complexity of modern economies and the involvement of governments in attempts to regulate them, and the modern responsibility of the state for social welfare. The quantity and difficulty of governmental decision making to which all this gives rise is said to make impossible the kind of detailed positive decision-making role for the people at large that is envisaged in radical democratic theory. This is a matter both of the organisational complexity of decision making by large numbers of people and of those people's inevitable lack of expertise and comprehension.

This type of argument overlaps with those based on studies of elites and of voting behaviour where, in effect, empirical evidence is said to confirm that there is no positive rule by the people. Some of the findings of twentieth-century sociology and political science have provided us with an account of the political systems of Western 'democracies'[29] in which they are shown in fact to be run by elites, with the mass of the electorate being ignorant and apathetic. This is clearly in stark contrast to radical democratic theory's model of a system which is run by an involved and politically rational citizenry.

To begin with, then, there was the study of elites, and a growing awareness of their existence and importance. Elites have come to be widely seen as playing a crucial role in all political systems. This includes the Western 'democracies', although whether, or to what extent, this amounts to elite control of the kind found in other political systems is something we shall take up shortly. Clearly, though, it amounts to something drastically at odds with the system of popular control portrayed in radical democratic theory.

But what are these elites that are said to be so important?[30] The meaning of the term 'elite' is hard to pin down, but roughly speaking we can say it means a minority group that is distinguished from the mass of the people by factors which give its members important advantages. Our concern here is with political or power elites where the particular advantage in question is the possession of, and/or an especial ability to obtain, political power. That is to say, a political or power elite is one that holds, and/or is especially likely to hold, political power – perhaps because it *is* an elite. There is a long tradition of thought which regards political elites as being of crucial importance.[31] In a sense Plato was an elitist. But organisational elitism – where elite power is seen as being required by the organisational needs of complex society – is relatively modern. It achieved its best-known expression in the works of the 'classic elitists' Pareto (1848–1923), Mosca (1858–1941), and Michels (1876–1936). Michels – with his famous iron law of oligarchy – is sometimes referred to as Mosca's disciple, but he was also profoundly influenced by the work of the sociologist Max Weber (1864–1920).[32] Today, many political scientists see the existence of political elites as inevitable. But, since rule by an elite is the very opposite of positive rule by the people, this means that the non-existence of radical democracy is also seen as inevitable.

The elitist critique of radical democratic theory was linked with, and further reinforced by, judgements about the nature of the mass electorate. These arose from studies of voting behaviour, which seemed to deny the capacity of the mass of the people for positive rule. Modern empirical studies of voting behaviour have been of various kinds, but the most relevant here are those using questionnaires and the sample survey method to obtain direct – and sometimes very detailed – information about why people vote as they do. The pioneering studies of the 1940s and 1950s (mainly, but not only, in Britain and the United States) apparently demonstrated that electors are largely ignorant of, and uninterested in, the issues and policies before them at elections; and, more generally, that they participate but little in politics.[33]

The evidence was, broadly speaking, of two main kinds. On the one hand voting behaviour was correlated with social and demographic characteristics. The conclusion frequently drawn was that voting was more or less 'socially determined': a person's voting behaviour was seen as a reaction to social and demographic position rather than as a response to issues and policies. As one of the earliest studies put it: 'a man thinks, politically, as he is, socially. Social characteristics determine political preference' (Lazarsfeld et al., 1968). Other studies drew back from quite such forthright conclusions but still implied a large measure of 'social determinism'. Social class (Britain and the United States), ethnic group, religion and urban or rural location (United States) were seen as the main determinants. On the other hand there was direct evidence of what this social determinism implied – that voting was not the product of political knowledge and interest. Voters, in fact, seemed to lack knowledge and interest: answers to survey questions revealed a massive ignorance of the issues and policy proposals facing them at elections. Many American voters knew 'the existence of few, if any, of the major issues of policy' (Campbell *et al.*, 1960) whilst of the British electorate it was said they are 'uninformed . . . The number who are well informed is probably no more than one-tenth of the whole electorate on the great majority of issues.' And 'the electorate is not only uninformed it is uninterested' (Abrams and Rose, 1960). The ignorance and apathy of the electorate was summed up in a leading study in these words: 'there seems to be widespread ignorance and indifference over many matters of policy. And even when opinions are held, many persons are not motivated to discover or are unable to sort out the relevant positions adopted by the parties' (Campbell *et al.*, 1960).

According to the conception of rational political behaviour indicated earlier, this evidence shows the electorate – the mass of the people – to be irrational. As such the people cannot be seen as capable of running the country, of holding positive power. This clearly supports the idea that elites must rule. Thus, to return to the basic issue, studies of elites and of voting behaviour clearly seem to demonstrate that in reality the Western 'democracies' are not at all like the democracies portrayed in radical democratic theory. In a word, radical democratic theory is shown as unrealistic.

The focus in modern political studies on the role and importance of pressure groups also contributed to the view that radical democratic theory was unrealistic. Pressure groups are bodies that seek to influence public policy by attempting to influence government: trades unions, business groups, farmers groups, campaign groups and the like (unlike political parties they do not seek to become, or become part of, the government).[34] Pressure groups have always been important, but they became more so with the increasing complexity of the economy, and growing government involvement with it. At all events, by the mid-twentieth century the study of their role in the political system had become a major concern of political scientists.

The implications of pressure groups for radical democratic theory are not, perhaps, so clear cut as in the case of elites and voting behaviour. This is partly a matter of some ambivalence in radical democratic theory: certain of the problems and differences in radical theories of democracy that we looked at earlier are central here. (In a sense this ambivalence is reflected in the fact that, as we shall see, pressure group operations are actually the inspiration of some modern theories of democracy.) Nonetheless, a clear critique emerges of a model containing only certain features of radical theories of democracy, but which is quite often taken as an exemplification of traditional democratic theory. Such a model is one in which the people have a single, definite and unproblematic will. This all-important will of the people is embodied in the electorate's unified decision on what they see – and want implemented – as being in the general interest (the clear influence of Rousseau can be seen in this widely accepted model).

The critique maintains that a political system in which pressure groups are important is crucially different from this model of democracy. There are two key points. First, pressure groups, in seeking to promote the particular interests of their members are thereby acting against the general interest as conceived in the model. (This point really relates only to those pressure groups which are interest groups, as distinct from those which promote a cause; but it is interest groups which tend to be the more influential.) Since, in the model, the government has been elected to implement the people's decision about what is in the general interest, to the extent that a pressure group successfully influences the government it is frustrating what the model sees as the will of the people. Second, pressure groups divert their members' attention away from the general interest and on to their particular group interests. To that extent, then, members ignore what the model conceives as the general interest and fail to express their view about it. In short, on this analysis, pressure groups frustrate the generation and/or the implementation of a 'will of the people'. And since, or to the extent that, studies show that pressure groups actually are key factors in the political process, government by the 'popular will' is shown not to exist. Again, the – or a – radical model of democracy is shown to be unrealistic.

Assessment of the academic challenge

The academic challenge to radical democratic theory has been powerful and fundamental. And this amounts to an undermining of traditional liberal democratic theory, since, as we saw, radical theory is its operative form. But there are, in any case, certain features of conventional theory that are also challenged by modern studies of politics, most particularly the stress on the importance in the political process of groups – elites as well as pressure groups – rather than individuals.

What are we to make of this challenge to traditional democratic theory? In answering this question we must consider both responses that reject, and those that accept, the validity of the challenge. We shall leave the second type till the next section and turn now to the first.

In fact there are two types of response that reject the challenge to traditional theory, although they do overlap to some extent. On the one hand there is the argument that, properly understood, the findings of modern political science do not actually constitute a challenge to traditional democratic theory. On the other hand there are denials of the validity of some of the findings themselves.

The denial that there is in fact a challenge hinges on a central contention. This is that democratic theory generally, and traditional democratic theory in particular, is primarily *pre*scriptive rather than *de*scriptive: its purpose is to prescribe what ought to be rather than to describe what is. As Duncan and Lukes (1963) argued in an influential article, those who criticise traditional democratic theory as being unrealistic miss the point that such theory does not purport accurately to picture, describe or explain political reality. On the contrary, it is meant to be critical and to picture what does not, but what ought to, exist; in short, to hold up an ideal. If the reality is not like the theory it is the reality rather than the theory that is at fault.

There is a good deal in this kind of argument. But there is an important rejoinder to be considered: it might be granted that a democratic theory is prescriptive but that it may nonetheless fail if it is greatly at odds with reality – even as prescriptive theory. Even Duncan and Lukes acknowledge that 'if such a theory seems intolerably remote from reality, it may be charged with utopianism' (Duncan and Lukes, 1963). And 'while idealised conceptions of our system may inspire both higher aspirations and performance in the real world, it is also true that too great a gap between democratic ideals and reality may inspire fanciful expectations whose frustration breeds cynicism' (Presthus, 1964).

Another, important and overlapping, type of argument centres more on the nature than the extent of the gap between ideal and reality. The principal contention here is that not only is there a gap but it is bound to remain, that is, the key factor is its permanence rather than its extent. It is not the difficulty of greatly changing reality that is focused upon, so much as the impossibility of changing it at all in the relevant respects: the nature of voting behaviour, for instance, is seen as a manifestation of the permanent nature of man.

These arguments raise issues that are also central to the discussion of the radical critique of liberal democracy in the next chapter, so we shall not try and assess them here. But before we move on we should notice that there is an issue of another kind that can be involved in considering whether the findings of political science constitute a challenge to traditional democratic theory. So far, we have focused on denying the existence of radical democracy. But its desirability can also be questioned. This arises mainly from considering the implications of the voting behaviour studies: in essence the question is whether a system is desirable where power is in the hands of irrational people.[35] Again, we shall leave this on one side for the moment since it becomes part of an issue discussed in Chapter 4: in effect demonstrations of the irrationality of voters can be taken as supporting traditional arguments against democracy which stress the need for rule by the wise few rather than by the irrational mass of the people. We should simply note here that any 'challenge' to traditional democratic theory that is involved in this form of argument consists in the contention that such theory is discredited for advocating that which is undesirable rather than for concerning itself with that which does not exist. (It might be held that it is not just traditional but *all* democratic theory that is challenged in this way. However, it is again radical democratic theory that is most vulnerable since it gives the largest role to the 'irrational' people; indeed, conventional and modern elitist democratic theory modify the role of the people specifically to cope with doubts about their rationality.)

The second way of attempting to refute the challenge to traditional democratic theory is to dispute the validity of the findings of modern political science on which it is allegedly based. Once more the issues raised are ones which become part of those discussed in the next chapter. Nonetheless, some questions relating to the voting behaviour studies are fairly 'self-contained' and should be mentioned here.

The point is that the validity of the findings about the electorate's ignorance and apathy can be questioned. This is partly a matter of looking critically at the pioneering studies, their findings and the interpretations put upon them. The essential argument here is that a re-examination of those studies shows that the picture they give of the electorate is not in fact quite so dismal as at first appeared. The voters are shown to have some interest and some political knowledge and not to be completely socially determined.[36] But this kind of argument overlaps into another, and rather more important one, to the effect that more recent studies of voting behaviour have given us a significantly different picture of the electorate.

In one of the seminal works it was asserted that 'the perverse and unorthodox argument of this little book is that voters are not fools' (Key, 1966). Indeed, Key discerned 'an electorate moved by concern about central and relevant questions of public policy, of governmental performance and executive personality' (Maas, 1966). Which view of the electorate is right – that of Key or the earlier voting studies – has continued to be a subject of controversy, but the weight of argument tends to favour Key. The critical factor in pro-Key analyses has been study of the electorate in periods other than the 1940s and 1950s when the original studies took place. Key himself included data from the 1930s and subsequent studies have focused, obviously enough, on the 1960s, 1970s and 1980s. Many points have arisen, both substantive and methodological; but the main one has been that the electorate's behaviour does vary over time. It is pointed out that the 1950s was a politically quiescent time, so it was quite natural for there to have been a low level of concern with politics. It is contended that the pioneering studies mistakenly extrapolated from findings concerning this atypical period to universal generalisations about 'the nature of the electorate'. The periods before and after the 1950s – especially the 1930s and 1960s – were less bland; political events made more impact on voters and they became more concerned and knowledgeable about politics.

Which *is* the typical period and what is the typical or natural form of behaviour (or whether, indeed, there is any such thing as typical or natural behaviour here) are questions that raise fundamental issues, some of which are touched on later. All we shall do here is refer to some of the more recent voting studies and then come back to the significance of all this for traditional democratic theory.

More recent studies have emphasised, on the one hand, a decline in the importance of social position and stable party identification as determinants[37] of, or influences on, voting behaviour, and, on the other hand, the growing impact of political issues. 'The rise of issue voting' (Nie *et al.*, 1976) in fact became a growing preoccupation of students of voting behaviour. Pomper (1975) concentrated on the *responsive* voter in America – the one who responds to issues. And a similar view of the British voter has been growing. The authors of one study in the 1980s, for example, said:

> The portrait that emerges from our study of the voter today is of someone who is not simply conforming to his or her own past or following other people's examples, but makes up his own mind. While little interested in politics and fairly unsophisticated in his or her political thinking, the voter is nevertheless quite aware of the parties' major policy proposals and has views about the parties' ability or willingness to implement them; he also has fairly definite views on a variety of political issues, particularly those that have a bearing on his or her own life. (Himmelweit *et al.*, 1981)

Some studies, on the other hand, have been more cautious, emphasising the *diversity* of influences on voting behaviour (Rose and

McAllister, 1986); some, indeed, maintain that there has been no increase in issue voting (Heath *et al.*, 1991). Others, again, though, continue to confirm a decline in stable party identification in Britain and that voters judge parties and governments increasingly by results (Crewe, 1991). And in an early 1980s book on British and American voting behaviour which 'attempted to show students where the balance of scholarly opinion' then lay, the author roundly proclaims 'a value-judgement which I believe the evidence justifies: that voters are not stupid. In this I share the views of V. O. Key' (McLean, 1982). This assessment – of at least American voters – has recently been backed up by a book on 'the reasoning voter' which asserts that:

> voters actually do reason about parties, candidates and issues. They think about what political parties stand for . . . they think about what government can and should do. And the performance of government, parties and candidates affects their assessment and preferences. (Popkin, 1991)

What are the implications of these newer studies' findings? They certainly modify the challenge to traditional democratic theory that we have looked at; but whether they go far enough to reinstate the theory is another matter. The point is that although the electorate is portrayed as more rational than it was by the earlier studies, the degree of rationality still falls far short of that assumed by radical democratic theory: there is no indication of the high level of political interest and the degree of detailed knowledge that radical theory assumes citizens to have.[38] The gap between theory and reality remains, albeit reduced in extent. The differing interpretations of the significance of such a gap have already been indicated and we cannot assess them all here. But it is right that we should look at one of them now. This is the viewpoint – roughly speaking that of modern political science – according to which no such gap should exist: a viable theory of democracy must be realistic. From this viewpoint traditional democratic theory remains deficient. Does this mean, though, that democratic theory as such is deficient? Can alternative theories be formulated that are viable? The answer, according to some, is yes. Such alternatives are 'modern' theories of democracy, and it is to a brief consideration of these that we now turn.

Modern democratic theory

Modern theories of democracy are a mid-twentieth-century creation. They were developed by modern analysts to fit the realities of the political systems of modern democracies.[39] By replacing what they saw as the discredited traditional theory they could rescue democratic theory.

There are, broadly speaking, two main varieties of modern democratic theory, although there is a significant overlap. The differences are quite important but, apart from any overlap in content, they share two common features. First, there is a full acknowledgement of those facts, about modern systems that are called democratic, systems that were seen as undermining traditional theory. Indeed, it is these very facts that form, as it were, the bases of the modern theories. This leads to the second common feature: an identity of purpose. The aim in both types of theory is to show that the very things which, from a traditional perspective, were seen as undermining democracy are more properly to be seen as *elements of* democracy. This means explaining how a system characterised by such phenomena is nonetheless still a democracy. It also involves – though this is not always recognised – showing that the phenomena themselves are desirable rather than regrettable.

Space forbids more than a very brief sketch of these modern theories of democracy (a fuller picture can be gained by following up the references). The two main varieties are 'elitist' and 'pluralist' democratic theory.[40] Essentially, the former considers the issues posed by scale and complexity, elites and the studies of voting behaviour, whilst the latter has pressure groups as a main focus.

Elitist democratic theory

In elitist democratic theories the implications of the work of Michels and Weber on the role of party leaderships (viewed as anti-democratic from the perspective of traditional democratic theory) is seen as 'pro-democratic'. Party leaderships are elites, but the presence and role of elites is accepted – indeed welcomed. At the same time, their presence is *reconciled* with the existence of democracy. In such theories' model of democracy,[41] the system is run by elites, thus coping with the scale and complexity problems. But, so the argument runs, the system is nonetheless democratic for three main reasons. First, the elites are 'open': people may rise readily from the masses to become members. Second, elites alternate in power. Systems in which but one elite remains permanently in power are quite clearly *not* democracies. But these are quite different from systems in which there is a plurality of political elites, with elites moving in and out of power. Third, the moving in and out involves a competition for power; moreover – and crucially – the competition is for the people's votes. The system is a democracy because the electorate decides which elite is to hold power: 'the result of the competition between [elites] is democracy. And this is because the power of deciding between the competitors is in the hands of the *demos* – the onlooker who benefits from a quarrel between other people' (Sartori, 1965).

This central idea was summed up in the well-known definition of democracy given by an influential exponent of elitist democratic theory, Joseph Schumpeter: 'the democratic method is that institutional arrangement for arriving at political decisions in which individuals acquire the power to decide by means of a competitive struggle for the people's vote' (Schumpeter, 1976).[42] And, it should be added, through the electoral process, the people can remove elites from, as well as appoint them to, power. In this way the ultimate power is in the hands of the people. Indeed, the people make, and are entitled to make, the ultimate decisions; hence the system is a democracy (but note the point about ambivalence in the next paragraph).

We shall not attempt any assessment of elitist democratic theory here since this is effectively subsumed under the discussion of participatory theory – itself a critique of elitist democratic theory – in the next chapter. But there are two points which should be noted now.

First, in order for the claim that it really *is* a theory of democracy to be substantiated, it must be envisaged that the people in appointing and removing elites will also be making the basic policy decisions. There is in fact some ambivalence in elitist democratic theory here, not least because the theory goes further than merely recognising the existence of elites and actually welcomes them for their superior decision-making capacity. For Schumpeter the voters should not make policy decisions at elections; rather, they should appoint elites to make these decisions for them: 'we reverse the roles of these two elements [as they occur in radical democratic theory] and make the deciding of issues by the electorate secondary to the election of the men who are to do the deciding' (Schumpeter, 1976); see also Miller (1983). But this is an extreme view. Indeed, even Max Weber (from whom much of the substance of Schumpeter's view was derived), besides contending that 'henceforth the people no longer chose between political issues and programmes but merely between political leaders', also held that those leaders 'have the task of convincing the masses of the righteousness of their cause' (Mommsen, 1974). And, in fact, most elitist democratic theorists impute at least a minimal policy-deciding role to the electorate, so that they are seen in broad terms as making the most basic or fundamental policy decisions. In short, the voters decide not only who shall have power but also, very broadly speaking, what they shall do with that power.

Moreover, the electorate affect, and ultimately control, the policy of the ruling elite by their power of removal as well as by their power of appointment. The elite in power must always think of the next election, and adjust their policy decisions accordingly, if they wish to remain in power: they are 'guided by "the rule of anticipated reactions", that is, by the expectation of how the voters will react at the next elections' (Sartori, 1965).

This brings us to the second point, which is that elitist democratic theory can quite properly be seen as fully realistic. Obviously it recognises the existence of elites but it is also in accord with studies of voting behaviour. As we saw just now, the more recent studies suggest that although they do not exhibit the kind of rationality required by radical theory, voters do in fact make just the kinds of broad and diffuse policy decisions – 'reactions' as well as forward-looking decisions – assumed in elitist democratic theory.

Pluralist democratic theory
Pluralist, like elitist, democratic theory transposes something which was held to undermine (radical) democracy into a *feature of* democracy. In pluralist theory this 'something' is the role of pressure groups as revealed by modern political science. Pluralist democratic theory is in fact, to a considerable extent, a democratic theory of pressure groups. It does, though, also tap and adapt a longer tradition of theory, a tradition which focuses on division and diversity within (the preferred kind of) society, the dispersal of power this involves and the contribution it makes to limiting the potentially dangerous power of a centralised state.

Pluralist theories of democracy are those in which the activities of groups are seen as operations on behalf of, and in some sense by, the people – so that the power of the people is manifested in the power of groups. Stated as simply as possible, the model typical of pluralist democratic theories can be outlined as follows. Elections, although important, do not properly express decisions by the people. The issues to be decided, and the various stands upon those issues, are too diffuse; above all there is a lack of correspondence between the multiplicity of electors' opinions and interests and the options available to vote on. This adds up to saying that no meaningful policy decision by the people is expressed at an election. Rather, the decisions of the people are expressed through the operations of pressure groups. This is because the groups effectively articulate the specific demands of their members and, in the model, all citizens are at least potentially members of pressure groups, or are catered for by them. Hence the actual views and interests of the electorate are precisely transmitted through the operations of pressure groups, and the outcome of the process is seen as a decision by all the people which has definite content.

In short, in this model the existence and operation of powerful pressure groups, far from undermining the liberal democratic process, actually constitute it. There are fundamental problems in this account which we cannot properly consider here (see Ricci (1971) for a useful discussion of the various criticisms of pluralist democratic theory). But there are some points we should note.

First, a crucial weakness in pluralist democratic theory lies in its account of a general collective decision in terms of the pursuit of separate particular interests. The problems here parallel those of utilitarian democratic theory, although now the particular interests in question are those of groups rather than of individuals. An associated point is that pluralist democratic theory gets into some difficulties about the role of government and the state. The key point is that the theory seems to lead to the odd and troublesome conclusion that where actions by the government are generated independently of, and are perhaps opposed by, pressure groups, such actions are somehow illegitimate and undemocratic. This is odd and troublesome because it is normally held that the government has the distinctive and important function of promoting the public's interest in contradistinction to the demands of particular interests. A final feature to note about the pluralist model is its congruence with the notion of *liberal* democracy. Power is 'pluralised' – dispersed, or divided up, amongst many groups – and this ensures that there is not too much left in the hands of the government: liberty is thereby protected. This brings us to the final point. Critiques of pluralist democratic theory in particular often merge into critiques of liberal democratic theory in general, which we consider in the next chapter.

The typical or basic model of pluralist democratic theory is, in fact, something of an ideal type and there are important variations of it. One of these involves a greater emphasis on the electoral process and is really a combination of elements of both elitist and pluralist theory. Indeed, one of the best-known and most sophisticated of modern democratic theorists, Robert Dahl,[43] has been called a 'pluralist–elitist' democratic theorist. Theories of this hybrid type have two key features. First, the focus is not just on pressure groups, but on groups as such – and the way in which society is naturally divided into, and is split among, them. Elites are seen as types of group, or as leading elements within groups. Elite competition tends to be assimilated to the pluralist scheme: elites are conceived as competing groups and power is accordingly viewed as being pluralised among them. But, second, this elite power process is also, to an extent, distinguished from – and modified by – the general group process. Elites win power through elections, but their exercise of such power is subject to, and modified by, the operations of pressure groups.

Consociational democracy

Another variation on the basic model is provided by the idea and theory of consociational democracy (Lijphart, 1968, 1969).[44] Here the general model of pluralist democratic theory is largely retained since the key feature remains the 'pluralisation' of power among various sections of society. But there are two main differences from the basic model.

First, the 'groups' concerned are not merely pressure groups; indeed they are not really 'groups' at all, but something more fundamental – segments of society. In fact a distinguishing feature of a consociational democracy is its existence[45] where society is deeply divided into various segments. These divisions are reflected in the political process in various ways, including the structure of the party system; and pressure-group activity on behalf of social segments is but one of them. The segments result from 'substantial cleavages in social structure in addition to those arising from socio-economic differences, cleavages founded on broad ideological and religious foundations' (McRae, 1974, Introduction). Such foundations typically include linguistic and associated cultural differences.

Here we should note a key aspect of the difference between the segments in consociational democracy and the typical groups in the basic pluralist model. In the basic model an important feature is the somewhat fluid and transient nature of the groups, with particular individuals belonging to many, and perhaps contrasting, groups. And particular groups have a variety of members, perhaps from many walks of life, with the same individuals sometimes turning up as members of various different groups. In the consociational model, on the other hand, the segments of society tend to be all-embracing so far as individuals are concerned: there is little or no intermixture of personnel and segments are stable blocks with permanent membership. In short, the divisions of society are deep, permanent and significant. (There are, of course, gradations between these two ideal types, and many of the groups in systems to which pluralist theory's basic model is applied have a nature rather more solid and significant than the model suggests.

Nonetheless the basic model's 'dilution' of group conflict, and the treatment of it as beneficial rather than threatening, remains an important feature of standard pluralist democratic theory.) This brings us to the second difference between consociational and standard pluralist democratic theory. In standard theory, group demands are not regarded as posing a problem. On the contrary, as we have seen, the interaction of groups is held to constitute a decision by the people, which is seen as some kind of aggregate or synthesis of group demands. In the consociational model, though, sectional demands, and how to reconcile them, are a, indeed *the*, key problem. Due to the fundamental nature of the sectional divisions and conflicts, demands cannot be simply aggregated or synthesised. In fact a very careful process of 'accommodation' is necessary. At times, indeed, it appears that consociational theory ceases to be about the nature of democratic decision making and becomes instead a theory about how such decision making remains possible in the face of grave difficulties. The nature of the decision making is then taken as given, democratic theory proper being assumed to provide the necessary analysis. This is a reflection of the fact that consociational theory is seen mainly as empirical theory concerned with explaining the functioning of actual political systems rather than as conceptual theory concerned with analysing the idea of a decision by the people. (The main empirical referents of the theory – the classic consociational democracies – are the political systems of The Netherlands, Belgium, Austria and Switzerland.)

Consociational theory does, nonetheless, at times also take on the role of democratic theory proper, providing an account of the nature of democratic decision making. Indeed, this is quite a sophisticated account, somewhat like Calhoun's theory of concurrent majorities mentioned in an earlier section of this chapter. In some ways it is rather better than the analyses found in standard pluralist theory and in discussions of majority decision making. In consociational democracy all important sectional demands have to be met. It follows that the only political decisions possible are those that go against no important demand and which will not therefore be vetoed by any section. In other words, while such decisions are not positively unanimous they do reflect a 'negative unanimity' or general consensus.

Decision making of this type raises its own difficulties, though. These are chiefly to do with the difficulty of getting sufficient positive decisions in the face of blocking vetoes, which means that a small minority can block a large majority's wish to change the status quo. But at least there is a clear sense in which any positive decisions are by *all* those involved.

And since, in consociational theory, the various sections together comprise the whole society, a decision by all the sections is a decision by the whole people.[46] In fact it is possible to argue that there is a significant sense in which policies or actions which fail to alienate any section of society are ones that really are in the general interest – as distinct from standard pluralist theory's typical and suspect notion that the general interest is some kind of positive aggregation of particular sectional interests. We have here, indeed, some approximation to Rousseau's notion of the general will, where the genuine will of all the people is for that which is in the general interest.

Corporatism and democratic theory

A further important variation of pluralist democratic theory is provided by corporatist theory. Whether 'variation' is the right description is debatable since corporatist analysis is often seen as an attack on, rather than as a variety of, pluralism; and corporatism is frequently viewed as undermining, rather than as being a form taken by, liberal democracy. And for this reason corporatist theory is better regarded as a part of the critique of liberal democracy we look at in the next chapter. Nonetheless, it should be mentioned here because it does have some clear affinities with pluralist analysis and when appropriately interpreted and developed it can be said to yield a corporatist theory of democracy (Cawson, 1983).

Corporatist theory is similar to pluralist theory in focusing on the extent to which power is 'pluralised' among various groups or sections. However, there are two important differences from standard pluralist theory.

First, power is not dispersed to the extent that it is in the pluralist model. And this is not just a matter of degree: there is a crucial intrinsic difference. A defining feature of 'corporatism'[47] is the extent to which interest groups – because their co-operation and collaboration is required by the modern interventionist state – become part of the centralised machinery of the state. The groups have a dual role of representing their members' interests and of being instruments of policy implementation – in a sense, arms of the state. They are then to a crucial extent, though not entirely, part of the power structure of the state. In standard pluralism, groups are autonomous organisations outside of the state – constituents of 'civil society'[48] – exerting pressure on it; in corporatism, groups are partially incorporated into the state and to that extent are no longer autonomous and dispersed centres of power.[49]

The second difference between corporatist and standard pluralist theory also concerns autonomy. In pluralist theory groups are conceived as voluntary associations, the object and reason for the formation of which is to promote objectives decided by individuals. Individuals form or join groups because they want certain objectives promoted, which may reflect an interest they discern themselves all to have. According to corporatist theory, groups are structured by external objective conditions – by the functions they perform in the economic and political system. Individuals find their situation in the economic and political system is structured in ways which *determine* their interests and actions. In pluralism a group 'takes its interest and derives its power from the individuals who comprise it. But for the functional group [of corporatist theory] the membership *takes its interest* from the function, and the power of the functional group in part derives from what are the objectives of state policy' (italics in original) (Cawson, 1983). This non-individualist basis of corporatism marks a crucial difference from standard pluralism. Indeed, it illustrates the way in which standard pluralism does fall within the basic individualism of traditional liberal democratic theory. The viability of such individualism, and its role in democratic theory, will be discussed in the next chapter.

Basic features of modern democratic theory

One final comment needs to be made before we leave modern democratic theory. We have seen that such theories are often said to be descriptive rather than prescriptive. However (and this is sometimes acknowledged by their proponents), modern theories are in fact prescriptive as well. Their models may seek to portray and to explain what actually exists, but those models are also pretty clearly recommended as the best type of political system. However, there is a further confusion which stems from the pre-occupation with descriptive analysis. This is a tendency to fall victim to the 'definitional fallacy' (see Chapter 1): because the theories' purpose, rather than being abstract analysis is conceived as explaining the workings of actual democracies, there is a tendency not to analyse the idea of democracy. Instead, it tends to be taken for granted that the systems being explained are democracies, without asking by what criteria they are counted as such. It follows from this that the theories tend to concern themselves with any salient aspects of the political systems concerned, without specifying whether they are characteristics of democracy. And this breeds considerable confusion regarding the nature of democracy, because it tells us little about it; rather as explanations, say, of the digestive systems of cats tell us little about the nature of cats.

We have looked at modern democratic theory in contradistinction to – as a replacement for – traditional liberal democratic theory. And yet there are crucial continuities and similarities. These are mainly to do with individualist assumptions. Despite the group orientation of modern theory, it is a group analysis which rests on an individualist foundation. We saw this just now when discussing the difference between corporatist and standard pluralist theory. The essential point is that the actions of groups are conceived and explained as the actions of individuals – that is, the members, or key members, of the groups. And it is straightforwardly the case that those members constitute (and in an important sense themselves decide to constitute) the groups, rather than the groups being aspects or products of pre-existing social structures. In the end, then, even in group-oriented modern democratic theory 'decisions by the people' are seen as decisions by individuals. When we put this basic individualism together with modern theories' reaffirmation of liberal ideas about the limitation of the state, and dispersal of power away from it, we have a clear continuation of liberal individualism. This continuity is arguably more important than the differences with traditional theory: modern theory is essentially a variety of liberal democratic theory. And it is to critiques of liberal democratic theory as a whole that we now turn – the main target of which is liberal individualism.

Notes

1. In fact there is considerable scope for confusion regarding Rousseau's meaning here; indeed, very different interpretations are possible. Thus it can be argued that Rousseau, far from being a direct democrat, is actually in favour of an 'elective aristocracy', very similar to conventional forms of representative democracy today, in which those in government actually make most of the decisions – although for Rousseau such decisions have to be ratified by the people. And it is true that Rousseau in his own words rejects democracy as undesirable and/or impossible of realisation (Rousseau (1968), Book Three, Chapter 4). However, this is in the context of his distinction between the government and the sovereign, which is always the people. When Rousseau rejects 'democracy' he means he does not believe in government, that is, *administration*, by the people (Rousseau (1968), Book Three, Chapters 2 and 3). This, however, is still compatible with his belief in *legislation*, that is, basic political decision making, directly by the people. This distinction – or, rather, the failure to attend to it – accounts for a good deal of the confusion and controversy over Rousseau's

meaning here. Unfortunately, it does not account for all of it since there is another aspect of Rousseau's theory which involves a tendency (a) to enlarge the role of government beyond mere administration and (b) to regard legislation by the people as ratifying rather than proposing decisions (although *that* ratification by the people is necessary is still a point of fundamental importance). Part of the point here is that, to an important extent, Rousseau's conception of the people is a juristic notion, as compared to Anglo-American theory's empirical notion. A key associated idea is that the legitimacy laws obtain from being ratified by the people is what is important, rather than the content of laws being actually decided by the people. Nonetheless, this is to push only one aspect of Rousseau's theory and it remains true that a widespread view is that Rousseau is a proponent of direct democracy. Part of the reason for this is the focus usually given to his best-known work, *The Social Contract*, in comparison to some of his other writings, where he departs from his stance in favour of direct democracy and against representation. In a very useful discussion, Fralin (1978, 1979) examines Rousseau's basic ambivalence regarding representation, and the changes in his ideas over time. See also Ryan (1983) and Miller (1985).

2. Birch (1972), in a lucid and concise analysis, argues the former, whilst Pitkin (1967) argues the latter. On representation see also Pennock and Chapman (1968) and Schwartz (1988) – a fascinating book which argues, among other things, that 'political representation is qualitatively superior to direct democracy'.

3. One of the issues to be discussed later is the extent to which traditional democratic theory is always liberal democratic theory. However, when the context makes the meaning clear the terms 'democracy', 'democratic theory', etc., will often be used instead of the longer-winded 'liberal democracy', 'liberal democratic theory', etc.

4. Rousseau is something of an exception here. But then, as we shall see, there is a question about whether Rousseau really is a traditional liberal democratic theorist.

5. In fact Locke does specifically recognise the *possibility* of democracy as a legitimate form of government. A good characterisation of the ambiguity of Locke's thought with regard to democracy is given by Seliger: 'Locke did not favour the permanent establishment of democracy. But its recognition as a legitimate and workable form of government enabled him to justify his advocacy of the right of revolt' (Seliger, 1968). For an argument to the effect that Locke's political theory is unambiguously democratic see Kendall (1941). See also Ashcraft (1987) who argues that Locke *does* focus on elections as a constitutional mechanism of popular power and that the masses *should* have the right to vote.

6. Whether or not J. S. Mill *should* be considered as a utilitarian is a controversial matter. At the very least, his is an importantly modified form of utilitarianism.

7. C. B. Macpherson sees J. S. Mill as important because he is a 'developmental theorist' (Macpherson, 1977a). For rather a different view of Mill see Pateman (1970).

8. The 'greatest happiness principle' is central in utilitarianism: that which is right is that which produces the greatest happiness of the greatest number. And (according to critics) this can imply that an individual should be used as a means to the end of producing general happiness (or, at least, diminishing general unhappiness) – as when, say, dangerous racial tension could be defused by the police charging any individual of the relevant colour (even though they know him to be innocent) in connection with the incident that gave rise to the tension. John Rawls is an important example of a theorist who criticises utilitarianism for subordinating justice for the individual to the general happiness (Rawls, 1972, for example Chapter 1, Section 5). On utilitarianism see further below.

9. Jefferson is, of course, the author of the American Declaration of Independence. On his democratic thought see, for example, Padover (1946) and Koch (1964). Price was well known in his own day as an English supporter of the American and French Revolutions. He praised the French Revolution in a celebrated sermon, *The Love of Our Country*, which provoked Edmund Burke into replying with the even more celebrated *Reflections on the Revolution in France* (Burke, 1968). On Price see, for example, Thomas (1959, 1992).

10. For an analysis and discussion of the concept of 'interests' see, for example, Barry (1965); Connolly (1972, 1983); Benditt, Oppenheim and Flathman (1975); and Oppenheim (1981).

11. Two points should be noted here: (a) notions of interests and of their representation also play a part in widely varying political theories which are not democratic; (b) such non-democratic theories focus typically on the interests of sections of society or groups, rather than on those of individuals (Birch, 1972, Pitkin, 1967). There are, though, also some varieties of democratic theory that focus on group interests: these are mainly modern theories (see Chapter 3), but some traditional theorists also have a similar focus – see the references to Madison and Calhoun below.

12. On utilitarianism, see for example Plamenatz (1958) and Smart and Williams (1973). On the utilitarian theory of democracy see Steintrager (1977), Lively and Rees (1978), Plamenatz (1973, Chapter 1), and Rosen (1983).

13. In fact the deployment of this idea leaves some room for a modification of the delegate view of representation: see Schwartz (1988, pp. 32–4).

14. J. S. Mill also has such doubts; but, as we have just seen, he is still confident that the general interest will be pursued by the *wise* representatives – that is, by the most enlightened representatives, who should hold the balance of power.

15. Although Bentham is ambivalent on this, within utilitarianism's thorough-going individualism, the notion of constituency interests should not

properly arise: it is individuals who have interests, rather than groups of individuals or entities such as constituencies.

16. For an extended discussion of utilitarianism in general, and of the relationship between the natural and the artificial identification of interests in particular, see Halévy (1954). There are, in fact, two very different arguments entangled here. First, there is the argument that whilst the 'invisible hand' works over a wide sphere, government is necessary in some, restricted, spheres. Second, there is the argument that there is no invisible hand, that individuals are always in mutually destructive competition and that government should not be narrowly confined to some restricted sphere.

17. See Pitkin (1967, especially pp. 203–5). Pitkin concludes that Bentham ends up with a view of representation like that of J. S. Mill and Burke.

18. On the doctrine of the mandate and the question of its validity see, for example, Birch (1964, pp. 116–22); Chapter 9 of this book contains a useful discussion of 'party democracy'. On democracy and political parties see also Ranney (1954), Ranney and Kendall (1956), Leiserson (1958), Duverger (1959), Rose (1974), Ware (1981).

19. For further discussion see, for example, Barry (1970) and Dunleavy (1991).

20. There is not the space here to discuss Rousseau properly. He is an extremely important and controversial political philosopher, and is very important in the context of democratic theory. It is well worth reading further about him: see, for example, Hall (1973), Grimsley (1983) and Cassirer (1989).

21. An important aspect of Rousseau's argument is that what might appear as being in an individual's interest (not having to give up time for jury service) may well not be so. And that which is for the common good may well be in his real, long-term (even if not his narrow, short-term) interests – living under a system of justice which is the better for having a jury system.

22. Besides the political systems of Britain and America the reference is also to other democracies (usually, but not always, English-speaking and members of the Commonwealth) whose structure and functioning have been heavily influenced by the British and/or American models. Examples are Australia, Canada, West Germany, New Zealand.

23. 'Idealism' with a capital 'I' refers not to an optimistic belief in the role of moral ideals in ordering life, but to the philosophical view – of which Plato is the originator and chief exponent – that ideas rather than matter constitute the ultimate reality.

24. Other important theorists include L. T. Hobhouse, Harold Laski (some of his work), T. V. Smith, Yves Simon, R. M. MacIver and C. J. Friedrich; see Thompson (1970, notes on pp. 190–2) for a list of relevant publications.

25. In fact an important issue in the historical development of the idea of citizenship has been the question of how many – and which sections – of those persons who are subject to a government should have the status of citizens; see, for example, Heater (1990). However, where they did exist – where the idea of citizenship was operative – citizens formed a significant

proportion of such persons; and, indeed, this marked a key difference from forms of government where there were no citizens, but only subjects. Moreover there is a 'major difference between the modern western and earlier times' (Oldfield, 1990) in that nowadays an important part of the notion of citizenship is the idea that *all* people (all adult – female as well as male – residents of a state) should be, or at least should have the opportunity of being, citizens. There is a complementary idea in Marshall's (1973) inclusion of social, as well as civil and political, rights in the concept of citizenship – an idea implying citizenship should bring genuine equality rather than just the partial or 'formal' equality which may be all that civil and political rights can bring. (This idea to some extent runs counter to the elevation of the political realm which is pivotal in the classic conception of citizenship; but Marshall *does* also see the political realm as central – he sees political reform as the way to ameliorate the injustices of the capitalist system.) Indeed, there is a firm connection between the ideas of citizenship and equality (see the main text). This development, of course, parallels and overlaps with the widening concept of 'the people' discussed in Chapter 1, and involves the integration of citizenship theory into democratic theory.

26. This revival has sparked 'lively debate between liberals and communitarians' (Oldfield, 1990); we shall be looking at aspects of this debate in Chapter 3.

27. It should be remembered that reference here is only to perspectives that recognise citizenship in the relevant sense. Mainstream liberal individualism, by contrast, tends to restrict public activity in terms of fields of activity – that is, it could be said that private life is defined in terms of fields of activity that are properly free of public control. But of course, this is, in part, precisely because there is no focusing on the idea of a political *community*. Indeed, there is an important sense in which mainstream liberal individualism does not recognise such concepts as a public sphere and *communal* life at all – or, rather, regards them as dangerous because they dress up, and thereby legitimate (an increased scope for) state activity.

28. One of the best discussions of this issue is Pateman (1985).

29. Quotation marks are used here because, as we shall see, the question can arise of whether, in the light of these studies, the Western 'democracies' can properly be counted as democracies at all.

30. On political elites see, for example, Parry (1969).

31. The reference here is both to beliefs that political elites exist and to judgements that they are desirable. These can be disconnected: some condemn the existence of political elites, and others, including some elite theorists, describe their existence without (allegedly) passing judgement on them. In fact, however, in elitist theories the desirability as well as the existence of political elites is normally maintained.

32. On Pareto, Mosca and Michels see, for example, Meisel (1958, 1965) and Lipset (1962); on Mosca, see also Albertoni (1987). On Weber see Mommsen (1974), Beetham (1985) and Held (1987, Chapter 5). The work

of Raymond Aron on elites and democracy should also be mentioned (see Aron, 1988).

33. Questions about participation, other than voting, will be left on one side here, and will be taken up in the next chapter. The main voting behaviour studies of this period were Lazarsfeld *et al.* (1968), Berelson *et al.* (1954), Milne and Mackenzie (1958) and Campbell *et al.* (1960). For further discussion of their significance see, for example, Burdick and Brodbeck (1959) and Holden (1974).

34. There is a vast literature on pressure groups, but useful introductions are: Alderman (1984), Ball (1986) and Schlozman (1986).

35. There are some tricky issues here, which are not always properly recognised. The point is that the same facts can hardly be said to demonstrate, at one and the same time, both the non-existence and the undesirability of radical democracy: if something is judged as undesirable, at least the possibility of its existence is surely presumed; at all events, it seems incoherent to contend that a factor which prevents something existing also makes that thing undesirable. The issues raised are quite complex, but one of the relevant points concerns the precise interpretation of certain 'facts': for example, is the nature and extent of voters' irrationality such that they are actually incapable of making political decisions; or is it that, whilst capable of making them, they can only make them badly?

36. Daudt (1961) provides a particularly thorough re-examination of this kind. One of his central concerns was to demonstrate that voters who changed their minds from one election to another – and thus, in a sense, 'decided' the outcome – did have some political knowledge and did exhibit rational voting behaviour, at least to some degree. (The early voting behaviour studies suggested that, contrary to what was generally thought, these 'floating voters' were the most irrational of all.)

37. In a fascinating discussion Dryzek (1990, Chapter 8) argues that the methodology of voting behaviour studies is inherently incapable of capturing the extent to which voting is an *autonomous* rather than a *determined* activity.

38. An illuminating characterisation of voter rationality is given by Popkin (1991): 'The term *low-information rationality* – popularly known as "gut reasoning" – best describes the kind of practical thinking about government and politics in which people actually engage. It is a method of combining, in an economical way, learning and information from past experiences, daily life, the media, and political campaigns.'

39. Perhaps one should write 'democracies'. It is very difficult to say anything here without begging important questions. An important issue, as we shall see, is whether in fact modern theories are not simply *assuming* what actually needs to be demonstrated, that is, that those modern political systems commonly referred to as 'democracies' or 'liberal democracies' really are democracies.

40. As with most such labels, confusion can arise from vaguenesses and

ambiguities. In the case of pluralist democratic theory, however, one should be particularly watchful. 'Pluralism', 'pluralist', etc., are terms that also have meanings more general than that involved in the use of the label 'pluralist democratic theory' to mark a distinction from elitist democratic theory. In a very general sense 'pluralist' distinguishes political systems which allow opposition to government – a *plurality* of viewpoints – to be expressed. In this sense 'pluralist' is roughly equivalent to 'liberal'.

41. There are complications – some of which are touched on later – arising from the fact that this model is itself very much built up from analyses of reality, that is to say analyses of actual political systems (above all the American system).

42. On elitist democratic theory, besides Schumpeter (1976) and Sartori (1965, 1987) see, for example, Bachrach (1967), Parry (1969), Kariel (1970), Ricci (1971), Graham (1986) and Held (1987).

43. R. A. Dahl is one of the most important of modern theorists and analysts of democracy. His main works are Dahl (1956, 1961, 1966, 1971, 1982, 1985, 1989, 1990). Dahl (1956) was a seminal work and was not just limited to outlining a 'pluralist–elitist' theory of democracy. His conception of 'polyarchy' (see Chapter 1) has become standard in analyses of political systems.

44. But note subsequent doubts about the idea: 'the coherence of the concept of "consociational democracy" and its empirical validity were much debated subsequently, and in the 1980s Lijphart produced a new typology of liberal democracies in which he drew a distinction between "majoritarian" and "consensus" governments' (Ware, 1992).

45. Unlike most theories of democracy, consociational theory is not so much an account of democracy *per se*, as an account of the form it takes in certain cases.

46. There is a problem here concerning the assumption that the expression of a sectional demand amounts to the same thing as a decision by all those *in* that section in favour of that demand. But this is an underlying problem in pluralist theory and is not unique to consociational theory; it will be commented on later.

47. 'Corporatism' is here used to mean the features of a, or the type of, political system outlined in corporatist analysis (and such analysis also contends that the political systems of the Western democracies in fact are, or do have features, of this type).

48. The meaning of 'civil society' derives from Hegel's separation of the state (which stands above society and embodies rationality and morality) and civil society (which is the area of private life and the pursuit of particular, especially economic, interests).

49. Even this is an oversimplification since corporatist analysis also focuses on the extent to which the state itself is *not* a monolithic organisation, precisely because of the extent to which its components have the character of dispersed power centres.

3

□

The radical critique of
liberal democracy

3.1
General nature of the radical critique

In this chapter we shall consider what can be called the radical critique
of the theory and practice of liberal democracy. This kind of critique
is less fashionable than it was: liberal democracy can now be said
to have triumphed (see the next chapter) and in so doing to have
vanquished its critics. Moreover, in an obvious sense this triumph
specifically involved the victory of liberal democracy over Marxism;
and this would seem to make the Marxist critique of liberal democracy
especially redundant.

However, as against this, there are three points to be made. First, as
indicated below, the discrediting of Marxism's own theory of democracy
does not necessarily invalidate its critique of liberal democracy.
Moreover, there is a growing contemporary communitarian critique of
liberalism which effectively pursues key points in the Marxist critique of
liberal individualism. Secondly, the very discrediting of the Marxist
alternative might mean that 'radical democracy is the only alternative'
(Mouffe, 1992, Preface) and that the non-Marxist radical critique is all
the more urgent. Thirdly, the very triumph of liberal democracy may
induce greater attention to its faults: 'the contradictions and blemishes
which democratic practice could easily getaway with [before], could not
escape critical gaze once the Berlin Wall had collapsed, nor be forgiven
simply by pointing to the horrors of the ostensible alternative' (Bauman,
1992). And as it is the radical critique that focuses on many of the
possible contradictions and blemishes it continues to be important.

In fact, as already indicated, two sorts of critique are brought together under this radical heading. Nonetheless, they share an important common theme that warrants the use of the unifying label; and, indeed, they are often interlinked. The connecting theme is the demand for radical change to existing ideas and/or practices in order really to achieve democracy. In other words, the basic argument is that liberal democrats are wrong in thinking that the ideas and practices to which they subscribe actually do bring about genuine democracy. It may be that practices do not actually realise liberal democratic ideals: that the Western 'liberal democracies', endorsed by liberal democrats, fail in fact to be democracies or properly to provide liberty. Or it may be that the ideas themselves are faulty; that the concepts, analyses and ideals of liberal democratic theories do not add up to a coherent or convincing picture of democracy or liberty. Or it may be a combination of both. But, whatever it is, in each case something radically different is required – be it a thoroughgoing change in social and political structures, or crucially different ideas, or both.

The radical critique, then, is far from being an attack on liberty or on democracy as such. It is in fact an appeal for more liberty and democracy. What *is* attacked is the notion that liberty and democracy can be achieved by orthodox liberal democratic theory and practice.

Very broadly speaking, we can say that there are two main forms of radical critique. There are those which are concerned with the restructuring of political ideas and practices, and those which look to wholesale changes in society. Such changes include the underlying economic and other social structures, and not just the political aspects. There are connections and overlaps between the two categories; but there are also real issues, to do with the nature and significance of political activity in the functioning of society, that divide them. In the first category are the critiques developed by the theorists of participatory democracy, while the second category comprises the various forms of Marxist critique. (In each category there are in fact various forms of argument, among which there are significant differences as well as similarities. Nonetheless it is the overlaps and similarities that are most important, and, in the interests of clarity, we shall usually refer simply to the participatory critique and to the Marxist critique.)

3.2
The participatory critique

Before we look at its nature we might first see what issues have provoked the participatory critique of liberal democratic theory and practice. Broadly speaking there are four main reasons for looking to participatory alternatives to liberal democracy and its supporting ideas.

First, there is a quite widely held view that modern Western democracies are so vast and complex that the ordinary person cannot relate to such systems or have any meaningful influence on their governments (Pranger, 1968; Ricci, 1971). Apathy and disillusion are an outcome of this. This is a matter partly of the nature of modern society, but partly also of the sheer numbers of people in 'The democratic leviathan' (Dahl, 1990). Bureaucracy, as a response to the organisational imperatives of modern society, is also seen as a threat to democracy that needs to be overcome (see, for example, Pollitt (1986)).

Second, it is often argued that the liberal democracies do not, and (short of complete restructuring) cannot, provide the kind of life they promise. It is sometimes the general quality of life that is at issue. Here the focus might be on such matters as pollution and the quality of the physical environment generally; or the imbalance between the paucity of public goods and the excess of private goods. Or the central concern might be with the dehumanisation of the work process or the poor quality of the cultural environment; and here there is an overlap with the Marxist critique. Sometimes it is the life of certain sections of society that is at issue. The general point here is that significant minorities, usually but not always ethnic minorities, are held to be excluded from the benefits enjoyed by more privileged groups; indeed, they are said not to have proper access to the democratic process. The liberal 'democracies' thereby fail to be properly democratic. Such arguments tend to merge into attacks which maintain that the actual inequalities, as opposed to formal equalities, in Western 'democracies' are too widespread and profound for them to be properly counted as democracies. Again, there is an overlap with the Marxist critique, but even a liberal democrat such as Dahl considers prevailing inequalities of political resources to be one of the most serious faults of Western democracies (Dahl, 1990; see also Dahl, 1985).

This brings us in fact to our third reason for the development of participatory critiques of liberal democracy. It is not just Marxists who are critical of the unequal distribution of power within liberal democratic societies. There are many, including Dahl, who still give primacy to political activity and structures but who nonetheless see the political sphere as subject to considerable influence. They see it as influenced by other aspects of society, in particular the organisation of industry and the economic structure generally. And such people argue that democracy is at best threatened, and at worst negated, by the inequalities inherent in the economies of Western democracies. However, the issues raised here – including those concerning 'industrial democracy' – are so heavily interrelated with the Marxist critique and its assessment that we shall consider them under that heading.

The fourth category of reasons for dissatisfaction with liberal democratic theory and practice are of a more theoretical kind. These include difficulties with providing a meaningful account of political obligation in the liberal democratic state – and the consequent serious implications for demonstrating and sustaining legitimacy – and philosophical problems connected with the justification of liberal democracy. They also include dissatisfaction with what liberal democratic assumptions imply for citizenship and the common good; and, underlying this, problems with the individualism of liberal democratic theory. We shall say something more about these topics when we look at the arguments supporting participatory theories of democracy (but we might note here that such dissatisfaction is, properly, with 'mainstream' liberal democratic theory rather than with neo-Idealist and citizenship theory).

Nature of the participatory critique

Let us turn now to the nature of the participatory critique itself. And first we should ask what is meant by 'participation', 'participatory theory', 'participatory democracy' and so on. 'Participation' means 'taking part in', and 'political participation' means 'taking part in politics or political decision making'; but this does not get us very far. The important questions concern the nature and the extent of 'taking part'; and, of course, it is *popular* participation that is at issue, that is, the ways in which the mass of the people take part in political decision making and the extent to which they do so.

There is a sense in which democracy necessarily involves pparticipation. If the people make the ultimate political decisions they are necessarily taking part in political decision making: 'democracy involves popular participation by definition. It is always a question of how much participation' (Pennock, 1979).[1] And indeed voting can be seen as a basic form of political participation. However, it is usually forms of participation over and above that of voting to which participatory theorists refer: indeed a central contention in such theories is that voting is not enough. This may not be simply a matter of quantity – the failure of the mechanism of voting to transmit information about people's views in sufficient quantity or with sufficient frequency. It may be held that there is a qualitative failure as well. This can involve more than the contention that voting fails properly to convey the information in the way intended (Burnheim, 1985, Chapter 3). It can also be argued that voting is 'an isolated, privatised act' inimical to the proper communal form of participatory activity; and, further, that it does not allow individuals autonomously to decide what views to express – and how – in a self-created activity. In liberal democratic states, indeed, voting is a fact of life that people have no choice but to accept (Pateman, 1985).

What, then, is the 'something more' that is held to constitute (genuine) participation? This is best conceived in two related dimensions. On the one hand there are the kinds of activity involved. Here the central idea is that of positively *doing* things, as against passively choosing among options presented by others. In existing liberal democracies joining political parties and engaging in their

Bill Clinton, Presidential nominee, and Al Gore, Vice-Presidential nominee, at the Democratic Party's National Convention in New York, July 1992.

activities are key forms of political participation. The presidential nominating conventions of the two main American parties provide spectacular examples of this. Participatory theorists, though, tend to look askance at political parties and to focus on more direct, unmediated, engagement in smaller scale policy-making activities.

On the other hand there is the function performed by such activities. The broad function is that of playing a part in decision making, but just what this amounts to varies. At one extreme there is simply the eliciting of views – the views of the rank and file to whom the decisions will apply[2] – by those who will make the decisions. Here participation amounts to no more than a process of consultation. If the 'consultation' is in fact really used to gain acceptance of decisions already taken we might call this 'pseudo participation' (Pateman, 1970). Genuine consultation, though, *precedes* the actual taking of decisions. And this merges into situations where even though the final power to decide rests elsewhere than with the rank and file, the views elicited actually have an influence on the decisions taken; this we can call 'partial participation' (Pateman, 1970). At the other extreme there is equality of power in the decision-making process; here the rank-and-file membership all have an equal power with the leaders in determining the outcome of decisions. Indeed, here there really ceases to be a distinction between leaders and rank and file: all are equal members of the decision-making body. This can be called 'full participation' (Pateman, 1970).

A participatory theorist is one who argues for more participation. And of course it is participatory theorists of democracy with whom we are concerned here: those who want more political participation by the people as the way of achieving proper – that is, participatory – democracy within the state.[3] We shall see that such theorists often further argue that in order to achieve such a democracy there must also be participation in spheres like the workplace, which a liberal would not count as 'political'.

Following on from our analysis of 'participation', we can say that a participatory democracy is one in which the basic determining decisions (and perhaps other decisions) are made by the people actively participating in the political process. Just what this involves, and the extent to which it is full rather than partial participation or consultation, varies with different participatory theories.

Participatory democracy and liberal democratic theory

The participatory critique implies, of course, that participatory democracy and its theory are crucially different from liberal democratic theory and practice. But there is not a simple clash here – the difference is not unqualified. As we have already indicated, there is an overlap; to a significant extent there is a sharing of the ideals of liberty and democracy. In essence, then, what the participatory democrat argues is that liberty and democracy are not in fact realised in liberal democracy. 'The major devices by which liberal theory contrives to guarantee liberty while securing democracy turn out neither to secure democracy nor to guarantee liberty' (Barber, 1984). And the corollary and converse of this argument is that liberty and democracy are only secured in participatory democracy. The differences inside the overlap thus remain crucial. They will be discussed at various points as we look at the pros and cons of participatory democracy, but, very broadly speaking, they involve three sorts of issue.

First, it has been argued that there is an underlying theoretical issue which gives rise to a fundamental, but largely unappreciated, difference between liberal democratic theory and practice and participatory theory. According to this argument it is only participatory theory that properly recognises and gives effect to the true liberal idea of voluntarism. The true idea involves individuals being conceived as voluntary members of a democratic community. This voluntarism, it is argued, was implicit in the origins of liberal democratic theory. It has, however, since been fatally obscured; and it is contradicted in the reality of the liberal democratic state (Pateman, 1985).

Second, and deriving from Pateman's argument, there are differing accounts of what is necessary for it to be said that the people make the basic political decisions. Essentially liberal democrats say that universal suffrage and voting at regular free elections is sufficient. Participatory theorists, though, require active involvement by the people in policy formulation; and this may well involve elements of direct democracy, or at least radical democratisation of the system of representation. A complication here concerns just what is included as liberal democratic theory. In the last chapter we included radical democratic theory. We saw, though, that there are important differences between radical and other liberal democratic theories, traditional as well as modern. Some might even *contrast* radical with liberal democratic theory. In the case of Continental democratic theory the relationship with liberal theory is even more ambivalent. And the key point here is that, with the emphasis on the positive, initiating role of the people, in radical and (even more) in Continental theory there are similarities with participatory theory. Indeed, to some extent participatory theory is inspired by, and is a modern manifestation of, radical and Continental theory. To that extent, then, it is an over-simplification to talk of a dichotomy between participatory and liberal democratic theory. In fact the division is clearest between participatory theory and conventional and modern varieties of liberal democratic theory. This is in fact the contrast that is usually drawn. Nonetheless, participatory theory is not simply a new version of radical and/or Continental theory. Apart from anything else key elements of participatory theory consist precisely in new responses to avoid old failures. That is to say, contemporary responses to what is seen as the failure in the twentieth century of pre-existing democratic theory – radical and Continental as well as conventional and modern theory. There is also an emphasis on pluralism in some recent participatory theory (Mouffe, 1992) that is absent in traditional radical, and is alien to Continental, theory.

The third kind of issue separating participatory and liberal democratic theory concerns notions of the individual and the community. Very roughly, participatory theory is communitarian in contrast to, and as a critique of, the individualism of (at least mainstream) liberal democratic theory. To put it that baldly, though, is to over-simplify. And we can best explain this aspect of participatory theory by understanding the way in which this is an over-simplification.

In fact participatory theory combines both individualist and communitarian perspectives: Pennock refers to 'the peculiar combination of the individualistic and the social or ... "collectivistic"' in theories of participatory democracy (Pennock, 1979). And whilst participatory theory is a critique of liberal democratic theory, it does to an important extent also uphold liberal ideas as against Marxist and other thoroughgoing communitarian theories. There is indeed, at least in important varieties of participatory theory, a 'dissatisfaction with the heritage of political theory, liberal and Marxist' (Held, 1987). Perhaps the key point can best be summed up by saying that while participatory theory gives crucial importance to the value of community and to the extent to which individuals and their activities are social products, 'the participatory democrat is' nonetheless 'distinguished by his insistence that individuals remain not only distinct and various, but "open", spontaneous and fluid' (Pennock, 1979). There is sometimes a convergence from the other side as well. Not only does participatory theory have its individualist aspect but some varieties of liberal democratic theory have a communitarian aspect. This was considered in the last chapter in our discussion of citizenship theory.

A related form of convergence is that between some forms of participatory theory and liberal pluralist ideas. As mentioned before, some participatory theorists are now balancing the importance of the unity of the overall political community with an emphasis on the extent to which modern polities have a plural character (Mouffe, 1992). Another point of convergence between participatory and pluralist ideas might be seen in pluralist democratic theory. Here it is not the individualist/communitarian distinction that is blurred,[4] so much as the distinctions involved in differing accounts of the nature of decisions by the people. The point is that on some interpretations, or in some forms, pluralist democratic theory may be construed as being about actively involving the people in policy formulation. Viewed in this way pluralist theory looks beyond passive voting at elections to the ways in which people become positively engaged in the policy formulating process through the positive political activity of the pressure groups of which they are members. It is true that critics of pluralist theory, amongst whom participatory theorists are prominent, see crucial fallacies in this sort of argument. The most important of these are said to involve the assumptions that the whole people are 'included' in pressure groups, and that their pursuit of group interests promotes the general interest and generates a 'will of the people'. But important counter-attacks in the name of 'pluralist participation' have also been made (Kelso, 1978).

This comparison of participatory and liberal democracy shows us broadly what participatory democratic theory is. We can learn more by looking at the main arguments for and against participatory democracy.

Arguments for participatory theory

Let us begin with the reasons for favouring participatory democracy. Some of these have already been indicated, but we should now bring these and others together to identify the main lines of argument in support of participatory democracy.

One sort of argument – or, more correctly, one aspect of some of the key arguments we are about to look at – concerns conceptions of the relationship between civil society and the state, or between economics and politics, or between the public and the private spheres. Two features of this kind of argument should be noted here.

First, there is the idea that democratisation of civil society can and should be achieved; and that this can overcome the negation of political democracy by the social and economic power structure. Such democratisation involves, principally, worker participation in industry, that is, industrial or economic democracy.

Second, and more generally, participatory theory can involve a radical critique of, and a means of overcoming, an artificial division in the liberal democratic order to which liberal democratic theory is blind, and which has profoundly undemocratic consequences. This is the division between the social and political realms which breeds and reflects corresponding and distorted conceptions of private and public (Pateman, 1985).[5] In short, participatory democracy can itself be conceived as transforming the structure of liberal bourgeois society and bringing about human emancipation without – or instead of – the revolutionary transformation which is essential according to the Marxist analysis.

To digress for a moment, we should note that this last statement, with its implication of a single form of 'Marxist analysis', is in fact something of an over-simplification. This is for several reasons. First, there are differences within classical Marxism concerning the question of the form that the revolutionary transformation could take; and in particular whether it could consist in the obtaining of power by the working masses through radical participatory democratic control. Second, some participatory theorists, notably C. B. Macpherson, have what amounts to a type of Marxist view of the necessity for a change in the structure of society *before* participatory democracy can become possible – see Macpherson (1977a, Chapter 5); for a discussion of whether Macpherson is a Marxist see Svacek (1976); see also the discussion of Macpherson in the next section of this chapter. Third, the idea of what a 'Marxist analysis' is had become excessively attenuated even before the recent eclipse of Marxism virtually ended it as a distinct form. At the extreme, contemporary quasi-Marxist analyses of socialism and democracy had at times become difficult to distinguish from mainstream liberal democratic, let alone participatory, theory. Witness their emphases on pluralism; the continuing need for the state, but at the same time the need to restrain it in the interests of liberty; and the associated hostility towards attempts to replace 'forms of representative democracy by exclusively direct democracy [which] will issue in statism' (Pierson, 1986).

Returning to the main arguments in favour of participatory democracy we can say these fall into four broad categories: instrumental, developmental, communal and philosophical. We shall look briefly at each of these.

The instrumental arguments, though important, are not the most distinctive. They are essentially an adaptation of typical liberal democratic – in this case utilitarian – arguments. The central idea is that people protect their interests best by participating in the making of decisions that affect them. And it is held that a participatory democracy is the best way for people to protect their interests with respect to decisions by the state. This is really to agree with the objectives of those who focus on voting as *the* democratic mechanism, but to disagree with the idea that voting alone will achieve these objectives. People must get involved and actually make themselves heard and felt if they want their interests protected. Participation is not an end in itself, but is instrumental to achieving another end – the protection of interests. Or, to put the underlying point another way, rule by the people as utilitarians envisage it can be achieved only in a participatory democracy.

The developmental arguments, on the other hand, are distinctive. They really derive from Rousseau and they are basically foreign to Anglo-American theory. (However, the variety of Anglo-American theory and the blurring of categories should be remembered. We should recall, for example, that John Stuart Mill uses developmental as well as instrumental arguments in the (albeit qualified) role he gives to participation in his theory. And we should remember that in neo-Idealist and citizenship theory, which have a significant overlap with participatory theories, key developmental ideas play a very important role.)

The central idea is that participation is valuable in itself and not, as in the instrumental arguments, just as a means to another end. It is valuable in that it develops the individual and his capacities. Rather as taking part in sport, and not just spectating, develops one's physical capacities, so taking part in political activity develops one's mental and spiritual capacities. At bottom this is to re-assert the view of man expressed in Aristotle's famous dictum – already noted in our earlier discussion of citizenship theory – that 'man is by nature a political animal': the view, essentially, that man needs to engage in politics, with all that it involves in human interaction, rational discourse and the exercise of autonomy, in order to develop into a fully human being. But this basic notion is filled out with a more specific account of the educative function of participation, where 'education' is used in a wide sense to cover the development of responsible, individual social and political action. One important aspect of this is said to be that political participation itself increases people's confidence in their ability to participate efficiently and meaningfully in politics: participation increases their sense of 'political efficacy'.

The communal arguments are in part extensions of these developmental arguments. It is held that an important aspect of how individuals are developed and educated by the experience of political participation is the way in which this teaches them about the nature and importance of the community and of their place within it; here there is an important overlap with key aspects of citizenship theory. This is valuable in various ways but above all it integrates the individual into the community. This has a dual aspect. On the one hand it benefits individuals, for example by giving them a true perspective on the communal aspect of life and how to relate to other individuals and their claims. On the other hand it develops and strengthens the community itself: the individual's subjective perceptions of, and commitments to, the community are at the same time objective bonds which bind the community together; and to strengthen the former is at the same time to develop the latter. Participation, then, strengthens the community and the individual's attachment to it.

An important implication of this with regard to political participation is that it increases the state's legitimacy by strengthening individuals' attachment to the political community. But the state's legitimacy is also increased by political participation because of what this means in terms of individuals' involvement in the making of the decisions carried out by the state. In a participatory democracy there is a real sense in which individuals can feel that the government's decisions are *their* decisions, and should therefore be accepted. This strengthening of legitimacy is particularly important in view of the 'legitimation crisis' that is said to be afflicting the liberal democratic state (Habermas, 1976) (for a useful summary see Held (1987, Chapter 7); for a critical assessment see Lawrence (1989)). Another significant aspect of the way participatory democracy can increase legitimacy is by means of the more coherent account it can be said to provide of political obligation. In her very important book on the liberal democratic theory of political obligation, Carole Pateman (1985) discusses the difficulties of providing a coherent account of political obligation in the liberal democratic state and argues that a satisfactory account can only be given in a participatory democracy.

This brings us to the fourth category of arguments for participatory democracy – the 'philosophical'. These relate to basic theoretical issues and contend that only in participatory democracy can they be satisfactorily resolved. In essence they are those posed by the individualism of mainstream liberal democratic theory. Arguably, fundamental theoretical difficulties are intrinsic to this individualism. These are central to the Marxist critique, and we shall be looking at this in the next section. But participatory theory, too, confronts some of these issues. At the risk of over-simplifying complex matters we could say that whereas Marxists see liberal democratic theory's individualism as an irredeemable fault, participatory theorists wish to preserve vital aspects of it and to overcome the faults it develops in liberal democratic theory.[6]

Pateman's discussion of political obligation can be seen in this light. She argues that the incoherence of the liberal democratic account of political obligation is part and parcel of the impossibility of giving a voluntarist account of the liberal democratic state – one that would accord with certain of liberal democratic theory's individualist premises. Only participatory theory, she argues, can adequately combine the idea of being obligated to obey the state with the idea of voluntarily undertaking such obligations. Participation fills the vacuum between the individual and the liberal democratic state by actively engaging individual citizens in the process by which it is run; and in a proper participatory democracy *all* adults would be engaged. In this way there is a genuine sense in which they can all feel they have individually contributed to, and are committed to upholding, the state's decisions (Pateman, 1985).

Participation, then, is seen as giving the fundamental nexus between the community and the individual (which is unrecognised by mainstream liberal democratic theorists), and the connection between the individual and the state, a rational and volitional character which generates or allows a genuine form of individual autonomy. This is to be contrasted with the bogus autonomy which, Pateman argues, character-ises the liberal democratic state.

Another, very interesting, philosophical argument has been put forward by Botwinick (1985). This, too, is a participatory response to theoretical problems within liberal democratic theory that arise, in part, from individualism. In this case the focus is on the nominalism and radical scepticism and relativism to which liberal individualism gives rise. Botwinick's argument has to be carefully read to be properly understood, but the key idea is that with an individualist analysis of social reality there are no 'supra-individual supports for knowledge and belief'. This involves a radical relativism such that in a society of 'epistemological equals' there is no warrant for the view of any person or group of people, including a majority, to prevail over that of anyone else. The only way out of the problem this poses for political decision making is for all individuals to be involved in reaching a consensus, via political participation. Where all views have equal validity, only a genuine consensus can have moral and political authority and only a participatory democracy can generate such a consensus (in fact neo-Idealist and deliberative conceptions constitute a bridge between mainstream liberal democratic theory and participatory theory – again, it is, properly, only mainstream theory that is the object of criticism). Once more, the argument is that participatory theory rescues rather than opposes liberal democratic theory: 'liberal democratic theory rests upon an historically unresolved paradox which has prevented political theorists from recognising the radical participatory implications inherent in classical democratic theory' (Botwinick, 1985).

Arguments against participatory theory

There are, then, strong arguments in favour of participatory democracy. But what of the counter-arguments? Let us try and indicate briefly the form that they take. Although there is a considerable overlap they can for convenience be divided into those that question the feasibility of participatory democracy and those that question its desirability. We can leave an assessment of the philosophical issues until we consider individualism again in the light of the Marxist critique.

Arguments challenging the feasibility of participatory democracy broadly take two forms: those that focus on people's political behaviour and motivations, and those that consider features of the logic of the situation within which political behaviour occurs.

The main burden of the arguments that focus on political behaviour is that the mass of the people do not have the inclination or the capacity to engage in the kind of political activity favoured by participatory theorists. We came across this sort of argument before when we looked at studies of voting behaviour in the last chapter. And as we saw then, any attempt to assess it raises fundamental issues. In the case of participatory theory there is an added dimension of difficulty: such theory sets out to challenge and go beyond the status quo so that the status of any empirical evidence about how and why people now behave is itself subject to radical doubt. For example, if people in existing political systems do not have the capacity or interest to participate in politics this, participationists argue, is precisely because in those systems they do not have a chance to participate properly. It is the experience of participation that breeds the capacity and interest to participate effectively.

The situational arguments against the feasibility of participatory democracy are more varied, but their common theme is the impossibility of participatory democracy in the face of the scale and complexity of modern society. The very factors which, as we saw earlier, have provoked a demand by some for participatory democracy are seen by others as making it impossible. And we should notice here that the issues, arguments and counter-arguments again parallel those involved in the appraisal of the critique of radical democratic theory by the modern democratic theorists. For example, on the one hand what is seen as the inevitability of elite rule is regarded as excluding the possibility of participatory democracy. On the other hand it is argued that radical social and political changes should be made which will prevent elite rule by establishing, or making possible the establishment of, participatory procedures and processes. Here we have again the same difficulty in assessing the empirical evidence, since it is that very evidence which is itself in question. However, this time there is a difference. Before, radical democratic theory was being challenged by factors beyond its cognisance, as it were; whereas participatory theory, although challenged by those same factors, is itself also a self-conscious counter-attack upon them.

This counter-attack has various features, but one of the main themes is a countering of the problems of scale and complexity with arguments for breaking down the size of political and social units. Such arguments still recognise the inevitability of some overall political organisation for large-scale modern society, even if this is only for 'co-ordination'. But the question is, how is this to be combined with the existence of small political units? Solutions offered to this problem vary from loose, federal and usually multi-stage combinations of political units, to the development of important, though subordinate, roles for community political organisations within the existing type of national institutional framework. There are important difficulties with proposals of this sort, however, which are admirably discussed by Dahl (1990). For example, what does 'co-ordination' amount to? If it is actually to be effective, will national co-ordination bodies be different from existing national states in any important respects? And if power *is* radically devolved to smaller units, this may bring the intended benefits of meaningful participation (as the individual is no longer swamped by sheer numbers), but at what cost? The smaller the unit, the less power it has to achieve what people want done in the modern world – control of pollution and unemployment, for example. The smaller the unit, the more the individual can participate; but the fewer or the less important are the matters in which that participation can occur.

We should notice here that the desire for smaller political units as a way of making participation more meaningful is closely connected with a fondness for direct democracy. Direct involvement by the individual in the actual decision-making body is seen as the most authentic form of political participation. Here there is a difference again between modern participatory theory and radical democratic theory (although Rousseau

*Learning about Maastricht: a Parisian reads the complete
text of the Treaty during the French referendum campaign
in 1992.*

in this, as in other ways, can be seen as a direct progenitor of
contemporary participatory theory). Radical theory saw representation
as the solution to the problem of scale and the impossibility of direct
democracy. Participatory theory, though, is in part a hostile response to
the actual experience of so-called representative democracy: 'representation destroys participation and citizenship . . . representative democracy is as paradoxical an oxymoron as our language has produced; its
confused and failing practice make this ever more obvious' (Barber,
1984).[7]

Direct democracy is clearly feasible where the unit is small enough –
the New England town meeting for example. But doubts about the
feasibility of small units is directly the point at issue. Such doubts have
contributed to a growing interest in modern communications technology (noted in the last chapter) as a way of making direct democracy
possible in large political units. But, as we indicated before, it is doubtful

whether the kind of participation possible would have the same quality as participation in a face-to-face meeting. Sheer numbers of participants and the qualitative difference between actual discussions and 'electronic interaction' are crucial factors. Nonetheless, as we saw, there are those who see communications technology as very important here. At the very least it could be seen as offering an improvement on, or a supplement to, that more traditional mechanism for achieving some form of direct participation in modern states, the referendum (on referendums see Butler and Ranney (1980) and Barber (1984, Chapter 10)). The question of the use of the referendum was, of course, highlighted by its use in some European Community countries in the process of ratification of the Maastricht Treaty. And we might note that its use here did show how the educative argument in favour of participation applies to referendums – in the way that people became motivated to gain some knowledge of the Treaty.

Judgement about the feasibility of participatory democracy must depend, in part at least, on one's judgement about its desirability. Apart from anything else (and in fact the reasons go further than this), if participatory democracy is regarded as desirable, the difficulties in the way of its realisation will be seen as obstacles to be overcome. Whereas if it is viewed as undesirable, such obstacles will be taken as crucial additional arguments for not seeking to achieve it, and indeed as sufficiently demonstrating that it is not feasible. So let us now see what sorts of argument can lie behind the contention that participatory democracy is undesirable.

One of these illustrates another dimension of the overlap between considerations of desirability and feasibility. Part of the facts-of-political-behaviour argument against the feasibility of participatory democracy was that people do not have the wish to participate more fully in politics. And it is reasonable to argue that it would be undesirable to have a system which required from people that which they do not wish to do. Either they would in some way be compelled to participate, which would seem to be clearly undesirable; or else decision making would be left in the hands of those who did wish to participate. In this latter case participatory systems would run the danger of becoming systems of minority rule rather than democracies, since it would be only a minority who would be interested. Moreover, it would probably be unrestrained minority rule since a guiding idea of participatory democracy – derived from Continental theory – is that the popular will should be unrestrained. The minority of activists, like the vanguard party of one-party democracy (see below), would be conceived as expressing and implementing the general will. Moreover, since the activists would probably be extremists, it is likely that the end result of participatory 'democracy' would be totalitarian rule by a minority of extremists – a vanguard state in fact.

Compare all this with the liberal democratic idea of representative government. This involves a system of defined and delimited governmental functions being performed by those who, having the inclination for the political life, are appointed and made accountable by popular election. This provides for a combination of popular, responsible and delimited decision making.

As before, using and drawing conclusions from empirical 'evidence' about people's present political behaviour and inclinations may be dismissed as beside the point by participationists. Nevertheless, one need not couch the anti-participationist argument in terms of evidence about what people's motives (presently) are, so much as in terms of what it is reasonable to expect of people, even in new circumstances. And in this connection it is noteworthy that the prominent participatory theorist C. B. Macpherson says that 'the price of participation' should not be 'a greater degree of activity than the average person can reasonably be expected to contribute' (Macpherson, 1966). (He is referring here to the possibility of democratic one-party systems, but the general point remains valid.)

But even supposing, or even when, more people do wish to participate to a greater extent, this itself would be undesirable, argue the anti-participationists. One of the key arguments is that participation by large numbers in the decision-making process clogs and slows that process and generally makes it thoroughly inefficient. The objections involved here clearly overlap considerably with the 'sheer numbers' objection against the *feasibility* of participatory democracy; and some of the same considerations and participatory responses apply. It should also be noticed that it is by no means clear that assessing this argument is simply a matter of weighing the value of efficiency against other values held to be realised by participation. It can be argued that, in some ways at least, popular participation itself increases efficiency by mobilising the knowledge latent and dispersed in the community. This is very similar to one of the traditional justifications of democracy as such, against the claims of rule by experts, which we shall look at in the next chapter. (On this, and other aspects of the pros and cons of participatory democracy, there is a very useful discussion in Lucas (1976).)

Another form of argument against too much participation has connections with one of the arguments about the threat posed to liberty by equality that we looked at in Chapter 1. This dwells not so much on the clogging up of the system as its general breakdown – a breakdown followed by a totalitarian takeover (this overlaps with the argument that participation leads to a totalitarian takeover by extremist minorities). Mass political activity is here regarded as too frenetic, as overloading the decision-making system and as leading to instability and a collapse into totalitarianism. 'The collapse of the Weimar Republic, with its high rates of mass participation, into Fascism, and the post-war establishment of totalitarian regimes based on mass participation, albeit participation backed by intimidation and coercion, underlay the tendency for "participation" to become linked to the concept of totalitarianism rather than that of democracy' (Pateman, 1970). Again, empirical evidence from political sociologists has been used to back up an anti-participatory argument. Voting-behaviour studies found not only that most electors were normally uninterested in politics, but also that the uninterested majority should not be raised out of their apathy since they tended to have non-democratic or authoritarian attitudes.

Critics of participatory theory, then, turn the participationists' case on its head. That case, it will be remembered, can be summed up by saying that only participatory democracy can realise the values and objectives of liberal democratic theory. The critics, on the other hand, say the opposite: participatory democracy – or rather the attempt to realise it – leads to results that are neither democratic nor liberal.

More lately, it is true, there has been worry about the threat to democracy and liberty from the top rather than from the mass, including the threat posed by the 'overloading' of – the pernicious effects of the excessive welfare demands upon – the liberal democratic state and/or the crisis in its legitimacy (see Held, 1987, Chapter 7). The latter is in fact a problem to which participatory democracy may be seen as a partial solution. However, the worries about the dangers of over-emphasising participation and unlimited democracy remain valid. Even as sympathetic a commentator as David Held thinks participatory theorists remain vulnerable to the criticism that they 'have attempted to resolve prematurely' complex matters involving liberty 'by allowing democracy to prevail over all other considerations' and have not asked whether there should 'be limits on the power of the *demos*' (Held, 1987).

This renewed concern with traditional liberal worries about individual freedom was also a hallmark of some later Marxist or neo-Marxist theorising (which in any case, as we have already seen, tends to converge with participatory theory). But before looking at this we must first understand the basic features of Marxist critiques of liberal democracy. And it is to these that we now turn.

3.3
The Marxist critique

The phrase 'the Marxist critique' of the theory and practice of liberal democracy is, perhaps, something of a misnomer. There have been (sometimes sharply) differing schools of Marxism and interpretations of Marx; and before its recent effective disintegration the distinction between what was or was not Marxism, or Marxist analysis, became increasingly blurred. Nonetheless there remains enough common ground amongst theories and analyses which made something of their claims to be Marxist for it to make sense to talk of *the* Marxist critique of the theory and practice of liberal democracy.

Although, clearly, the two are heavily interrelated it is convenient to consider the critique in two parts – the critique of theory and the critique of practice. And we shall begin with the latter.

The critique of liberal democratic practice

The critique of practice consists in showing that the practice of (what are called) liberal democracies does not accord with liberal democratic theory's account of it. The critique of the theory, though, in a sense goes one step further and contends that the theory is faulty in the first place.

The central argument in the critique of practice starts from the association of liberal democracy with capitalism: liberal democracy – or what liberal democrats maintain is such – occurs where there is a capitalist system. But such a system, it is argued, actually prevents the realisation of liberal democracy. Capitalism, contrary to what liberal democrats suppose, makes it impossible for liberal democracy to exist. 'For Marx and Engels the reality of liberal democracy appeared systematically to curtail its pretentions' (Levin, 1983). What actually exists is said to be a sham democracy – called 'bourgeois democracy' by Marxists – in which freedom and democracy do not in fact exist.

'Formal' freedom exists, but not genuine freedom. This is basically due to the inequalities that characterise capitalist society, so that the position of the proletarian 'wage slave' is in fact one of lack of freedom, despite possession of the same civil liberties and political freedoms as the bourgeoisie. 'In its implementation abstract freedom emerges as bourgeois freedom. Seek for the content behind the form and this freedom reduces itself to private property and free trade. It is not men who are set free but capital' (Levin, 1983). Or, as Pierson (1986) puts it, writing of the noted Marxist, Rosa Luxemburg (1871–1919): 'like Marx, [she] sought to develop an analysis which would reveal bourgeois democracy's "hard kernel of social inequality and lack of freedom hidden under the sweet shell of formal freedom and equality".' There is also another, and rather different, argument about the lack of freedom in capitalist systems – and therefore in liberal democracy. This Marxist argument is not always focused upon, and its significance is rather different because it shows that *all* are unfree, 'proletarians and capitalists alike'. Their lack of freedom consists 'in their domination by an economic system which has its own laws and logic' (Gray, 1986a).

Democracy, too, is said not to exist. This is because, it is argued, the mass of the people are not in fact in control. The underlying thesis here derives from Marx's class analysis, according to which the class that controls the means of production dominates society. Under capitalism this class is the bourgeoisie; and so it is the bourgeoisie – the capitalists – and not the mass of the people, who have power in bourgeois democracy. This basic thesis has been interpreted and developed in different ways.

One leading interpretation sees the state as the instrument of the ruling class. This received its best-known expression in the famous statement in *The Communist Manifesto* that 'the executive of the modern state is but a committee for managing the common affairs of the whole bourgeoisie'. A well-known modern formulation is to be found in Miliband (1969).

A frequent argument, here, is that the ruling class control the state machine, by providing the personnel who staff the governmental machinery. But it has to be explained how it is that contested elections and universal suffrage do not place the control of the state in the hands of the mass of the people. One key thesis is that so-called free elections do not in fact express the will of the people, and the elected politicians rather than being the agents of the popular will are members or instruments of the ruling class. This might be a matter of *de facto* restriction of choice at elections, so that there is no option which offers the voters a radical, anti-capitalist policy. Or it may (or may also) be that the ruling class, by controlling the mass media and the education system for example, can mould public opinion in such a way that there are no anti-capitalist views to be expressed. In this case elections simply 'echo back' the ideas or ideology of the ruling class and leave them undisturbed in their control of the state.

The argument that public opinion may be moulded by control of the instruments of communication and socialisation can merge into different kinds of argument, which we shall consider in a moment. These maintain that it is the effects or requirements of the system, rather than the deliberate or conscious exercise of power, which promote the bourgeois cause. The contention is that the whole socialisation process imbues the mass of the people with a pro-capitalist outlook. This sort of argument may extend to the contention that not only ideas but also desires are the result of indoctrination or socialisation, and that 'false needs' are created (Marcuse, 1968). But whether it is needs or ideas, and whether it is an exercise of power or a result of the system, the outcome is the same: the electorate are the victims of 'false consciousness' and unable to express an authentic will of their own.

This idea is of profound importance in – and in assessing the validity of – the Marxist critique of liberal democracy, and we shall be returning to it later. It also overlaps with a key idea of Gramsci's. Antonio Gramsci (1891–1937), one of the founders of the Italian Communist party, 'is probably the most original political writer among the post-Lenin generation of Communists' (Kolakowski, 1978).

According to his conception of hegemony, the ruling class secure their power not so much by the use of the state as by control of society's intellectual life – and therefore of the people's ideas – by purely cultural means. 'The privileged classes . . . secured a position of hegemony in the intellectual as well as the political sphere; they subjugated the others by this means, and intellectual supremacy was a precondition of political rule' (Kolakowski, 1978).

Domination by the ruling class need not, then, centre on their control of the state. Indeed, the state may well act autonomously to some extent – perhaps even acting against the short-run interests of capitalists.

The idea of relative autonomy points to, and can be a part of, another and rather different form of Marxist analysis. Here bourgeois domination of society is seen not so much as an exercise of power by a ruling class as a matter of the system operating to the benefit of the bourgeoisie, or, one might say, in the interests of capitalists. (It might be more accurate to say 'in the interests of capitalism'; or, if this is thought to be circular, one might talk of the system operating 'in such a way as to maintain its capitalist character'. The presumption would be, of course, that it is only capitalists who benefit from capitalism; however, as we shall see, one of the liberal democratic responses to the Marxist critique is to question this presumption.[8])

The argument might be in terms of 'structural determination', where the state is seen as constrained by the structure and functions of the capitalist system, including the international capitalist system, to pursue only policies that benefit capitalists. Or the argument might focus on the nature of the state itself, and the way it functions, in capitalist society. Here the essential argument is not so much that the state is *constrained* by something outside itself – the capitalist system – as that the state in capitalist society *is itself* necessarily of such a nature that it naturally promotes the interests of capitalists. For example, its revenue and the criterion by which its performance will be judged, could both be said to involve the successful operation of the capitalist economy. Such an argument might be developed in terms not just of the nature of the state but also of the regime in which the state is embedded (Elkin, 1985). (For further excellent analyses of the nature and role of the state in capitalist societies see also Benjamin and Duvall (1985) and Braybrooke (1985).)

In either case – structural determination or the necessary role of the state – the system is not democratic since public policy is not the outcome of decisions by the people. Again, there is the failure of actual systems to be democratic as prescribed by liberal democratic theory. But let us turn now from arguments concerning the failure of the practice to the alleged failure of the theory itself.

The critique of liberal democratic theory

We shall focus here on only one part of the Marxist critique of liberal democratic theory: the critique of individualism. However, it is, perhaps, the most fundamental part. Moreover, key aspects of it overlap from *passé* Marxist analysis into the burgeoning communitarian critique of liberalism.

We have already several times remarked that individualism is a key characteristic of liberal democratic theory. And it is time now to draw these points together; to see just what is postulated and assumed in liberal democratic theory and to look at the way in which Marxist theory calls it into question.

The issue is actually a little more complex than at first appears. It is easy to assume – and it often is assumed – that it is a matter of a straightforward clash: individualism on the one side and the Marxist critique of this on the other. But, because of the complexity of the notion of individualism and the richness of Marxist theory, this is not really the position. The best way, though, to clarify matters a little is to start with the over-simplified, and commonly assumed, account and then see how this has to modified. In this account, what we described in Chapter 2 as 'ontological individualism' is taken as central to liberal democratic theory. Marxist theory is then seen as mounting a fundamental attack on this. This attack has two interrelated aspects.

First, there is a rejection of what is seen as an outcome of ontological individualism, the blindness to the reality and value of community. Liberal democrats, it is held, are unable to perceive the existence – and are therefore unable to appreciate the value – of community because ontological individualism involves seeing social collectivities merely as collections of individuals. (In fact this statement of the case is over-simplified, even as a general view of liberalism (see Kymlicka, 1989). In any case, liberal democratic theory includes some theories that involve explicit rejection of such crude individualism: even if we exclude Continental theory, we still have neo-Idealism, where the reality and value of community is clearly important – compare Tucker (1980) who includes A. D. Lindsay amongst 'liberal humanists' – and citizenship theory, where it is central. It is even arguable that John Stuart Mill's thought gives significant recognition to the importance of community. However, as a statement about key aspects of Anglo-American democratic theory it is true enough to make it important.)

We cannot here go into the very important idea of community. Suffice it to say that from classical Greece onwards there has been a tradition of thought in which the community that individuals inhabit is seen as having, in an important sense, a reality of its own – quite apart from the individuals who inhabit it at a particular time. In this sort of conception the focus is on such things as institutions, customs, traditions, language and, more generally, culture. Indeed, before the growth of individualist ideas in early modern times, the notion that individuals could be conceived as separate from the character they had as part of a society or community did not really make sense. And, to an extent because individuals gain their character from the community they inhabit, community is seen as having very great moral worth. It is the community (or the properly ordered community) that develops an individual's capacities, gives a sense of belonging and identity, and provides the focus for motivation and activity. Liberal democratic theory, it is argued, being blind to all this is unable properly to evaluate social and political activity. In particular it fails, on the one hand, to see the true inhumanity and alienation that the capitalist system involves; and on the other hand, it is unable to give a proper account of a collectivity, and hence of a collective – a democratic – decision.

As we have just indicated, Marx was not the first exponent of a communitarian perspective. But he was particularly important in turning this perspective, as a critique, on liberal democratic theory. Although to some extent he was using and developing Rousseau's and Hegel's thought here, Marx added his own ideas and, what is more, combined these with the other aspects of his wholesale and fundamental critique of liberal democratic theory and practice. Now, as we have seen, although Marxist theory as such has perhaps disintegrated – or, at any rate, suffered a grave setback – the critique of individualism is very much still alive and kicking. Varieties of many of the above forms of argument, and those developed below, are the subject of lively current debate and are being deployed in a developing communitarian critique of liberalism.[9]

The second aspect of the challenge to ontological individualism is a direct attack. Here the target is the very notion that society is composed only of individuals, and that its character is determined by the characteristics of those constituent individuals. A variety of telling arguments derive from communitarian theory, and receive their most penetrating development from Marx. There are perhaps two main ones. First, that '*man* is not an abstract being squatting outside the world' (Marx, 1844). Rather, he takes his character from his historical and social context. That is to say, individuals are social beings and their character and behaviour are, to a crucial extent, the product of their particular social environment. The second main argument is that social phenomena are not explicable simply as the product of the character and (at any rate the intentional) behaviour of individuals. Rather, social structures have, in a crucial sense, an existence of their own; and, indeed, they structure the behaviour of individuals. (Consider, say, the Indian caste system, the market and, more generally still, language.)

These arguments raise profound and complex issues in political and social theory. In unravelling them one would need to look more carefully at the conception of 'ontological individualism', and perhaps divide it into component features. In particular, it would be helpful to distinguish between the idea of what Lukes calls the 'abstract individual' and 'methodological individualism' (Lukes, 1973). Our purpose here, however, is not to engage in a full analysis of individualism, so much as to focus on issues crucial to an understanding and appraisal of liberal democratic theory. One key issue – and perhaps the most fundamental – that arises is this: if the character and behaviour of individuals are the product of their social environment, can (or to what extent can) we say that they are making decisions of their own, expressing their own will? Similarly, can we say that the people make their own decisions – that there is any such thing as an authentic will of the people? This connects up with the kind of Marxist critique of liberal democratic practice we have already looked at, that sees the people as the victims of false consciousness. We shall come back to this issue at the end of the chapter, when we attempt to assess the Marxist critique.

Another issue that arises concerns the relationship between ontological and what we earlier called 'moral' individualism. The liberal democratic assumption is that there is a tight connection between the two so that the latter is dependent on the former. In other words, the assumption is that the proper kind of moral importance can be given to the individual only if individuals are seen to be independent entities rather than social products which are merely pieces of the social fabric. Here the Marxist critique is turned back against itself, as it were. For the liberal democrat the Marxist arguments issue forth in, or imply, unacceptable moral conclusions.

Again, though, it is necessary to look more carefully at the notions of individualism involved, and matters are not so straightforward as at first appears. It may well be that any close relationships here, involving the values of moral individualism, are with only some of the components of ontological individualism. Or, to put the point another way, it is arguable that these values can be held without subscribing to all that is included in ontological individualism. In particular, it can argued that a commitment to 'respecting persons, to maintaining and enhancing their autonomy, privacy and self-development . . . does not . . . imply the adoption of . . . the abstract conception of the individual' (Lukes, 1973). But this is more than a hypothetical argument: the point is that Marxism – despite what its critics might say – arguably does subscribe to these values. 'There can be little dispute over whether Marx was an individualist, for he places great value on the achievement of autonomy' (Tucker, 1980).[10] And arguably most Marxists, with the possible exception of Lenin and Mao, are individualists in this sense.

This brings us back to the point that there is not a straightforward clash between individualism, seen as a distinctive feature of liberal democratic theory, on one side, and Marxism on the other. In fact the Marxist critique can be seen not so much as an attack on the values of individualism as an attack on the theory and practice of liberal democracy for not implementing them. Again, then, the criticism of liberal democracy is not of its ideals but of its failure to realise (or worse, its negation of) them. 'Marx's individualism goes further than that of most liberals' and 'his critique of liberalism arises out of his claim that the prevailing conditions in liberal society actually serve to frustrate our efforts to be self-directing' (Tucker, 1980). Marx, then, does not 'reprimand liberal philosophers . . . for failing to articulate the true nature of these ideas [true human autonomy, true political liberty and equality]; rather, he is concerned that they do not see how difficult it is for these goals to be realised under capitalist relations of production' (Tucker, 1980).

Possessive individualism

Arguably, then, Marxists are not critics of individualism as such. But it must be remembered that they are, as already pointed out, fundamentally critical of an aspect of ontological individualism. They completely reject 'abstract individualism' – that is, they reject the idea of the abstract individual, the idea of man as 'an abstract being squatting outside the world'. And we shall come back to this. It can also be said that Marxists are critics of what is, in a sense, a 'perverted' variety of moral individualism. And this *is* held to be distinctive of liberal democratic theory because of that theory's association with capitalist society. This is what C. B. Macpherson calls 'possessive individualism' (Macpherson, 1962). Briefly, this consists in the idea 'that each person is the sole *proprietor* of his own person and capacities, and that each person has an infinite desire to *appropriate* resources (human as well as natural)' (Levine, 1981). This involves a sanctification of the idea of private property and its accumulation that leads to the iniquities of capitalist society. And it is also said to involve the invalid assumption 'that individuals owe nothing to society for the skills which they acquire when they are trained to accomplish sophisticated tasks' (Tucker, 1980).

Whether possessive individualism is, in fact, a central feature of liberal democratic theory is arguable. First, there is the liberal humanist or neo-Idealist strand to be remembered. In fact Macpherson does explicitly recognise the different nature of some liberal democratic theory: neo-Idealist and citizenship theory. He regards J. S. Mill as a major figure in this category of 'developmental democracy' (Macpherson, 1977a). Indeed, Macpherson's aim is to separate 'out the developmental from the possessive elements of liberal individualism' (Lukes, 1979) and incorporate the former into a 'non-market' theory of liberal democracy. However, he thinks J. S. Mill's theory was also contaminated with Benthamite assumptions,[11] and that both he, and later the neo-Idealist and early twentieth-century citizenship theorists failed to come to grips with the class nature of capitalist society. And in any event, Macpherson argues, it was purely possessive individualist theories that came to predominate in twentieth-century liberal democracy. This may have been so; but, arguably, the picture is now changing. Spragens (1990) refers to 'what until fairly recently had *been* the prevailing account of liberal society as a concatenation of possessive individualists who muddle through' (emphasis added). Even if what we earlier called 'modern democratic theory' – and what Macpherson refers to as the 'equilibrium model' – has been dominant, there is now rising dissatisfaction with its narrowly individualist foundations. This is fuelling an increasing challenge – witness the new interest in citizenship theory and the recent concern with basing liberal democratic theory[12] on rational discourse rather than calculating individuals (Dryzek,1990; Spragens, 1990; Miller, 1992).

Even if we insist that the equilibrium model does still predominate, there is a second argument to consider: it is actually doubtful whether, *pace* Macpherson, utilitarian varieties of liberal democratic theory – on which the equilibrium model is said to be based – can properly be regarded as embodying possessive individualism. As Tucker points out, utilitarians have generally defended the principle of preserving an area of individual freedom similar to that sanctified by natural rights theorists (pre-eminently Locke) and which 'possessive individualists regard as a principle of justice' from which an entitlement to accumulate property follows. But utilitarians:

> have done so only because they were convinced by the argument that human happiness will be maximised by a policy which allows people to do what they choose. They certainly have not regarded the principle as a natural entitlement which can be claimed regardless of the social consequences which might be thought to follow. (Tucker, 1980)

And, where necessary, utilitarians would justify state interference in what possessive individualists would regard as areas of sanctified individual liberty: such state action could be justified if it were to produce a greater sum total of happiness.

Nonetheless, Macpherson's argument has been influential. And it is true that it is a plausible interpretation of the implications of the natural rights strand in liberal democratic theory – which is, after all, a major strand. Macpherson's critique here is broadly Marxist. And his general stance towards liberal democracy is very similar to Marx's, as interpreted above:

> he places himself among 'those who accept and would promote the normative values that were read into the liberal-democratic society and state

by J. S. Mill and the nineteenth and twentieth century idealist theorists, but who reject the present liberal-democratic society and state as having failed to live up to those values, or as being incapable of realising them.' (Lukes, 1979, quoting Macpherson, 1977b)

However, Macpherson is not, perhaps, fully a Marxist since he does not subscribe to a Marxist account of what is necessary to transform capitalist society. This is associated with what can be argued is his 'failure' to free himself from ontological individualism in his criticism of liberal theory's possessive individualism: he does not complete 'his penetrating critique of its possessiveness' with 'an abandonment of its individualism' (Lukes, 1979). Macpherson, in fact (and this is part of the reason for his importance), straddles the Marxist–liberal democratic divide:

> Remaining faithful to the truth of the central maxim of liberal-democratic theory which affirms self-realisation as an end in itself, while drawing inspiration from the Marxian critique of capitalism, Macpherson proceeds to reform liberal-democratic theory. His [theory is a] synthesis of the two traditions, liberal democratic and Marxian. (Kontos, 1979, Preface)

It will be remembered, indeed, that Macpherson was earlier cited as a participatory theorist. And it might be taken as a characteristic feature of participatory theory that it combines a radical critique of the actuality of liberal democracy (perhaps, but not necessarily, Marxist inspired) with a commitment to its fundamental ideas and to working within its framework to reform it. But although its ambivalence with regard to ontological individualism and its commitment to working within the framework of liberal democracy perhaps makes it importantly different from Marxist theory, there are also important overlaps. Apart from the particular case of Macpherson and the difficulties, which we have already mentioned, of separating off a distinctive form of analysis in later Marxist writing, there are in Marx's own thought important elements of participatory democratic theory which we should now consider.

Marxist democratic theory

After the revolution, control is in the hands of the mass of the people – the proletariat. And at times Marx envisages that control being exercised by processes and mechanisms of a sort that would be approved by democrats. It is his account of this that is often taken as exemplifying his theory of democracy, though, as we shall see in a moment, there is considerable uncertainty about whether this is meant to indicate his final, preferred, form of society, or even whether it is a likely form at all – final or transitional. Be that as it may, in this account he focuses on the Paris Commune as a model, where all officials were elected by universal suffrage 'responsible and revocable at short terms'. The commune was to serve as a model for the rest of France where:

> [the] commune was to be the political form of even the smallest country hamlet... The rural communes... were to administer their common affairs by an assembly of delegates ... and these district assemblies were again to send deputies to the National Delegation in Paris, each delegate to be at any time revocable and bound by the *mandat impératif* (formal instructions) of his constituents. (Marx, 1970, quoted in Held, 1987)

Marx, in fact, has – or utilises – here a theory of participatory democracy; although, like the participatory theory discussed earlier, it is not a theory of *liberal* democracy: boundaries are not drawn round the sphere of public activity to protect a wide sphere of individual, private activity. We have in fact already seen that in the Marxist critique of liberal democracy it is not democracy that is criticised but its non-realisation – so Marx's theory must include an account of what this democracy is that ought to be realised. We mention this here to explicate further the nature of the critique of liberal democracy, although as a *political* theory, over and above the social theory and philosophy, Marxism is widely held to be deficient. As such it may be considered to have little to contribute in the way of a theory about the institutions and processes of democracy. Nonetheless, it raises some quite complicated questions concerning the fundamental ideas embodied in democracy, and the way in which Marx's account of it fits into his underlying social theory; and we shall briefly indicate one or two important points (for further analysis of Marxist democratic ideas see, for example, Pierson (1986), Graham (1986) and Levin (1983, 1989)).

To begin with, it is not entirely clear how far Marx's theory of democracy is a theory about the character of the transitional phase, and how far about the eventual communist society in which the state has withered away. In the latter case, complex issues arise concerning the conception of the state and its relationship to the conception of democracy. The usual, and certainly the liberal democrat's, view would be that democracy is a *form* of state. However, apart from the apparent

Marxist view that true democracy may require the absence (in at least some sense) of the state, it has recently been argued from a non-Marxist standpoint that the state is unnecessary and that 'a democratic state is a dialectical contradiction' (Burnheim, 1985). There is also the anarchist tradition which is not unlike aspects of Marxism at times. Here again there is an ambivalence between on the one hand treating democracy as a form of the rejected state, and on the other hand seeing stateless anarchist society as the most perfect (or the only true) form of democracy. William Godwin (1756–1836) is the key figure here. But as radical a theorist as Carole Pateman regards the state – albeit a reformed state – as necessary to democracy (Pateman, 1985; Chapter 7 contains an illuminating discussion of anarchism and democracy). And certainly in this book we have treated democracy as a form of state.

We should, though, now return to the uncertainties in Marx about the *stage* at which democracy will exist. These uncertainties are troublesome in understanding Marx; and they have been the source of a deep ambivalence, and endless controversy, within subsequent Marxist theory. (And this is apart from, or superimposed on, controversies concerning whether the proletarian takeover, which ushers in the transitional phase, could itself be effected by democratic means. On both types of controversy see Pierson (1986).) In particular, such uncertainty has intermeshed with arguments about the difficulty of getting a proletariat imbued with false consciousness to see its own interests. This double ambivalence has generated doubt about whether the transitional phase should itself be democratic or whether it should be seen purely as a necessary step towards true democracy. Or perhaps there can be some amalgam of the two via the notion of the real will, as against the apparent will, of the proletariat.[13]

We shall see in a moment how the theory of 'people's democracy' grew out of Lenin's interpretation of Marx here. And many see Lenin's views on democracy as crucially different from those of Marx. In essence the two crucial points are these. First, Marx is more concerned with characterising the communist society as democracy while Lenin is preoccupied with the business of getting there. Second, despite some oscillations in Lenin's view, Marx is unlike Lenin in being prepared to see the transitional phase as democratic in a sense that a participatory democrat would endorse (but see note 13), principally because the proletarians themselves are conceived by Marx as developing a revolutionary consciousness.

There is a common view, then, that there are crucial differences here between Marx and Lenin. It is also commonly held that these differences have too often been obscured because it is Lenin's (distorted) interpretation of Marx's ideas in the form of Marxism–Leninism that was manifested in the communist regimes which were for so long the enemies of liberal democracy. As Graham (1986) puts it: 'the terrible fate which befell Marx was that he was Leninised.' And because of this fact, it can be argued that liberal democrats, on the whole, paid less attention than they should have done to what Marxism had to say about democracy. The iniquities of Marxism–Leninism tend to be viewed as self-evident; and with this the whole of Marxism is frequently dismissed by liberal democrats. This, of course, is a tendency that has been greatly reinforced by the downfall of communist regimes which can be seen as confirming the iniquities, as well as demonstrating the present irrelevance, of Marxism–Leninism.

The ambivalence in Marx should not, however, be forgotten. And there is another view according to which Lenin gave an authentic interpretation of Marx, and that Marx himself is as anti-democratic as Lenin. Nor can Marxism–Leninism be absolved by blaming Stalin for hijacking it (once a common view on the Left). This view is well-stated by Harding:

> Stalin, not Lenin, it is argued, is really responsible for the anti-democratic face of subsequent Communism. These attempts to salvage the reputations of both Marx and Lenin from responsibility for the anti-democratic ethos of modern Communism are unconvincing and misleading. Leninism was an authentic Marxism. As an ideology it faithfully reflected . . . Marx's own deep ambivalence towards and suspicion of democracy. (Harding, 1992)

But even though the 'positive' Marxist account of democracy may now be thoroughly discredited, the 'negative' critique of liberal democracy remains profound and cannot be ignored. We shall turn to an assessment of this shortly; but first we need to say a little more about the Leninist development (whether authentic or otherwise) of Marx's account of democracy.

Leninist theory and one-party democracy

One of the reasons for the ambivalence of the relationship of Lenin's to Marx's theory of democracy is the shifts that occurred – often in response to changing Soviet circumstances – in Lenin's theory. We should particularly note that for a short period after the Revolution in

1917 Lenin expounded a theory of soviet democracy which was a form of Marx's Paris 'Commune democracy' (see, for example, Harding, 1992). However, this period was very brief and following the usual understanding we shall locate Lenin's theory of democracy primarily in the 'post-Soviet' phase of his theory, leading principles of which 'were to inform Soviet practice for the next seventy years' (Harding, 1992). Here the notion of rule by a party – a *single* vanguard party – is central. Indeed, we have in this theory *the* basic model of one-party democracy.[14] We shall see in a moment that there is a Third World variant of one-party theory. But this drew much of its inspiration from the Leninist model, and is really parasitic upon it – as demonstrated by the fact that when the Leninist model collapsed with the downfall of the communist regimes embodying it the Third World variant effectively lost all credibility (see Chapter 4, section 3 below).

But let us start with the general form and significance of the one-party model of democracy before we come back to its Leninist foundations. The key point here is that until very recently it was held, in some quarters, that we had in this model a general alternative to liberal democracy. In fact it was seen as a powerful and challenging alternative, existing not just in the realm of theory but also being embodied in the political systems of states, some of which were powerful and many of which were hostile to liberal democracy. These were the 'people's democracies' of the communist world and the one-party democracies of the Third World, which until recently made up a hefty proportion of the world's states.

In his influential little book *The Real World of Democracy*, C. B. Macpherson stated that 'democracy is not properly to be equated with our unique Western liberal-democracy, but that the clearly non-liberal systems which prevail in the Soviet countries, and the somewhat different non-liberal systems of most of the underdeveloped countries of Asia and Africa, have a genuine historical claim to the title of democracy' (Macpherson, 1966). Its validity we can leave on one side for the moment, but it is certainly true that there exists here a claim that is – or was until recently regarded as – important; and the ideas involved require to be understood.

The two forms of this non-liberal democracy Macpherson calls the 'communist variant' and the 'underdeveloped variant' (Macpherson, 1966). We shall be looking at each of them (the first in a moment, and the second in the next chapter). But first, what do they have in common: what are the distinctive features of non-liberal democracy?

The most visible feature is the single party: non-liberal democracies are (or were) one-party systems. This finds its basis in, and is an expression of, a social unity that produces and is maintained by what amounts to a Rousseauean general will. Perhaps this is more apparent in the case of the 'underdeveloped' than the 'communist' variant, but essentially the basic idea is that there is a general will which expresses itself through, and only through, a single party. As it is the general will – the single genuine will of the people – that the party expresses, it follows that there is no legitimate democratic function for any other party and that there is no limit to what the governing party can properly and democratically do. For critics, this is the notion of totalitarian democracy again (see the discussion of Continental democratic theory in Chapter 2).

'The people', then, is conceived as a social unit. There are some differences between the variants here but, in contradistinction to liberal-individualist conceptions, they share the idea of the people as some kind of communal, corporate entity. The differences are in the nature of the entity focused upon, but in each case there is something of the original, Aristotelian meaning of 'the people': the common people, the hitherto oppressed.

We shall be looking at the variants – in this chapter and the next – but first there are two important general points to be dealt with. Both arise in Macpherson's analysis. First, part of Macpherson's argument is that even if, or where, non-liberal democracy does not qualify as democracy in the narrow sense of a system of government, it does qualify in the 'broader social sense' of a kind of society (Macpherson, 1966). Now this may or may not be so, but as we have already suggested, although Macpherson would not agree, this broader sense is but a secondary meaning of democracy. And in any case the really important and interesting question is whether non-liberal 'democracy' qualifies as democracy in the narrower, primary sense.

This brings us to the second point. With regard to the narrow meaning, Macpherson states that for non-liberal democracies 'democracy has had something like its original meaning, government by or for the common people' (Macpherson, 1966). But democracy does not mean, and never has meant, government *for* the people (the 'common people' or otherwise); rather it means government *by* the people (see, for example, Sartori (1987, Chapter 15, section 5)). And to suggest that 'government for' is the 'original meaning' as in Aristotle, is wrong:

Macpherson is, quite simply, untrue to Aristotle. As has been correctly observed, 'Macpherson's view that democracy means originally "rule by or in the interests of the hitherto oppressed class" is doubtful. It would be a truer account to say that it has meant rule by and *therefore* in the interests of the poor' [Lively, 1975]. Aristotle ... said that democracy was a rule in the interest of the poor (and/or the many) *because* democracy – the direct Greek democracy – was government *by* the poor ... Hence, Aristotle said what has been said ever since: The interest of the poor, or the many, is affirmed when the poor or the many can themselves affirm it. (Sartori, 1987)

And in fact the key question about non-liberal democracy – the question on which the significant controversy and the deep theoretical issues centre – is whether in any sense it *is* government by (even if it is government for) the people. This is certainly the question we shall ask here about one-party democracy.

People's democracy

Let us now look briefly at the first – the chronologically and theoretically antecedent – variety of one-party democracy, the 'communist variant' (we shall look at the 'underdeveloped variant' in Chapter 4, section 3). What we are essentially considering here is 'people's democracy'; the democracies that existed behind the former Iron Curtain in Eastern Europe, and in communist countries elsewhere. (As we have already mentioned – and as we shall discuss further in the next chapter – the model of people's democracy has effectively collapsed. Nonetheless, one or two instances of people's democracy do still exist – this includes the hugely important country of China – and we shall continue to talk of it here in the present tense.) Strictly speaking the term 'people's democracy' does not refer to the former Soviet Union itself, but only to its satellites and to China. One of the differences here is that the satellites allegedly had multi-party governments, a number of parties united in a coalition. However, 'the decisive characteristics of the ... governmental form [of the people's democracies] was the leading role of the working class, represented by its "vanguard", the communist party.' And there was an 'essential identity between the ... patterns of government' of the Soviet Union and its satellites (Kase, 1968). We shall therefore treat 'people's democracy' as including the former Soviet Union.

In people's democracy the single will of the people is elicited and implemented by a single vanguard party, the Communist Party. We shall sketch in the nature of the system by indicating the key features of these ideas – the people, the vanguard party and the eliciting of the people's will.

These are Leninist ideas; and here we come back to the Leninist theory of democracy. It is essentially this that constitutes the theory of people's democracy. We have already seen that, arguably, Marx equated democracy with the final, classless communist society, but that the dominant idea in Lenin is that democracy occurs before that. For Lenin democracy is achieved when the proletariat comes to power after the revolutionary overthrow of the capitalist power structure, that is, during the phase of the 'dictatorship of the proletariat'. And people's democracy is seen as being the form taken by the dictatorship of the proletariat (Kase, 1968).

The idea of the people, then, is in this theory essentially a class concept. There are some complications and modifications – which we shall look at in a moment – but the basic notion is of the people as the working class, the proletariat. Two overlapping reasons are usually given for counting one class only as equivalent to 'the people'. First it is pointed out that the proletariat is (at least in the sort of societies Marx originally had in mind) the most numerous class, the majority. And since, it is argued, rule by the people in a democracy actually means rule by a majority, the proletariat is operationally equivalent to the people. 'The dictatorship of the proletariat . . . will, for the first time, produce a democracy for the people, for the majority' (Lenin, 1960).

In fact, as we saw earlier, the whole idea that democracy amounts to rule by a majority is fraught with difficulties, but these do not come within the purview of Leninist theory. Indeed, the existence of what the liberal democrat sees as the strange and obnoxious idea of democracy being constituted by the *dictatorship* of the majority – the dictatorship of the proletariat – is related to a failure to focus on the proper qualifications to the idea of democracy as majority rule. The second reason, however, for the one-class concept of the people is that the proletariat is seen straightforwardly *as* the people, in the traditional Aristotelian sense of the poor or 'the hitherto oppressed classes'. Here rule by the proletariat simply *is* rule by the people, without the qualifications and difficulties of saying it is merely rule by a majority of the people.

There is an overlap between these two ideas since the traditional Aristotelian sense of the people connects up with the (now) dominant meaning of the people via the assumption, made also by Aristotle, that the poor are nearly always the most numerous. There is also another dimension to this connecting up of the people-as-proletariat with the primary idea of the people as the whole population. In Marxist theory the overthrow of capitalist society by the proletariat – the proletarian revolution – is the decisive step towards the communist, classless society which will be for the benefit of everyone. Action by the proletariat, then, frees, and is on behalf of, not just the proletariat but the whole of humanity; or, at any rate, all the humans in the state in which the revolution occurs (Marxist theory originally held that the proletarian revolution would transcend state divisions). Rule by the proletariat, then, is on behalf of the whole people.

One complication is that Leninist theory recognised that the proletariat was not necessarily actually in a majority. In this case either the proletariat was the vanguard of the rest of the people ('the non-proletarian working masses', mainly the peasantry); or else the proletariat jointly constituted the people: 'On the continent of Europe, in 1871, the proletariat did not in a single country constitute the majority of the people. A "people's revolution" . . . could be such only if embracing both the proletariat and the peasantry. Both classes constituted the "people"' (Lenin, 1960). However, it was later said that the people's democracies have 'all, including the Chinese people's democratic dictatorship . . . reached the stage of full proletarian dictatorship' (Kase, 1968). In the Soviet Union itself, the official view became that the dictatorship of the proletariat had been superseded by a state of the whole people, but this seemed to make little difference to the basic ideas of people's democracy (see Reglar and Young (1983) for a useful discussion).

For Marx, as we have just seen, it seems the rule of the proletariat (and incidentally he himself uses the phrase 'dictatorship of the proletariat' very infrequently) can involve rule by the whole proletariat through radically democratic processes. In Lenin, however, the dominant idea is that of the dictatorship of the proletariat being exercised in the form of rule by the vanguard of the proletariat – the Communist Party. This is necessary partly for organisational reasons, but also because Lenin, unlike Marx, does not really think the proletarians, unaided, are capable of developing a revolutionary consciousness and discerning their true interests. Instead they will have induced in them, as victims of capitalist society, a 'false consciousness', a 'trade union consciousness'. This will lead them merely to attempt to ameliorate their position under capitalism, by trade union activity and so on, rather than trying to overthrow it.

It is the vanguard, then, that actually exercises power – on behalf of the proletariat. This is government *for* the proletariat, government for the people. But is it government *by* the people? This is a crucial but tricky question. There is, it is true, often a tendency simply to talk of government for the people. Macpherson, as we have seen, talks of government 'by or for' the people. However, he also admits that in the narrow sense of democracy a vanguard state is not a democracy, since it is not government by the people (Macpherson, 1966, Chapter 1). And we have already argued that for democracy to exist there must, indeed, be government by the people.

In fact, there are also arguments to the effect that rule by the vanguard party *is* government by the people. One of these plainly will not do, though. This is the argument which points to rule by the vanguard being essential for bringing about a situation – the eventual communist society – in which people are truly emancipated and in which they really do rule themselves in the fullest possible sense. This could be a very important argument, but the most it could establish is that vanguard rule is a necessary condition for the establishment of, not that it actually *is*, rule by the people.

The more fundamental argument makes use of what is very like a variant of Rousseau's idea of the general will; and it is here that we come back to connections between Continental theory, totalitarian democracy and the theory of people's democracy.[15] The basic general idea involves distinguishing between people's apparent and true wills, and focusing on the true will for what is in the real interests of the people. Now, in Marxist–Leninist theory, the people is constituted by a class; and what is in the real interests of a class, and therefore of the people, can be objectively identified by those with the necessary knowledge, including knowledge of Marxist theory. The real will of the people can, then, be identified by those with the requisite knowledge. Lenin, as we just said, thought that only the vanguard party, rather than the mass of the proletariat, had the necessary knowledge. And in taking action to realise the true interests of the people we could say the vanguard party is doing nothing other than implementing the true will – the general will – of the people. In fact in Lenin's own thought there is a certain ambivalence between a 'hard' and a 'soft' version of this theory: in the hard version the vanguard party simply tells the proletariat what its will is;[16] but in the soft version there is the idea that through mass participation under the leadership of the party – and such leadership *is* vital – the proletarians come themselves to know their interests correctly.

Perhaps a synthesis of the two versions best expresses the essence of Lenin's thinking: the vanguard party knows the 'correct' policy to implement, but the masses must come to realise that this is the correct policy, through direct political participation in which they are led and educated by the party. There is here still a connection with Rousseau's own insistence that for the general will to exist the people must at some point actually, overtly, will what is in their real interests.

Be that as it may, however, the experience of people's democracies has been one in which rule is actually by the party and only the hard version of the theory can be said to apply. Here, unlike in Rousseau, one is required to accept that there is a meaningful sense in which people can be said to will – decide in favour of – that which is in their true interests, even when they do not themselves actually, subjectively, do so. This raises important issues, some of which will be discussed later, but two points need to be made now.

First, the liberal democrat cannot accept that there is any sense in the notion that people will or decide things which they do not actually, empirically, will or decide. (The hard version of the Leninist theory ultimately turns on the conception of the proletariat as an objectively defined social entity; whereas the liberal democrat sees essentially autonomous individuals who can be only what they themselves conceive themselves to be. Again this raises deep issues which will be taken up later.)

Second, the liberal democrat will very sensibly insist that whatever is to be made of the theory of people's democracy, the practice amounts to unbridled power being in the hands of the vanguard party, or its leading organs or individuals. Not only is this undemocratic, it is illiberal and dangerous. One need not accept without qualification Lord Acton's dictum to the effect that all power tends to corrupt and absolute power corrupts absolutely. But one can still recognise that self-interest, and/or particular individual ideas on the use to be made of power, will tend to exert a dangerous influence on those whose power is not effectively limited, and that the liberty of citizens is likely to suffer accordingly.

For a time, after the accession of Gorbachev to power in the former Soviet Union, it looked as though people's democracy might be reformed and become more genuinely democratic. Particularly significant was Gorbachev's talk of the importance of democracy and his attempt, originally, to democratise the internal structure of the ruling Communist Party. We should bear in mind here Macpherson's account of how a one-party state could be democratic. He argued that the then existing vanguard states were not democratic in 'the narrow sense', that is, the primary sense, but that 'a one-party state can in principle be democratic even in the narrow sense' provided that certain conditions are fulfilled (Macpherson, 1966). One of these is that there should be full intra-party democracy – that the party itself should be democratically controlled by its members. A liberal democrat would not accept this as sufficient[17] since choice is restricted within a party ideology, and is made only by party members. Although another of Macpherson's conditions is that membership of the party should be open to all, this seems paradoxical: either there would be some ideological limits to membership – in which case choice is still restricted – or else there would be no such limitation, in which case a *single* party is pointless, and effectively ceases to exist.

Of course, in the event, such argumentation turned out to be beside the point. There was no stopping the logic of democratisation. In the Soviet system (including in this phrase Russia, effectively the successor state to the Soviet Union) the Communist Party lost its leading role, and elsewhere in Eastern Europe there was a sudden and dramatic transformation from one-party systems to multi-party liberal democratic systems. Effectively, people's democracy had ceased to be a serious alternative to liberal democracy (see also the next chapter).

Assessment of the Marxist critique

Let us now return to the Marxist critique itself, and ask what we are to make of it. This is obviously a large and complex question and in the space available we can only sketch in an answer by making a few points about some of the more salient issues. We shall start with what we called the critique of practice. Leaving aside for the moment arguments about an exercise of power by a ruling class, let us look first at the more general line of argument to the effect that the system operates in the interests of capitalists.

There are powerful arguments here and, although it might be possible to take issue with them to some degree, let us accept their cogency. But let us also be clear about just what it is that is being accepted. It is accepted, then, that the system operates in the interests of capitalists; but the crucial point is that this does not of itself imply that it operates *against* the interests of the mass of the people. Or, rather, it is only an accompanying theory about the nature of capitalism that implies this. So a crucial issue then becomes the validity or otherwise of this theory. Marxist critics of liberal democracy naturally take the validity of this accompanying theory for granted. It never occurs to them, at this point, that it can be challenged. The question of this challenge we must leave hanging in the air for the moment, for the point to get clear here is this. *If* it is the case that capitalism is in the interests not just of capitalists, but also the whole people, then a demonstration that the system operates in favour of capitalists does not, of itself, show the system to be necessarily undemocratic. And if the system not only operates in the interests of the whole people, but the people (because of this) subjectively approve of the system, then there is every reason to call it democratic – assuming, of course, that the other necessary conditions of a democracy (free elections and so on) are present.

To go a bit deeper, it must be acknowledged that the above argument rests on the assumption that *if* the people ceased to approve of the system then they could change it – through the mechanisms of liberal democracy. Or, to put the point another way, the assumption is that the approval of the people is a necessary condition for the continuance of the system. This raises the issues that we left on one side just now, concerning the power structure within the system, and we shall come back to these in a moment. One of the arguments relating to those issues was that the people are the victims of false consciousness. And this argument is also a direct challenge to the point we are trying to establish at the moment. That is to say, if the people approve of capitalism only because of their false consciousness, then we are back to square one: the people's approval would then be one of the mechanisms by which the system maintains itself and would not be an authentic expression of their own will. Again, we shall come back to this shortly.

We return now to the argument that, irrespective of whether or not the system itself prevents rule by the people, power within the system is not exercised by the people but by a ruling class. We shall not attempt here to go into the essentially empirical question of whether, or to what extent, in the various Western political systems, government has failed to respond to demands which go against the interests of those who hold economic power. But it is certainly arguable that the evidence does not seem to bear out the proposition that such demands are systematically ignored or flouted. For example, Boreham *et al.* (1989), assessing the view that the capitalist state 'has little capacity to to be able to respond positively to working class demands', argue that 'empirically . . . this view must be regarded with little credence'. And, citing Korpi (1983) as exemplifying support, they say the state 'may become an instrument for translating the interests of labour into redistributive and egalitarian practice. It is becoming increasingly common for post-war struggles over economic policy and welfare-state provision to be seen in this way.' (See also Turner (1986).)

But whatever conclusions we come to here, the more theoretically interesting, and the more fundamental, arguments to consider are, in any case, those that we left on one side a short while ago. These maintain that the electorate is unable to make anti-capitalist demands as decisions in the first place. The most basic argument here is that pro-capitalist views are produced by controlling or moulding public opinion. This is an aspect of the 'false consciousness' argument. The idea of the deliberate control of opinion is importantly different from the notion of automatic socialisation. And both are different from the idea of being subjected to cultural hegemony or the ideology of the ruling class. Nonetheless, there is a significant overlap, and we shall deal with the control-of-public-opinion argument as part of a general assessment of the common element in all these arguments. (Again we shall not attempt an assessment of empirical evidence – evidence about the control of the media in different countries, the processes of socialisation and so on. Rather we shall concentrate on the theoretical question of whether it is plausible to argue that people's views *can* be completely determined in this way.) Moreover, the issues here link up with some of those raised by the Marxist critique of abstract individualism.

The critical part of the common element is that the ideas individuals have are not generated by themselves but are in some way externally induced in them. The question of the validity of this notion is of profound importance in assessing the viability of liberal democratic theory and practice; and we shall come back to it shortly when we look again at the Marxist critique of individualism, where some of the same, or directly relevant, issues are raised.

Even if we reject the Marxist argument that the people are not in control of political decision making in capitalist society we are still left with other important criticisms. There are still the arguments about the inequalities and injustices of capitalist society, and the lack of real freedom behind the formal freedom provided by the liberal democratic state.

Broadly speaking there are three forms of counter-argument with which to defend liberal democracy here. The first largely overlaps with the contention above that the liberal democratic state *can* be used by the people for their own ends. It is to the effect that *if* the people wanted to change the system to rid themselves of its alleged iniquities then they could in fact do so (and to the extent that they do not do so then these 'iniquities' are not regarded as such by the people). This is the argument of social democracy and reformism. There are many issues here but the key ones for our purpose have already been covered in considering whether the people can in fact use the liberal democratic state for their own ends.

The second form of argument provides, as it were, the reasons why the people do not want to change the capitalist system. In other words, we have here justifications of those features of the system that are alleged to be iniquitous. These include the arguments of perhaps the best-known of recent liberal political philosophers, John Rawls (1972, 1985) and Robert Nozick (1974). Both hold that what a Marxist would call 'formal' freedom is profoundly important and that its significance is not negated by inequalities, provided that those inequalities benefit the least well-off (Rawls)[18] or that they result only from holdings to which people are entitled (Nozick). We cannot here get into a discussion of the issues raised; there is in fact a burgeoning literature in this whole area. (For a useful survey of this, and other aspects of the debate about the application of liberal values, see Gray (1986b) and Plant (1991, Chapter 3).) We must stick to what the people can do rather than why they should – or should not – do it.

Nonetheless, that justifications of this kind exist is relevant to an argument put forward a little earlier. This was to the effect that the validity of aspects of the Marxist critique turns on the assumption that capitalism is not in the interests of the people. And though we cannot enter into an assessment of rival arguments about the justice, or otherwise, of capitalism, the very fact that rival arguments exist shows that there is an issue to be settled. It is not, therefore, indisputably the case that capitalism goes against the interests of the people (further relevant points are taken up below when we consider capitalism and democracy generally). Moreover, a democrat would argue that it is the people who should settle the issue.

The third form of argument, which is perhaps the most important and convincing, is rather different in that it half accepts the Marxist case. Here it is acknowledged that there is a great deal wrong with the capitalist system, but that it can be put right without a total transformation of the system. In particular the economic inequalities, and accompanying injustices and lack of freedom, can be remedied without changing the structure of the liberal democratic state and the market system. This can be done by changing the economic power structure itself in such a way as to give control of capital to the mass of the workers, rather than to just a few managers and owners: in other words a system of industrial democracy.

Industrial democracy
This subject is large and controversial. Many questions arise concerning what exactly is meant by 'industrial democracy', its feasibility and its desirability. There are many objections to be overcome

in defending a system of industrial democracy, workers' control or economic democracy; and there are many difficulties, both theoretical and practical, in the way of instituting and running such a system. Many of these – and other theoretical and empirical issues – are lucidly discussed in an excellent book by R. A. Dahl (1985; see also Dahl, 1990 and 1989, Chapter 23) which also contains a useful survey of the relevant literature. Aware as he is of all these issues, Dahl is nonetheless firmly in favour of economic democracy. In fact he builds up an extremely strong case for it. Here, though, we shall simply point to one or two of the more important issues involved.

The general idea behind economic democracy, as Dahl sees it, is to provide an 'alternative to corporate capitalism' which strengthens 'political equality without sacrificing liberty'. Arguably, then, it retains key virtues of a liberal democratic and capitalist system without its main defects. And this is a crucial point: economic democracy (at least of the type Dahl is talking about)[19] constitutes a modification, not a complete rejection, of capitalism. The free market and the profit motive are retained but the control of economic enterprises is changed so that the mass of the workers, rather than just a few dominant people and groups, are in charge. Another way of putting the central point is to say that we have here the free market without the iniquities that a certain rendering of the notion of private property gives to it (see further below). In a lucid and devastating analysis, Dahl shows the mistake in thinking that corporate capitalism – private ownership of (sometimes vast) corporations – can be derived from the notion of private property rights (Dahl, 1985).

Another important point is that economic democracy is a central element in most participatory theories of democracy (Pateman, 1970). Participatory theory, it will be remembered, wants society as a whole to be firmly under the control of the people (to the extent, indeed, that liberal democrats see some dangers here). And we referred earlier to the idea that such control properly involves control of economic structures. This clearly connects up with socialist ideas, but where it differs from (at least traditional mainstream) socialism is in the stress on direct democratic control of industry. This is to be contrasted with the notion of control of industry by the state, albeit a democratic state (see also note 19). It further connects up with those aspects of the Marxist critique which decry the nature of the distinctions liberal democratic theory draws between political and social, public and private.

Part of the participatory theorists' case, roughly speaking, is that the structures, processes and activities in what the liberal democrat wrongly regards as the separate sphere of social and private – particularly economic – life ('civil society'), have just as much to do with determining the nature of collective existence as do those in the sphere that the liberal democrat marks off as the 'political'. As we saw earlier, this idea that there are, in effect, political power structures outside the liberal democrat's restricted vision of the formal political realm, is linked with a critique which sees the public realm as much wider than the liberal democrat supposes. (Dahl, however, does not really push his theory in this direction: his remains a liberal democratic theory, albeit one that has strong affinities with participatory theory.) Here again we see the overlap between the participatory and Marxist critiques. But, unlike the Marxist, the participatory democrat argues that these bogus divisions of liberal democracy can be overcome by democratisation of the economic, as well as the formally political, power structures; and this can be done without – or rather, instead of – a wholesale transformation of the system.

Discussion of key liberal democratic concepts brings us again to the Marxist critique of liberal democratic theory. In assessing this we shall focus on just one aspect: the critical analysis of the idea of the abstract individual. Other issues are no doubt important, but their relevance is really for a critique of (albeit prominent) varieties of liberal democratic theory, rather than of the theory *per se*. For example, as we have already seen, the criticisms concerning blindness to the importance of community are not applicable to all forms of liberal democratic theory. Nor are the criticisms of possessive individualism.

This is not to deny that these criticisms are important. Nor is it to deny that prominent varieties of liberal democratic theory, in the Anglo-American world at least, suffer from these criticisms. For example, the kind of individualism which is the corollary of the blindness to community, lands most accounts of collective decision making in the kind of mess we referred to in the appendix to Chapter 1. However, the answer to this mess is to be found in the modified individualism of theories that lie within what is arguably the spectrum of liberal democratic theory itself, if we include not only neo-Idealist and citizenship theory but discursive or deliberative conceptions of democracy (see note 12). What we need to do here is to focus on that aspect of the Marxist critique that applies to *all* varieties of liberal democratic theory. And this is the critique of abstract individualism, which applies alike to theories characterised by a thoroughgoing, and a by modified, individualism (it even applies, as we saw, to Macpherson's participatory theory).

Critique of individualism pushed too far

It will be contended that the nub of the argument in defence of liberal democratic theory here is this. It should be acknowledged that the criticism of abstract individualism has much force and that liberal democratic theory is largely guilty of not seeing this, but that the critique in the end fails because it tries to prove too much.

The fundamental point is that, although overall the notion of the abstract individual is faulty, still it has at its very core a conception that is valid. And while it is true that liberal democratic theory in its usual formulations can be faulted for containing the full, defective conception, it must nonetheless be endorsed for incorporating the valid core conception. Moreover, this conception is crucial to any theory of democracy.

The faults in abstract individualism are indeed those we focused on as part of the Marxist critique. Man does not 'squat outside the world'. Individuals are in the social world: they are social beings in the sense that their characters and behaviour are to a very large extent a product of their social environment. Moreover, to an extent that liberal democratic theory does not normally recognise, individuals' lives, as well as their characteristics, are social. Their behaviour consists in the part they play in the various *social* practices in which they are enmeshed, and can only be understood as such (just as the behaviour of an individual playing cricket cannot be understood simply by analysing him as an individual without understanding cricket).

However, this line of argument can be pushed too far. Despite the extent to which individuals are social beings, and activity is social rather than purely individual, there is also a crucial and irreducible extent to which individuals are independent of their social environment and their activity is voluntary. This has several aspects, or can be expressed in several ways.

First, to say that individuals are socially constituted does not imply that they are socially *determined*. They can still be separate autonomous beings with human capacities that are innate and not the product of their social environment.[20] And this connects up with moral individualism – which the critics of liberal democracy theory also wish to uphold here. Indeed, it may be that a proper recognition of the social constitution of individuals, rather than the blindness of abstract individualism, is necessary for a proper connection to be made. Lukes expresses all this very well:

the principle of respect for persons requires ... that we regard and act towards individuals in their concrete specificity, that we take full account of their specific aims and purposes and of their own definitions of their (social) situations. And ... that we see them as the (actually or potentially) autonomous sources of decisions and choices . . . Respecting them as *persons* . . . involves the kind of understanding of both their social and individual aspects which the abstract view of them precludes. For, on the one hand, such respect requires us to take account of them as social selves – moulded and constituted by their societies – whose achievement of, and potential for, autonomy, whose valued activities and involvements and whose potentialities are, in large, socially determined and specific to their particular social contexts. On the other hand, it requires us to see each of them as an actually or potentially autonomous centre of choice (rather than a bundle composed of a certain range of wants, motives, purposes, interests, etc.), able to choose between, and on occasion transcend, socially-given activities and involvements, and to develop his or her respective potentialities in the available forms sanctioned by the culture – which is both a structural constraint and a determinant of individuality. (Lukes, 1973)

Gould (1988), in developing her social ontology, also argues that a proper account of individuals' autonomy involves recognition of 'the nature of individuals as agents and as *social* beings' (emphasis added).

Pateman makes similar or complementary points in arguing that a voluntarist understanding of politics is not incompatible with, and indeed requires, a recognition of the faults of abstract individualism. Abstract individualists – because they see all social practices as external to, and as constraints upon, the individual – necessarily see obligations as limitations on individual autonomy. (And thoroughgoing communitarians are no better because they are liable to interpret social constitution as social determination.) It is only by a *proper* appreciation of the ways in which individual life is a social phenomenon that one can really see where autonomy lies. Pateman argues that 'if individuals are separated from their social relationships . . . it is then impossible to give due weight to the fact that individuals are, at one and the same time, both superior to and bound by their rules, rights and obligations' (Pateman, 1985). Individuals cannot escape social life, which is constituted by such practices; but individuals can *decide* which obligations to enter into. Again, as Pateman states:

[it] is true that no one comes into the world fully mature, free and equal and free from all social ties, but it is only abstract individualists who argue as if they do. The fact that humans are social creatures, born into a network of social relationships, is the foundation for, not a barrier against, the construction of a democratic association. (Pateman, 1985)

Another aspect of this argument about the way in which the case against abstract individualism overshoots itself can be put in terms of a false deduction of particular conclusions from a general proposition. There is, in fact, very often an invalid move from the proposition that individuals are socially constituted to the conclusion that they are fully constituted by the *particular* social environment that they inhabit. Socialisation theories tend generally to commit this fallacy because, in their empirical particularity, they necessarily focus mainly on the mechanisms of particular societies. But Marxist arguments are especially prone to this because they are enmeshed in a general theory, the polemical purpose of which is precisely to show the particular effects of a *particular kind* of society – capitalist society – on individuals. (The full story is more complex, however, since the implications and assumptions of Marxist conceptions of the nature and role of the individual in the future communist society are very different – see the discussion of Marxist individualism above. However, Marxist analyses of capitalist society do have a tendency to over-simplify and fall foul of this fallacy.)

There is another way of making the point that to admit that individuals are socially constructed does not amount to accepting they are socially *determined*; and, indeed, that by insisting on the latter the critique of abstract individualism fails because it overreaches itself. This concerns the status of individuals' own thinking, where the argument that individuals' ideas are always socially determined is one that becomes incoherent (see below).

In fact this point is crucial because the social-determination-of-ideas argument must be refuted if it is to be possible to demonstrate the existence of democracy at all. Meanwhile, while accepting the role of the social environment, the task of the liberal democrat must be to show that individuals' thinking is not socially *determined* in capitalist society (Holden, 1983). This connects up with the issue raised by the false consciousness and cultural hegemony arguments that we looked at earlier.

If people's ideas are induced in them by – are simply a product of – their socio-cultural environment then there is a crucial sense in which their thoughts, and hence any decisions they make, are not their own.[21] (In fact there are various complications here, but this statement remains valid; see Holden (1983).) It follows that there cannot be any real decisions by the people – no authentic will of the people – but only a processing of people's cultural milieu, rather as prisms refract but do not generate light. If there cannot be decisions by the people, there can be no democracy. And this is not just a theoretical point (albeit a momentous one): any such invalidation of the notion of decision making by the people can have fateful practical consequences. If the views the people express are not really their own then no particular importance attaches to the 'will of the people'. And indeed, as in Leninist vanguard theory, the view is justified that the expressed will of the people should be ignored in favour of objective assessments of their real interests. In practice this can mean that the expressed wishes of the people can be ignored in favour of anything rulers wish to do, and we end up by justifying pernicious forms of tyranny, as in Stalinist Russia.

Of course, simply showing the unfortunate consequences of the people's ideas being socially determined does not in itself prove that they are not (although it may cause us to ponder the matter very carefully instead of easily accepting the notion). To go into all the issues involved would demand a book in itself and we shall focus on just one point, arguably the most fundamental. This arises from the *relativism* which is a corollary of the notion that ideas are socially determined. It is a general point but it crucially undermines any attempt to show that the voters' ideas are socially determined in the particular case of the existing liberal democracies. To cut short a somewhat complex argument (Holden, 1983) the key element is this. Any particular argument that ideas are determined in a certain sort of way, or that the ideas of a particular group or historical period are determined in a certain way, implicitly rests heavily on the notion that *all* ideas are socially determined. And this underlying and crucial presupposition is simply taken for granted. But as we have already suggested, this notion is, arguably, incoherent. And if this is so, any particular argument about social determination collapses because a key part of its foundation crumbles away.

The argument that the notion of all ideas being socially determined is incoherent, turns on a central issue. This is that true ideas are generated by something more than social context – something other than social causation. Ideas which are socially determined do not express truths, any more than nightmares caused by – but only statements resulting from investigation of – indigestion, express truths about the digestive system. Thus the contents of ideas which are socially determined – or, more precisely, the statements in which these contents are expressed – are not true. And, conversely, ideas expressed by statements which are true, have not been socially determined (they, or their occurrence, may well have been subject to social influence – but it is social *determination* of ideas that is antithetical to their being true).[22] Hence to say that all ideas are socially determined is to say that no statements are true. But this is self-defeating or incoherent: it is like the Paradox of the Liar. Either the claim that no statements are true is itself untrue, or else all statements are not untrue. Either way, the notion that all statements are untrue is nullified: and this nullification destroys the notion that all ideas are socially determined. It thus drastically weakens – by destroying the presupposition of – arguments that particular (sets of) ideas are socially determined. But, further, it lets in the conception of true ideas: and it is then extremely difficult to resist the contention that some ideas are held *because* they are true. Indeed, another way of putting this argument is to say that if ideas are true then their existence, and their presence in people's minds, has been explained – or at least a crucial part of the explanation has been given – without bringing in social determination. (Who would invoke social determination to explain why people have, say, the idea that war or famine bring misery?)

Marxist arguments that people's ideas in capitalist societies, and hence in liberal democracies, are socially determined thus loses its main support – for, to repeat, powerful support is derived from the presupposition that *all* ideas are socially determined. But, more than this, we can see how the particular Marxist arguments can be challenged. We have already looked at this line of reasoning, but to bring the threads together let us say again that it is at least, at the very least, arguable that the beliefs of the people in capitalist liberal democracies are true or valid.[23] But, as we have just seen, to the extent that this is the case we have the reason, or one of the key reasons, why they hold these beliefs. And, conversely, Marxist explanations in terms of partisan socialisation, ideology of the ruling class, or cultural hegemony are thereby rendered redundant. It should be noticed that the contention is not that such Marxist explanations are *never* valid, but rather that frequently they are not; in any case they should be scrutinised with a great deal more rigour than is usual. Moreover, as was previously suggested, the democratic response to the difficulty of deciding which ideas are valid – and hence not socially determined – is to let the matter be decided by the people themselves. Another way of putting this is to say it must be recognised that popular opinion should be treated as valid. It might be objected there is a circle here that is impossible to break out of: if people's ideas are invalid then they will not themselves be able to see this. But, again, there is no getting away from the fact that whether there *is* a circle is problematic, that is, deciding what ideas *are* valid remains fundamentally problematical. Given this is the case, the argument that it is popular opinion which is valid – or should be treated as valid – at the very least should not be ruled out. And a traditional justification for democracy is that there are good reasons for treating popular opinion as valid (see the next chapter).

A final reason for objecting that the emphasis on the social character of individuals and their activity – which is proper enough in itself – can be pushed too far, involves another form of concern with the anti-voluntarist implications of social explanations of individual minds. Again, it is the implied impossibility of decision making by the people that is crucial, but this time the focus is on the notion of decision making itself. A democracy is a political system in which the basic determining decisions are made by the people. But this idea of a decision has individualist implications. Part of the very concept of a decision is the notion of an *act* of a human mind. Such an act can only take place within an individual: only an individual (or an individual's mind) can act. Indeed, only an individual has a mind. True, individual minds are crucially influenced – structured even – by their socio-cultural context, subject to the limitations implied by our social determination of ideas argument. But the notion of minds *acting* has irreducibly individualist implications. A collective decision can be conceived only in terms of a combination of individual decisions; so the notion of a decision by the people also has irreducibly individualist implications.

It is true, as we have seen, that there are fundamental problems in the way of interpreting a collective decision as a combination of individual decisions. And it may be that overly individualist mainstream Anglo-American democratic theory, with its focus on preferences, has to be modified along the lines of neo-Idealist theory and discursive or deliberative conceptions of the democratic process. This may be necessary to give proper weight to the shaping effect of rational interaction, the communal context and individuals' views of the common interest. However, though such a process of integrating views may be a necessary condition for the making of decisions by the people, it does not itself constitute the making of such decisions.

Decisions by the people, then, can only be decisions by individuals. Moreover, only non-socially determined individuals *act* and make decisions: a consequence of viewing individuals as socially determined is to see them as passive transmitters of socio-cultural influences rather than as decision makers. In this view there can be no decisions by individuals and therefore no decisions by the people.

As before, though, we should beware of assuming that simply showing its unfortunate consequence – the impossibility of popular decision making – in itself disproves the existence of social determination. But again, it should at least cause us to ponder carefully. Having pondered, it is true that it is difficult to claim that one comes up with a definite, final answer. Apart from anything else we are here entrapped in the venerable free-will versus determinism controversy. Nonetheless, it is arguable that one's own experience amply demonstrates the absurdity of supposing that individuals are not decision-makers.

3.4
Liberal democracy and capitalism

In considering the Marxist critique of liberal democracy two assumptions have remained largely unquestioned. These are that there is a special connection between liberal democracy and capitalism;[24] and that this connection is problematic for liberal democracy. We ought now to query the validity of these assumptions.

The two are in fact intermeshed to a considerable extent. Whether, and in what ways, capitalism is (or is not) regarded as problematic for liberal democracy depends to no small degree on the way in which they are seen to be connected. That there *is* a connection is strongly suggested by the empirical evidence: overwhelmingly, liberal democracies exist in capitalist societies[25] (the converse, however, is not true: there are, and have been, plenty of capitalist societies that do not have liberal democratic political systems). However, whether or not there are exceptions is not simple to determine. This depends on such things as the definitions of the terms involved and interpretations of the nature of particular societies and political systems.

But even if all occurrences of liberal democracy so far have been in capitalist societies, it is conceivable that future occurrences might be in a different socio-economic context. And this ties up with aspects of the preceding discussion since it could be argued that at least some participatory theorists and Marxists are in favour of 'true' liberal democracy which could exist only in a non-capitalist system. C. B. Macpherson certainly sees his argument this way. (All these theorists are in favour of 'true' democracy; the only point which can be at issue here is whether the system they favour is meant to be, or can properly be called, *liberal* democracy.) But it is not just radical critics who regard liberal democracy as possible in non-capitalist contexts. Even Schumpeter, who maintains there is 'a natural affinity between capitalism and democracy', thinks 'it is also true that democracy can survive and even thrive in a socialist state' (Coe and Wilber, 1985).

But let us assume that liberal democracy does occur only in broadly speaking capitalist systems. (The qualification 'broadly speaking' is inserted here because, as we shall see, one important issue concerns the definition of 'capitalism' and whether a market system is necessarily capitalist.) The reasons for this connection are partly historical and contingent. But there are, arguably, also inherent connections between liberal democracy and capitalism. A good part of the Marxist critique, indeed, assumes or argues exactly this. But the opposite sort of case is also commonly argued: that there are inherent connections between liberal democracy and capitalism such that capitalism is a necessary condition (or, at the very least, highly favourable) for liberal democracy.[26] It may be said that:

> both systems are based on the belief that freedom of individual choice will result in socially desirable outcomes ... A capitalist market economy relies on the maximising decisions of individual consumers and producers to achieve an efficient allocation of resources. A democratic political system relies on the decision of individual voters[27] to achieve the proper resolution of political disputes. In both cases power is widely dispersed. Thus each system reinforces the other. (Coe and Wilber, 1985)

See also Usher (1981) – but note the critical analysis by Berg (1986) – and Beetham (1992), who lists five liberal arguments contending that capitalism is necessary for democracy (but also lists five socialist counter-arguments). For a powerful argument connecting liberal democracy and capitalism see Novak (1991). See also the July 1992 issue of the *Journal of Democracy* which features 'a special symposium on capitalism, socialism and democracy'.

It should be realised that the connection discerned is specifically with *liberal* democracy. That is to say, capitalism is seen as being inherently connected not just with democratic control – via the notion of consumer/voter sovereignty – but also with freedom. Even an author who insists there 'are all sorts of limits to political toleration that the state imposes for the sake of economic order' in capitalist liberal democracies, nonetheless points out:

> the one grimly unshiftable fact that must make all socialists pause: 'There is one striking generalisation that can be extracted from the otherwise indeterminate history of democracy. It is that political freedom in modern times ... has only appeared in capitalist states.' (Ryan, 1986, quoting Heilbroner, 1986)

And this is the view that was a contributory factor in – and has in a sense been vindicated by – the downfall of communism in the 'democratic revolution' of 1989 (see the next chapter).

Now, it may be that there are compelling arguments here. But it may also be that the radical critics are nonetheless right – as Heilbroner's qualifications suggest – in stressing the illiberal and anti-democratic implications of the power structure of corporate capitalism. As we have already seen this is, essentially, the position now taken by Dahl (1985), in contrast to his earlier stance (Dahl, 1956). Charles Lindblom, a fellow exponent of 'neo-pluralism' (McLennan, 1984; Held, 1987), graphically expresses the viewpoint in these words: private corporations are 'disproportionately powerful . . . the large private corporation fits oddly into democratic theory and vision. Indeed, it does not fit' (Lindblom, 1977).

Whether this concession to the radical critique amounts to admitting that capitalism and liberal democracy are, after all, antithetical, depends partly on one's definition of capitalism – in particular, is it equivalent only to corporate capitalism in the sense indicated by Dahl? But this definitional question is less interesting than the underlying point that an inherent connection can be seen between *the market* and liberal democracy. In other words, the key connection discerned concerns that aspect of capitalism referred to as 'the market'; so the contention is that if capitalism is divested of its structure of corporate power it remains closely connected, and perhaps is a necessary condition for, democracy.[28] (However, whether Lindblom is arguing this, or its contrary, is another matter. It is not entirely clear whether the essence of his argument is that corporations are inherently favoured by the market, at the expense of democracy, or whether it is the market itself that is the culprit. Besides Lindblom (1977), see Lindblom (1982, 1991) and Elkin (1982). There is a similar issue in interpreting Levine's argument about freedom and its tensions with capitalism and the market (Levine, 1981, Chapter 9).)

The relationships between democracy and the market constitute a large, important and complex subject in its own right, not least because it overlaps with fields in political economy which are also large, important and complex in their own right – such as the relationship between the state and the market in individualist economic analysis and, indeed, the whole field of public choice analysis. All we can do here is point to a few of the key issues (see also Dahl, 1990, Chapter 3).

As just indicated, the organising assumption at issue is that, broadly speaking, the relationship between the market and liberal democracy is the same as that which pro-capitalist democrats see as obtaining between capitalism and democracy. In other words, the assumption is that there are inherent connections between the market system of distribution and exchange and liberal democracy, provided that units of production are internally democratised. Another crucial assumption, also one attacked by latter-day Marxists, is that we are dealing with a genuine market system. In other words the proviso is that the market is not rigged or dominated by a few disproportionately powerful enterprises, as in monopoly capitalism.

Points that could be made against this assumption of inherent connections between the market and liberal democracy would centre on the allegation that a market system, with its intrinsic competitiveness and pursuit of private gain, is destructive of the kind of community which can be seen as necessary for democracy. As against this, though, it can be pointed out that (a) 'private' gain and the pursuit of profit have a different significance in a non-(corporate) capitalist market, and (b) some kind of market system is necessary even in overtly communal systems. And this point about the sheer efficiency of the market is of crucial importance. It is noteworthy that even as radical a critic of orthodox liberal democracy as Burnheim, who is by no means wholly in favour of the market, still sees it as having a vital role (Burnheim, 1985, Chapter 4). Again, the events of 1989 are widely taken as a decisive vindication of the viewpoint.

On the positive side, then, one of the main factors is efficiency – not least, efficiency in generating outcomes from myriads of individual decisions.[29] This is a factor which is stressed by Hayek and Friedman, who also focus on the connection between liberty and the free market (Hayek, 1960, 1976, 1982; Friedman, 1962). And if one were to try and summarise the connections between liberty and the free market, the following would be the main points on which to focus.

The free market can be seen as necessary to preserving liberty, since it disperses decision making and therefore power. But it can also be seen, in itself, as a key liberty, or system of liberties.[30] The important ideas here are that crucial individual liberties are necessary for, or presumed by, the operation of a free market, that freedom of trade is itself an important liberty and, more generally, that the whole notion of *laissez-faire* can be seen in terms of the most extensive form of liberty possible. Moreover, the market provides for – and enlarges in the most practicable way – freedom of choice. This last point can be extended into positive or developmental ideas of liberty since it can be argued that freedom of choice is a necessary condition for self-development. Indeed, this can be pushed further, since it can be argued that:

> 'self-development' ... may essentially require, market incentives and competitive striving. Thus many contemporary liberal thinkers, among them John Rawls and Robert Nozick, argue (in different ways) for *both* a market system based on incentives and a Humboldtian/Millian[31] vision of the maximal development of human personality. (Lukes, 1979)

A forceful exposition of the connection between the market and freedom, in both senses, is developed by Novak (1991). And it should not be forgotten that material prosperity, even though it may not figure directly in characterisations of 'self-development', *is* a necessary condition for it. Here we come back to the efficiency of the market, and what is argued to be its indispensable role in providing material prosperity. (We might also recall that Marx himself saw capitalism as necessary for the material development without which the eventual communist society could not exist.) In all these ways, the market could be said to be strongly connected with *liberal* democracy. And we should remember here that the market operating in the context of economic or industrial democracy is perfectly compatible with many forms of, or ideas about, participatory democracy.

Having now discussed a particular kind of defence of liberal democracy we shall turn, in the next chapter, to the general question of the justification of liberal democracy.

Notes

1. A full statement of the point would be a little more complex. A key element in the participatory critique is that the liberal democrat's account of democracy is faulty, and that what is assumed to be ultimate decision making by the people is really not such – precisely because there is not enough participation by the mass of the people in the decision process. Perhaps the point is better made by saying that a genuine democracy necessarily involves participation, and by allowing that there are different accounts of what a 'genuine' democracy is.
2. The term 'rank and file' is used because the idea of participation is applied in various contexts – for instance in industry, as we shall see, 'rank and file' means the workforce. With regard to participation in a democratic state, of course, it means the mass of the people or the people as a whole.

3. There are really two arguments here (though they are not necessarily always clearly distinguished): that participatory democracy is the best, or the only worthwhile, form of democracy; and that a system is not a democracy at all unless it is a participatory democracy.

4. Although less frequently, pluralist theory is also sometimes seen as 'bridging' the individualist/communitarian divide. Here the individual is seen as being integrated into the total community via membership of ('partial') groups. This is a perspective that derives ultimately from Hegel (Pateman, 1985).

5. A critique of liberal democratic theory's division of public and private, summed up by the slogan 'the personal is the political', is an aspect of feminist criticisms of liberal democracy. For feminist analyses of liberal democracy see, for example, Phillips (1991, 1992) and Mendus (1992).

6. This is an over-simplification since, as we shall see, the place of individualism in Marxist theory is complex and controversial, and on some interpretations Marx was committed to individualism. However, the dominant view – and the one most influential in Marxist confrontations with liberal democratic theory – is that Marxism involves a fundamental critique of liberal individualism (although, as we shall see, what is meant by 'individualism' here needs specification).

7. The significantly different radical approach of Burnheim should also be noticed here. He, too, despairs of representation as it exists in the liberal democratic state, and indeed goes so far as to argue for the dissolution of the state; but instead of looking to direct participation he argues for a system of 'statistical representation', with selection of representatives by lot, on functionally defined, autonomous decision-making bodies (Burnheim, 1985).

8. Of course, from a Marxist viewpoint, there is an important sense in which there can be nothing which benefits capitalism or capitalists in the long run – for in the long run capitalism is doomed to extinction. However, the run may be very long indeed, and the nature of the present system and who benefits from it remain matters of profound importance.

9. For coverage of this debate see Kymlicka (1989), Walzer (1990), Avineri and de-Shalit (1992) and Mulhall and Swift (1992). For a good introduction, placing it in a wider philosophical context, see Plant (1991, Chapter 9); for another good introduction see Kymlicka (1990, Chapter 6).

10. But see Carver (1992) who contends that 'Tucker's work falls short of a full account, because Marx's individualism has peculiarities he does not suspect. These lie in the way that the individual is socially constructed.'

11. Not only was J. S. Mill's thinking 'contaminated' in this way, but, according to Macpherson, it was necessarily so: 'In the nineteenth-century economy of scarcity', possessive market ideas and developmental ideas 'were, rightly, seen as necessarily linked together: the only way to free all individuals to "use and develop their human capacities fully" was "through the productivity of free enterprise capitalism"' (Lukes, 1979, quoting

Macpherson, 1977a). In the modern world, though, a post-scarcity form of liberal democracy is possible (this seemed more plausible in the 1960s and 1970s than it does today).

12. It can be debated whether discursive, or deliberative, theories of democracy are alternatives to, rather than examples of, liberal democratic theory. Both Dryzek and Miller, for example, take the former position; but this is to use a conception of 'liberal democratic theory' that identifies it with narrowly individualist forms. Here the latter position is taken since we are using a wider conception of liberal democratic theory where the focus is simply on the idea of limited public authority as the defining feature of the liberal component.

13. Some light can be shed on this by arguing that there are in fact *three* criss-crossing sources of uncertainty or ambivalence in the writings of Marx and Engels. Firstly there is ambivalence concerning whether the Paris Commune model is a form of, or an alternative to, the dictatorship of the proletariat (arguably it is the latter); secondly there is ambivalence about whether the Commune model is or is not an instance of final communism (arguably it is not); and, finally, there is ambivalence about whether, or in what sense, the Commune model is a form of state (although it is clear that it is the negation of the hitherto existing state form). For an illuminating discussion of these points see Levin (1989, Chapter 6). On balance it would seem the best interpretation is as follows. The Commune model is a radical democracy, which is a form of the transitional phase to the final communist, stateless society and is therefore distinguishable from it. The dictatorship of the proletariat is an alternative, and more probable, form of transitional phase. But the latter can only be seen as democratic (in the way developed further in the Leninist model of democracy) by invoking the notion of government by a Rousseauean 'real will' of the proletariat, which does not require liberal – or participatory – democratic structures for its manifestation.

14. 'One-party democracy' is put in quotes to indicate that it is not accepted here that this is a viable conception of democracy (see below for a substantiation of this view). However, for the sake of simplicity quotes will not normally be used hereafter.

15. Whether Lenin consciously made use of Continental democratic theory is another matter, although, for example, Harding comments (with reference to some of Lenin's arguments about the democratic role of revolutionary dictatorship) that, 'no doubt, Lenin had in mind the experience of France and the classic example of the French Revolution' (Harding, 1983). And in Marx's original analysis it is said that 'we find a teleological variant of Rousseau's theory of the general will' (Levin, 1983).

16. In its extreme form, in the last phase of Lenin's thought, the party remains as the true embodiment of the proletariat and its interest even where the masses, having been subverted by circumstances and become actively

hostile to policies advancing the proletarian cause, in effect cease to be the proletariat (Harding, 1983).

17. And, indeed, it seems that Gorbachev did not espouse what a liberal democrat would recognise as democracy: see Sakwa (1989).

18. One of the main justifications of capitalism has always been that by raising the general level of prosperity more than any other system, even those who benefit least are better off than they would be under any other system.

19. If developed in a different way, economic democracy can become part of a socialist theory – cf. the guild socialism of G. D. H. Cole (Pateman, 1970; Glass, 1966). But it is instructive that mainstream 'state socialists' have always been uneasy about industrial democracy precisely because of the extent to which it implies something other than state planning for the overall allocation of resources, and there is a very strong tendency for this 'something other' to be the market. For an excellent recent analysis of the relationship of industrial democracy to socialism see Pierson (1992).

20. There is a fundamental issue of social and political theory involved in, or lying behind, those being considered here: whether there is a constant or identifiable 'human nature'; and, if so, what it is.

21. The notion that individuals' ideas are determined in this way is widely based. There are theories of socialisation in modern sociology and political science, there is the sociology of knowledge and behind this the historicist tradition which feeds into – and which Marx combines with – ideas about the nature and role of ideology (see, for example, Benewick *et al.* (1973)).

22. Fundamental issues are, of course, raised here, which we cannot go into. The extent to which rationality and criteria of validity and truth, if they exist at all, can be viewed as transcending socio-cultural contexts and influences are matters which are the subject of socio-philosophical analysis and debate – much of it recent – and which are deeply controversial (for a good overview see Bernstein (1983); for a recent brief discussion see Spragens (1990, Conclusion)). The 'anti-relativist' stance – exemplified in the line taken here – has often been attacked, but just as often defended. One very important theorist who is, in an important sense, an anti-relativist, is Jurgen Habermas (for a recent introduction see Williams and Fearon-Jones (1992)). Compare, also, the 'epistemological "causal theory of knowledge" ' (Cunningham, 1987, p. 262).

23. Ideas which are not actually true may nonetheless be 'valid' in the sense of being 'rationally acceptable'. As such, it is arguable that they have the same status in this context as true ideas (Holden, 1983).

24. Strictly speaking, in order to avoid question-begging we should say that the connection is between *systems that are called* liberal democracies, and capitalism. However, the interests of clarity make it desirable to avoid such circumlocutions and either the proviso can be taken as read, or we can accept that the preceding argument has sufficiently demonstrated that democracy can exist in a capitalist society.

25. Novak (1991) argues that '*democracy* and *markets* [he is referring to capitalism] do not mutually entail each other in the world of conceptual logic. . . . But in the real world of actual experience, a polity which recognizes individual rights is bound to be drawn to an economic system which empowers individual agency. Similarly, an economic system based upon markets and individual incentives is, over time, bound to be drawn to a political system recognizing individual rights and liberties.'

26. It is possible to see connections running the other way as well, but it is difficult to see these as inherent since, as we have said, few would dispute that capitalism can exist under non-liberal democratic systems.

27. There is, indeed, a literature on the 'economic theory of democracy' – which is really a modern elaboration of the classical utilitarian theory of democracy – that seeks to analyse the voter-attracting behaviour of political parties on the model of the consumer-attracting behaviour of producers. This really began with Downs (1957); for a critical review of some of this work see Barry (1970), Aranson (1981, Chapter 7) and Dunleavy (1991, Chapter 5). One important sector of this literature is a branch of political economy specifically concerned with developing a theory of democracy in which the democratic process is seen as the analogue of the market, with elections viewed as exchange mechanisms in which the currency is votes and the commodity is political power. Especially important here is Buchanan and Tullock (1962); for comment, besides Barry (1970), see, for example, Cornford (1972).

28. Many, including Marxists, would argue that this kind of separation cannot be made and that a market system necessarily leads to, or is accompanied by, concentration of ownership of resources. For a Marxist, also, there are other 'capitalist evils' connected with alienation and the exchange relationship which are rooted in the market system as such. We cannot enter here into a discussion of these issues; but it does seem that many of them are defused when control of economic enterprises, instead of being vested in a few managers or owners, is put into the hands of the mass of the workers. There is, in fact, an increasing interest in non-capitalist forms of the market (see, for example, Burnheim (1985, Chapter 4) and Gould (1988, Chapter 9)); an important aspect of this is the current concern with 'market socialism' and 'the social market' (see, for example, Sartori (1987, Chapter 14, section 4) and Miller (1989)). For a recent, incisive, survey and analysis see Pierson (1992). See, also, the discussion of market socialism in Przeworski (1991).

29. This, of course, is to bypass the whole question of the nature of public goods – and the way collective decisions about them are generated from the decisions of individuals – which so exercises public-choice theorists. However, there are two key points which remain valid. First, where it is private goods that are desired, the market is very efficient at providing them; and this is because the market mechanism copes efficiently with the interplay of the myriads of individual decisions relating to private goods.

Second, because the market does this efficiently it leaves channels freer for coping with collective decision making about public goods.

30. It is the 'negative sense' of liberty to which reference is being made here, but as the text shows, there are also implications in terms of 'positive' conceptions as well.

31. The reference here is to Wilhelm von Humboldt (1767–1835) (Humboldt, 1969) and to John Stuart Mill (1982).

4

□

The justification of liberal democracy

In this chapter we are concerned with the question of how liberal democracy is to be justified. Or, to put the emphasis slightly differently, the question is whether, and if so why, liberal democracy is a good system of government. In fact the question is usually put in the stronger form of asking whether, and why, liberal democracy is the *best* system of government.

4.1
Questions about the justification of liberal democracy

Before we address the question directly there are two preliminary issues to be cleared out of the way. These arise from considering what 'justification' consists in, and what precisely is to be justified.

The main point about the first issue is that the nature of justification is a controversial matter. This is a large subject, but the most important thing as far as we are concerned is that some would deny that justification as such is possible at all. Someone might, for example, *prefer* liberal democracy to other systems of government; but this would be a matter of subjective preference, relative to that particular individual, rather than a matter of objective, rational justification. This view was especially prevalent in mid-twentieth century Anglo-American thought and had its main bases in fundamental assumptions or positions in philosophy and social analysis. In brief, it was held that value judgements – especially moral judgements – could not be validated or proved correct in any sense. And in particular they could not be scientifically validated, a position dubbed 'scientific value relativism' (Brecht, 1967).

All this, of course, left the justification of liberal democracy in a sorry mess.[1] Indeed, it seemed to leave the whole justificatory project of political philosophy in a mess. However, matters began to change in the 1970s. The publication of *A Theory of Justice* (Rawls, 1972) which contained a systematic theory, including a justification of liberal democracy (see below), was hailed as marking the revival of political philosophy. Also, scientific value relativism was undermined by developments in philosophy, including the philosophy of science, which questioned the notion of a significant divide between objective science on the one hand and moral judgement on the other. Arguably, an implication of such developments is that moral judgements can be rationally defended, at least to the extent that scientific theories can be.[2]

However, the idea that liberal democracy could be given an objective, rational justification had not yet been saved. Rawls's theory was attacked as ethnocentric relativism masquerading as objective justification – and even Rawls himself, in later writings, seems to go some way to accepting this (see note 8 below). And the logic of the developments that undermined scientific value relativism were increasingly pushed further to the point where many now argue that even scientific theory cannot, properly speaking, be rationally defended. Paradoxically, then, the very developments which undermined scientific value relativism have contributed to a more fundamental form of relativism. This has bolstered an increasingly rampant general relativism, stemming in modern times from Marx and Nietzsche and manifesting itself most lately in post-modernism, and an aspect of which is a critique of the role of reason in the generation of ideas about politics. Still very influential then is the contention that justification as such is not possible – that moral judgements about liberal democracy are not based upon reason but are relative (in this case to particular cultures rather than to particular individuals). To this extent, the justification of liberal democracy would still appear to be in a sorry mess.[3]

Or, at least, this was true until very recently. Even in the world of theory, relativism had not completely swept the board. The pendulum had begun to swing back and the project of providing rational foundations for liberal democracy survived: an example mentioned below is Gould (1988), who, although merely describing her project as 'quasi-foundationalist', does, crucially, distinguish this from anti-foundationalist relativism. Indeed there has been a 'recent reawakening of interest in the philosophical basis of liberal democracy' (Spragens, 1992). Spragens gives us a valuable account of this, besides providing such a basis himself (see below). But it is developments in the world of practice that have been the most dramatic; and these have had a profound impact upon theory. The theoretical developments have, then, been subsumed by – or swept up in – the dramatic changes that are discussed in section 3 below. As we shall see, it is argued that these imply, or lend support to the notion, that liberal democracy has triumphed and that it is universally accepted as the best system of government. And to the extent that there is such universal acceptance the idea that moral judgements about liberal democracy are relative to particular cultures is radically undermined (see also Fukuyama, 1992, p. 338).

It is arguable, then, that the project of justifying liberal democracy has been reinstated.[4] But this brings us on to the second preliminary issue: just what is it that we are seeking to justify? For an important point to remember here is that liberal democracy itself is to be justified and not something that *fails to be* liberal democracy. Critics of complacent liberal democrats have in fact often been developing the kind of critique we looked at in the last chapter. That is to say they have been attacking the American and other Western political systems for failing to realise the liberal democratic ideal, for failing to embody the idea or model of liberal democracy in practice. But it is with the justification of the model itself that we are concerned in this chapter and not with systems that fail to embody it.[5] Having said this, though, we should also recognise that the 'failure arguments' tend to flow over into attacks on the liberal democratic model itself. We saw this in the case of Leninism and the idea of one-party democracy. And even participatory theory was seen to have a certain ambivalence or blindness about the idea of needing checks upon popular power, which could be construed as a rejection of a key element actually in the liberal democratic model.

The justification of liberal democracy – of the liberal democratic model – thus requires a double aspect. It needs to be justified against traditional attacks from the right, to the effect that the people should not have the power it ascribes to them. But it also needs to be justified against attacks from the left, to the effect that this power is given insufficient scope.

But we now come to another point that arises in settling what exactly is to be justified. In Chapter 2 we saw that there were many different theories and models of democracy. It is arguable, indeed, that in the face of such diversity we should not seek a justification of democracy, or *the* model of democracy, as such. Rather we should focus on justifying a form, or *a* model, of democracy (Nelson, 1980). And though we are here crucially reducing the amount of diversity by concerning ourselves specifically with *liberal* democracy, the amount we are left with is still very significant. Nonetheless, there are common elements in this diversity: these are the very elements by virtue of which the single label liberal democracy is appropriate and which figure in the definition given in Chapter 1. In other words it makes significant sense – very significant sense – to talk of a general model of liberal democracy here, and to ask about the justification simply of 'liberal democracy'. This is not just a point about definition. The more important point, or implication, is that there are good reasons for favouring a governmental system of a certain general form – and this form corresponds with the general model of liberal democracy. This can perhaps be better appreciated by focusing on the importance assigned by these reasons to the difference between this general form and others that are held to be *un*desirable.

There are, though, two partial qualifications to be made to this notion of an overall justification of a general model. First, one of the types of justification referred to below does not apply to all forms of liberal democracy. This is the 'developmental' justification which is held to apply specifically to participatory democracy. We mentioned previously the ambivalence of participatory theory, and it may be that the developmental justification is not to be counted as a justification of liberal democracy at all, since participatory democracy is sometimes seen as a *contrasting* form of democracy. But this is to over-simplify the subtle relationship between participatory and orthodox liberal democracy; and it should also be remembered that the developmental justification can apply to indisputably liberal democratic theories such as John Stuart Mill's. Even so it is absolutely clear that there is one type of liberal democratic theory in respect of which this form of justification is not applicable. This is elitist democratic theory, which is explicitly criticised by participatory theorists for rejecting the developmental idea. Elitist democratic theory is also explicitly defended by its advocates for rejecting more than the very minimum of participation – that is, voting. Indeed, it is by virtue of this that participationists see what is called elitist democratic theory as ceasing to be a democratic theory at all.

The second partial qualification to the notion that we shall be considering justifications of a general model, concerns the characterisation of that model as *liberal* democracy. Traditional justifications often tend to be of democracy as such, and whether the democracy spoken of is (or is intended to be) necessarily liberal democracy may not be clear. But at least the application of such justifications to specifically liberal democracy is not ruled out, and we shall treat them as having this application. And anyway, part of the case for liberal democracy that informs this book is that genuine democracy must necessarily have key features of the liberal democratic model. One type of traditional justification, though, must be looked at a little differently. This is where democracy is favoured because it ensures liberty. How far this is applicable as a justification of democracy is contentious (Chapter 1). But it is clearly a central justification of *liberal* democracy: indeed, liberal democracy can be seen as a system specifically designed to ensure liberty – even, if necessary, at the cost of some diminution of democracy.

4.2
Justifications of liberal democracy

Having cleared the ground, and having established that the justification of liberal democracy can be seen as a valid project, it is time now to sketch in the main types of justification of liberal democracy. (Referring back to the previous remarks about the nature of justification, we shall not really be focusing on the logical form these take; but at least looking at their substance will illustrate this form.)

Starting with justifications against the 'challenge from the right', there are a number of different types of argument in support of liberal democracy. It is, though, fruitful to group them into three categories. These focus respectively on the underlying principles, the inherent virtues and the beneficial results of liberal democracy. From another perspective one might divide justifications into those which focus merely on legitimacy – that in order to be legitimate government must take the form of liberal democracy – and those which focus on the merits of the actual substance of government in systems of this form. However, there is a great deal of overlap between the reasons for saying the substance of government is good in a liberal democratic system and the reasons for ascribing legitimacy to such a system. It therefore becomes confusing to try and keep them separate, and we shall stick to our threefold categorisation.

Underlying principles

Let us look first at the 'underlying principles' category. Here liberal democracy is viewed as giving expression to fundamental moral principles, and is seen as the way of ensuring or facilitating their operation. These principles may in turn be based on fundamental theoretical or philosophical analyses of the nature of man and reality. We might call these 'philosophical' justifications.

An important type in this category is the 'Christian justification' of liberal democracy. Key theorists are Jacques Maritain and Reinhold Niebuhr (see, for example, Maritain (1945) and Schram (1976)). In fact to treat this as a single type is to over-simplify and merge together different arguments. Nonetheless, there are important common elements.

Perhaps the best way of characterising the Christian justification is by saying that it consists in a religious expression of, or provides a religious underpinning for, moral principles typically seen as the bases for liberal democracy (and at which we shall look in a moment). For the Christian, it can be argued then, these principles, which other theorists regard as secular, have their proper expression or foundation in Christianity. The principles in question are primarily those of equality and liberty, so important in philosophical justifications of liberal democracy (see below), although other important principles and ideas can be involved as well.[6] The Christian underpinning or expression is chiefly concerned with the dignity of man and the equal status of individuals in the sight of God. More generally still, we see here a religious foundation for the liberal democrat's belief in the supreme worth of the individual. And ultimately, perhaps, it is only a Christian conception of the individual that really secures individualism from its critics: even the minimal individualism that we saw in the last chapter is necessary for liberal democratic theory may be vulnerable to the kind of fundamental (but not specifically Marxist) communitarian critique of liberal individualism advanced by, for example, Sandel (1982). A flavour of the Christian justification is given by Maritain's approving quotation from a speech by an American Vice-President, Henry A. Wallace, in 1942: 'The Idea of Freedom . . . is derived from the Bible with its extraordinary emphasis on the dignity of the individual. Democracy is the only true political expression of Christianity' (Maritain, 1945).

A secular equivalent of the transcendental foundation for the belief in the individual provided by Christianity is to be found in the philosophy of Kant, although it is specifically attacked by Sandel (1982). As in the case of the Christian justification this can be developed into a justification of liberal democracy. It is true that Kant is in no straightforward way a liberal democrat. In fact his position is rather complex and can, perhaps, be best summed up as involving a belief in government by those who are representatives of, but who are not necessarily answerable to, the people (Williams, 1983). Nonetheless his underlying philosophy gives an account of the human individual in which autonomy and respect for persons is of supreme importance.[7] His distinctive pronouncement on the moral importance of individuals is that people should never be treated 'simply as a means, but always at the same time as an end' (Kant, 1964). And he is usually counted as a liberal philosopher.

Moreover, what is perhaps the most comprehensive recent justification of liberal democracy, John Rawls's *A Theory of Justice*, can be seen as an application of Kantian philosophy (Rawls (1972, section 40); Rawls (1980); Darwall (1976); Williams (1983); but see Höffe (1984)). There will be no attempt to summarise Rawls's justification here, other than to say that the conclusion that liberal democracy is the appropriate form of government for free and equal individuals is derived from the idea that this is the form of government to which entirely free, equal and rational individuals would agree.[8] (The literature on Rawls is now very considerable but Daniels (1975) and Blocker and Smith (1981) are useful collections of papers, while a useful recent introduction is Lassman (1992).) They would agree to it because it satisfies principles of justice. These principles give priority to the maintenance of equal basic liberties. At another level, then, Rawls provides a version of justifications of liberal democracy in terms of equality and liberty, and these we shall now indicate.

Such justifications ascribe fundamental importance to the principles of equality and liberty and seek to show that liberal democracy is necessary for their realisation – and is to be valued because of this. We have already discussed the connection between democracy and the principles of equality and liberty (Chapter 1) and hence we have looked at some of the ways in which liberal democracy can be said to realise these principles. Only one or two further remarks need to be made here.

These stem from the observation that if a case for liberal democracy is to be made because it realises these principles, any such justification will also have to show why the principles themselves are to be valued. In the Christian and Kantian cases this was a major part of the justification. But what other sorts of reasoning are there?

An aspect of scientific value relativism had been that it is impossible to validate basic principles. This impaired 'pre-Rawlsian' justifications of democracy. One such allegedly impaired justification in terms of equality is nonetheless lucidly presented in Cohen (1971). He takes the view that the validity of the basic principle cannot be demonstrated. This principle is the contention that people are in an important and basic sense equal. (In an earlier idiom this would have been a 'self-evident truth': 'We hold these truths to be self-evident, that all men are created equal' – American Declaration of Independence, 1776.) In fact, though, he provides persuasive argumentation in its support. Democratic decision making, he contends, is necessary to give an equal say to all individuals. And the provision of an equal say is, in turn, necessary to give proper recognition to the basic equality of all men, deriving from an essential quality they all have beneath their undeniable differences. More recently there has in fact been less ambivalence, and an overt re-engagement, in some quarters, in rational authentication of first principles. As already pointed out, there is in effect a renewed interest in providing what scientific value relativists would have dismissed as 'metaphysical' foundations for democracy. Gould (1988) is a good example: here there is a justification of democracy[9] as the realisation of the freedom and equality of individuals, grounded in a philosophical validation of the worth of such freedom and equality.

Justifications that focus on liberal democracy as the means of protecting and promoting liberty have, apart from the Christian and Kantian foundations already mentioned, three main bases. These are the ideas of natural law and natural rights and the classic defence of individual liberty given by John Stuart Mill in *On Liberty* (Mill, 1982).

A natural law justification is given by Hallowell (1954) in which he connects natural law, liberty and equality. He argues that the natural law tradition stemming from Cicero (106–43 BC), and transmitted to the modern world via Christianity, shows people are equal in their capacity to reason and thereby to determine right from wrong. Freedom requires that they all should know and will the good; and this in turn requires that they all should share in the control of government. Lord Devlin makes a very similar point when he says that all men 'have at their command – and in this they are all born in the same degree – the faculty of telling right from wrong. This is the whole meaning of democracy' (Devlin, 1965).

We saw in Chapter 1 how democracy – although some see it as threatening individual liberty – can be regarded, and valued, as the form of government which will secure areas of individual liberty. (And the notion of liberal democracy can be seen either as expressing the idea of an automatic connection between liberty and democracy, or as a modification of democracy needed in order, on occasion, to protect individual liberty against democracy.) Natural rights theories and Mill's defence of liberty are accounts of why there ought to be areas of individual liberty, where individuals are free from governmental interference. It will be remembered that although the accounts are different, the areas of individual liberty sanctified are broadly similar (Chapter 1). The natural rights justification of democracy given classical expression (by implication at least) in Locke's *Second Treatise* was embodied in Paine's *Rights of Man* and in the American Constitution. And today it is frequently argued that in parts of the world where it does not yet exist liberal democracy is needed to prevent abuses of human rights (the world-wide advance of liberal democracy is discussed in section 3 below). John Stuart Mill, it is true, was very worried about the propensity for individual liberty to be threatened by democracy, nonetheless he is important here as a champion of both democracy and liberty (and he seeks to limit democracy's threatening propensities).

And it remains true that one of the most widely held justifications of democracy (which can find expression by stressing the notion of *liberal* democracy) is to the effect that democracy is desirable because it preserves freedom. As Hallowell states:

> When we talk today about the preservation of democracy, what most of us, I think, are concerned about is the preservation of freedom. We realise that democratic forms and institutions find their essential and ultimate meaning in the presentation and enlargement of human freedom. They are not ends in themselves but means to an ultimate end. They are not identical with freedom but the means through which freedom may find its best political expression. (Hallowell, 1954)

Inherent virtues

Let us turn now to the 'inherent virtues' justifications. These are justifications which centre on the value of the liberal democratic process itself, in contrast to those in the third category which focus on the value of the results obtained by, the outcomes of, that process (though there is not always a clear division between the two).

One of the most important of these is the 'developmental justification': the argument that democracy is to be valued because it develops the potential of the individuals involved to become fully rounded human beings. As we have seen, this is essentially an argument connected with participatory theories of democracy; for it is political participation that develops those engaged in it (see the remarks above about the admissibility of this as a justification of liberal democracy).

The main ideas, including those that connect individual development with integration with the community, were covered in the discussion of participatory democracy in the last chapter.[10] One interesting argument which we mentioned but did not consider in depth, however, is that developed by Botwinick (1985, 1990). This, in a sense, takes as its point of departure the relativist justification discussed below. He argues that there is a radical scepticism and relativism involved in the individualism of liberal democratic theory, such that the possibility of objective validation of belief is denied: 'supra-individual supports for knowledge and belief are knocked out'. This causes deep problems that cannot be resolved by theorising. The only answer is political: since there is no theoretical basis for agreement[11] amongst individuals they must reach a consensus by action – political action. This can be done only by political participation. One of the problems to be solved is that:

> the fact that we are all as it were epistemological equals [implies] industrial and governmental power cannot legitimately be invoked in furtherance of any particular individual's conception of the good unless that conception has managed to attract to itself what we might call a participatory consensus. (Botwinick, 1985)

The other problem is that scepticism (or relativism) is self-defeating (as we noted in the last chapter when we saw that relativism was implied by the notion that ideas are socially determined). Now, Botwinick continues, it is important to understand the relativist thesis and the importance of its consequences. It might be held that *because* it is self-defeating it is impossible to specify its consequences. Botwinick, however, maintains that the problem applies only to theoretical statement and that there are practical consequences:

> If skepticism can only be shown, or intuitively perceived, but not stated, then perhaps the way out of this dilemma is to create a participatory society in which epistemological equals interact with each other in fashioning the institutions and decisions that affect their lives. If the philosophical quandaries pointing towards skepticism and yet inhibiting a consistent formulation from being put forward are indeed irresoluble, then in this negative, indirect sense we will have provided an objective ground for political participation. (Botwinick, 1985)

Besides those that focus on participation there are other justifications which can be classed as valuing the liberal democratic process itself. One such is that the process is rational – embodying 'the civilising power of reason'. This view has been restated in a sophisticated way by Spragens, who argues that liberal democracy should still be properly understood, and justified, as a manifestation of reason, but with reason itself properly understood in terms of a conception of rational practice that 'is implicit in the recent philosophy of science and language' (Spragens, 1992). A related view is that the liberal democratic process is the best way of managing conflict. Liberal democracy allows the sources of conflict to be expressed – thereby acting as a safety valve. But besides allowing disagreement and dissent, it defuses their consequences by providing and 'ceremonialising' processes of conflict resolution. 'The ultimate claim of a democratic government to authority is that it permits dissent and survives it' (Frankel, 1962, quoted in Cohen, 1972). But besides managing conflict, liberal democracy can be said to reduce or minimise it, at least if the democracy in question is not in the process of breaking down. The argument is that such things as freedom of discussion, freedom of association and the opportunity to attempt to convert people to one's own point of view tend to lessen frustration and thereby to minimise violent conflict. They also facilitate peaceful change. But, above all, the electoral mechanism provides a peaceful solution to one of the key problems of modern political systems: the problem of succession. A significant justification of democracy, then, is that it provides for an orderly succession of rulers.

Another set of arguments in the 'inherent virtues' category comes back again to scepticism (although this time they are not just linked to participatory theory and apply generally to liberal democracy as such). One of these is called by Wollheim 'the completely sceptical argument for democracy':

> According to this argument, it is impossible for anyone to discover what is the right course of action for the community, or where the true interests of its inhabitants reside. From this it follows that everyone in the community should be allowed to do what he wants to do as far as is socially possible. The only society in which this can happen is the one in which everyone has some control in the government: therefore Democracy is favored. (Wollheim, 1958)

The relativist justification

A variation of this kind of justification is one to the effect that relativism implies liberal democracy. If it is the case that there are no absolute standards of right and wrong, then, it is argued, all viewpoints are equally valid and all should be tolerated. Moreover, all ought to have an equal chance to compete and to be adopted as public policy. That is to say, in the absence of absolute standards the only criterion left by which to decide which policy ought to be chosen is popularity: that policy should be adopted which can attract the most votes.

Superficially, this form of justification may seem convincing. However, it is fundamentally misconceived. At a crucial point the argument contends that the absence of absolute standards implies the non-existence of moral judgements; yet this is denied by the very judgement asserted by the argument itself. Indeed, the whole argument is self-contradictory: a moral judgement asserting that democracy ought to obtain is derived from what amounts to a contention that no moral judgements can be made.

The so-called relativist justification of liberal democracy is, then, fundamentally flawed (whether Botwinick's argument in this context is more convincing is debatable). However, this defective relativist justification has, in fact, been extraordinarily influential. This is partly because it appears to connect up with the liberal value of tolerance – although, in fact, as Fukuyama points out, because relativism attacks all values and 'is not a weapon that can be aimed selectively' it must end up attacking the value of tolerance itself (Fukuyama, 1992)[12]. But it is also because it 'made a virtue of necessity'. As we indicated earlier, moral relativism left the intellectual defence of democracy in a sorry mess; but, paradoxically, via the relativist justification the cause of this mess became itself the justification of democracy! (See the brilliant survey and analysis in Purcell (1973); for an excellent short analysis, see Spragens (1973, pp. 95–9); Thorson (1962) provides an explicit and lucid example of the relativist justification – but its very lucidity serves to expose its central weakness.)

Another argument in favour of democracy that we should mention is, to an extent, a combination of the previous two. Even if the relativism argument is mistaken, it can still be acknowledged that liberal democracy might be said to cope well with the existence of a diversity of values. Within certain limits, it allows for the expression of, and influence upon, policy by many different viewpoints. In this way, it could be argued, dangerous frustrations are avoided. And here we come back to the justification indicated earlier: that liberal democracy minimises conflict. If it is presumed that in modern societies there is likely to be a substantial diversity of values and interests, and there is much to support such a view, then a justification can be formulated to the effect that liberal democracy is the only system of government likely to be viable in modern society. Wollheim includes another dimension when he writes of the argument that:

> under modern conditions [democracy] is the only working possibility. No member of an emancipated industrial society will put up with political tutelage. He insists on having a fair chance of influencing the government in

accordance with his own desires and ideas; and by a 'fair' chance he means a chance 'as good as the next man's'. This argument was succinctly summarised in the nineteenth century by the conservative James Fitzjames Stephen who said that in Democracy we count heads to avoid breaking them; and it remains today one of the best arguments in favor of democracy on account of its extreme economy. (Wollheim, 1958)

This is surely an excellent argument for liberal democracy, quite apart from any virtue of 'economy'! And it complements another argument which we can put under the heading of the inherent value of the liberal democratic process, albeit in a negative sort of way. The argument just indicated is of the form: even if democracy has nothing else to commend it, it is at least likely to work. The justification complemented by it adds that democracy is at least better than other systems of government. This was exemplified in Winston Churchill's remark in the House of Commons in 1947: 'it has been said that democracy is the worst form of government except all those other forms that have been tried from time to time.'

Beneficial results

The final category of arguments was justifications of liberal democracy in terms of its beneficial results or outcomes. The key point in some of the most commonly cited of these arguments is that a democracy allows the opinions of the 'common man' to prevail. From the Greeks onwards one of the reasons traditionally given for regarding this as a good thing is the contention that 'true opinion on political and moral matters is the privilege of the common man. Accordingly, power in a community should reside with him: and this it does only in a democracy. Hence the superiority of democracy' (Wollheim, 1958). Variations on this theme have included the idea that 'true opinion' is the possession of a majority of people, even if not of all of them, and that therefore the majority should rule. Another variant is the argument that wisdom is scattered throughout the community, and hence that wise policies can be obtained only by tapping as much of it as possible in the decision-making process. This can only be done – or, at least, it is only practicable to do this – by involving everyone in the decision-making process. A stronger form of this argument is the one developed by Aristotle to the effect that, although each individual may be deficient in the qualities necessary for political decision making, the people collectively are not deficient in this way: they are, indeed, better endowed than any experts, since the *combined* qualities of all the individuals add up to a far from deficient totality (Aristotle, 1981).

Whether or not such contentions about the 'true opinion' or the wisdom of (many or all) ordinary people are valid is a matter about which there has been dispute down the ages. Indeed, it has been one of the main issues upon which 'right-wing' critics of democracy focus. It might be objected that it is one thing to accept that the common man has a certain amount of wisdom – or common sense – but quite another to accept that he has greater wisdom than those who might be specially trained or otherwise specially qualified to rule. Or, to put it another way, it might be said that the common man is not devoid of wisdom, but that he does not possess true knowledge. From Plato onwards, a powerful stream of thought has asserted that the common man is insufficiently qualified to rule (see, for example, Spitz (1965)). But here we must bring in the main argument that has been adduced in support of the view that the opinion of the common man should prevail.

In its strongest form, this additional argument is the one especially associated with utilitarian democratic theory. This is the idea that whether or not common men – or all individuals – are wiser than the select few (or one) in some absolute sense, it is at least the case that each individual knows his or her own interest better than anyone else. And a specifically utilitarian justification of democracy builds on this conception to reach the conclusion that a democracy is the best system of government, since it secures the greatest happiness of the greatest number. (Individuals achieve happiness by pursuing their interests; democracy is the system of government in which it is assured that the interests of all, or a majority of, individuals – 'the people' – will be pursued; therefore democracy secures the greatest happiness of the greatest number.) Now, as we have seen before, there are great difficulties that stand in the way of a theory of democracy in terms of self-interest alone. And this greatly complicates – if not entirely frustrates – any attempt at a straightforward utilitarian justification of democracy. But it can be argued that a more sophisticated justification, which focuses on individuals' judgements about what is in the common interest, can overlap with utilitarian theory. In any case there is an important core to the argument from individuals being the best judges of their own interests that remains valid. This is simply the notion that whatever else goes into the making of communal decisions, in the end such decisions are only justifiable if the mass of the people judge their experiences of them to be acceptable. And a democracy provides the means whereby the mass of the people can effectively overturn policies that they find unacceptable.

This type of argument, developed from an argument of Aristotle's, is stated in terms of a 'shoe-pinching' analogy. It is found in Lindsay (1943), and we have already come across it in Pitkin's characterisation of the 'Liberal' theory of representation: only the wearer (the people) knows where the shoe pinches (the effect of governmental policies). As Lindsay points out – and Pitkin in effect makes the same point – this idea is quite compatible with fairly elitist conceptions of democracy (although this is not his terminology). The expert could be said to propose and the mass dispose: the shoemaker makes the shoes and the people decide whether to accept them or call for others, and perhaps for other shoemakers, according to whether they pinch or not. This is, indeed, a powerful argument for liberal democracy.

Significance of the justifications

These arguments for liberal democracy against 'right-wing' attacks add up to a powerful, convincing justification. They are perhaps not so often focused upon now because criticisms from the 'right' are seldom heard today. But they have often been voiced in the past. And in some parts of the world this past is very recent indeed: where military coups and authoritarian governments have been frequent, so have such criticisms of liberal democracy (today, though, because of the recent success of the *idea* of liberal democracy the use of such such criticisms to bolster non-democratic governments is effectively ruled out – see section 3 below). Nor should it be forgotten that in the Western world, too, quite recently there were military or authoritarian dictatorships: in Spain, Portugal and Greece.

Also not so long ago, Europe was the scene of the greatest challenge to liberal democracy, with the triumph of totalitarian dictatorship in Nazi Germany and Fascist Italy. These were in effect right-wing (in our sense as well as the usual one) challenges to democracy, although their own rhetoric, it might be said, was more similar to 'left-wing' criticism. In fact the main target of criticism was the specifically liberal element in liberal democracy, both the ideas about restricting the state and the underlying liberal individualism. In this respect, Fascist criticism of liberal democracy had important affinities with Leninist criticism. And, of course, many would argue that in terms of the totalitarian challenge to liberal democracy Leninist–Stalinist Russia was on a par with the Fascist dictatorships. This brings us back to the challenge from the 'left' to liberal democracy. It might be disputed whether Leninist criticism and the theory and practice of people's democracy really amount to 'left-wing criticism' in the sense defined earlier. But it is, of course, true that elements of the Marxist critique, with which Leninism is connected (even if perversely), fall into this category.

Defending the other flank

In fact, as we said earlier, the radical critique generally oscillates between accusing liberal democracy of not realising its ideals and attacking those ideals themselves. It is the latter that constitutes the 'left-wing' attack. More implicit than explicit, it amounts essentially to the contention that liberal democratic ideas about defending individual liberty involve un-acceptable – undemocratic – limitations on the power of the people. It might be said that the founding father of this line of criticism is Rousseau. And this harks back to the difficulties encountered in deciding whether Continental theory should be counted as liberal democratic theory. But the modern radical critique of liberal democracy is more pointed because it has the actual experience of the (alleged) deficiencies of the theory and practice of liberal democracy on which to sharpen itself.

There are two main sorts of justification in the face of this kind of attack. These are reiterations of traditional arguments in liberal democratic theory, but they are none the worse for that. First, there is the stress on the importance of individual liberty in the classical liberal, 'negative' sense. Areas of individual life should be preserved from regulation by the state, or invasion by the community, even, or perhaps especially, where the state or community in question is fully democratic. Many of the issues here have already been discussed and we shall not go over them again. But the essence of the matter is the strength of the case for protecting areas of purely individual autonomy – areas of life within which each individual decides what activities to pursue; moreover, these are areas of private life, and such activities can legitimately include those which fulfil purely individual, as distinct from communal, objectives. It is true that the validity and extent of such private areas continues to be much debated by critics of liberalism. But we might recall Held's (1987) concern with 'discussion about the desirable limits of collective regulation ... *if* the model of a more participatory society is to be adequately defended. Such an engagement might well have to concede more to the liberal tradition than has hitherto been allowed by left-wing thinkers.'

The second form of justification here focuses on practical consequences of ideas and theories. The main point is that the liberal democratic idea emphasises certain sorts of institution and process as a way of both expressing and limiting the popular will. Above all, there is the stress on the importance of free, competitive, contested elections. And theories involving critiques of the liberal democratic model tend to issue forth in systems that dispense with free, contested elections. The results are nearly always undesirable and can be disastrous. Neither Hitler nor Stalin would have remained in power if either had had to face his people in free elections (it is true that Hitler came to power by winning an election, but he subsequently abolished them). A knockdown justification of liberal democracy remains that it prevents tyranny because the people can – through peaceful, constitutional means – kick the rascals out. And this is a justification against 'left-wing' as well as 'right-wing' attacks because, as Leninist–Stalinist theory and practice so graphically illustrate, it is *theories* about the need for the supremacy of unlimited popular power that are *in fact* most likely to lead to pernicious tyrannies.

There are, then, powerful and convincing justifications of liberal democracy against attacks from both the 'left' and 'right'. It is true that there remain compelling 'left-wing' criticisms of liberal democracy. Carole Pateman's (1985) book, for example, is profound and important. When all is said and done, however, the attacks that are most convincing are those that criticise the liberal democratic state for not realising the liberal democratic ideal. The ideal – the liberal democratic model itself – is to be rescued or retrieved rather than attacked. This is true of both Pateman and Macpherson. To be sure, both do mount critiques of liberal democratic theory as well as practice. But, essentially, these amount to attacks on misconceptions which prevent orthodox liberal democratic theorists from comprehending the true nature of the liberal democratic ideal – the authentic liberal democratic model. Again, the model itself is acclaimed rather than attacked.

Indeed, as we shall see in the next section it is arguable that the model is now *universally* acclaimed.

4.3
The triumph of liberal democracy?

In the previous two sections we considered how liberal democracy may be justified. But we now need to ask about the generality of the justifications. Do they have universal application? Do the arguments for liberal democracy apply across space and time or do they show only that liberal democracy is the best form of government in some sorts of circumstances, but not in others? In fact, as we shall see, the universality of application of the arguments for liberal democracy is now quite widely accepted: indeed, it may be that this – together with the associated acceptance of the validity of those arguments – marks the triumph of liberal democracy.

This broad endorsement of the idea of the universal validity of liberal democracy is a very recent development. True, such an idea was a presupposition of much traditional liberal democratic theory, and continued as such in the beliefs of many citizens of liberal democracies. However, the argument that liberal democracy is the best form of government in only some circumstances has also had wide currency. It has even been advanced by some key liberal democratic theorists. J. S. Mill, for example, argued that although representative government is the ideal form of polity it may not be suitable for underdeveloped societies (Mill, 1912, Chapter 4). And Rawls (1972) argues in a similar way that until a certain level of wealth has been attained in a society his principles of justice do not fully apply.

In arguments of this sort, however, it is presumed that societies go through stages of development, with liberal democracy being seen as suitable for the later, and better, stages. Liberal democracy, therefore, *is* still seen as the ideally best form of government – the best form of government in the best form of society – and so we still have, in a key sense, an unqualified justification.

It is, though, easy to confuse this sort of argument with another, where liberal democracy is no longer seen as ideally best. Here, although liberal democracy is regarded as the best form of government for societies of a certain sort, there is no contention or implication that these are the better forms of society. Liberal democracy may be the best system of government in certain circumstances, but it is not necessarily the best system *per se*. Indeed, those who maintain that liberal democracy is simply the best system, and not just in Western societies, are accused of ethnocentrism, the elevation of 'the Western European and North American ... experience to the level of a universal truth, without recognizing its own "culture-boundness"' (Fukuyama, 1992).

Clearly, the anti-ethnocentric and the liberal-democracy-is-ideally-best lines of argument are importantly different. However, there remains a common element in the idea that the desirability of establishing liberal democracy is limited by circumstances. We shall go on to assess this idea in a moment, but we should first note the extent to which it tends also to involve assessments of the limited *possibility* of establishing liberal democracy. That is to say, the idea of the limited range of liberal democracy's desirability has been firmly bolstered by perceptions of the limited range of conditions under which it is possible in the first place. For example, the contention that liberal democracy is the best system only in Western cultures – which is involved in the anti-ethnocentric argument – often merges with the argument that liberal democracy is only possible in such cultures. In fact, questions about the conditions under which liberal democracy is desirable, and under which it is possible, tend to merge into a question about its feasibility, suitability or appropriateness. Thus Huntington (1991) says that the 'cultural thesis' – in one of its two forms – 'states that only Western culture provides a suitable base for the development of democratic institutions and democracy[13] is, consequently, largely inappropriate for non-Western societies.'

It has often been argued, then, that liberal democracy is only appropriate for some – notably Western – societies. And, although things have now changed, until very recently this argument was widely accepted. But what are we to make of this argument – this repudiation of the traditional idea of the universal validity of liberal democracy, this challenge to the contention that it is simply *the* best form of government? Consideration of this question will bring us on to the reasons for the recent change.

The limited suitability argument has been underpinned by analyses of the necessary conditions for liberal democracy. Many of these apparently demonstrate the limited possibility of liberal democracy. The absence of the requisite culture and the necessary level of economic development have been the factors most often emphasised.[14] As we shall see below, attention focused particularly on underdeveloped countries and it was widely maintained that liberal democracy was unsuitable for the Third World. But there was also the question of the regimes of the communist world, which not only differed from liberal democracy but actually challenged it (see Chapter 3, section 3 above). A common response to this was, of course, a robust assertion of the superiority of liberal democracy but this was often undermined by the limited suitability thesis. As Fukuyama (1992) points out, 'many of the peoples of Eastern Europe were held to be either incapable of or uninterested in the liberal democratic traditions of Western Europe.'

All this highlights how very common regimes other than liberal democracy have been. And, in fact, the limited suitability argument was powerfully boosted by the limited incidence of liberal democracy: the argument that liberal democracy often was not suitable seemed to be confirmed by the fact that liberal democracy often did not exist. There is the underlying point that democracy itself is historically rare: 'throughout recorded history hierarchy has been the rule, democracy the exception' (Dahl, 1989). Indeed, apart from in ancient Greece it hardly existed before this century. But liberal democracy has seemed rare even in the twentieth century. At times, in fact, it looked as if it were being squeezed out. There was the failure of liberal democracy in the Third World, which has already been referred to. But there was also the rise of brutal totalitarian regimes. Those of the Fascist Right required military defeat; but those of the Marxist–Leninist Left, as already mentioned, continued their challenge into the post-war world. Totalitarianism constituted both a dire physical threat *and* a head-on challenge to the value-system of liberal democracy.

All this 'had a devastating effect on the self-confidence of liberal democracies, whose isolation in a world of totalitarian and authoritarian regimes led to serious doubts about the universality of liberal notions of right' (Fukuyama, 1992). This persisted beyond the defeat of Fascism. In 1975 Daniel Patrick Moynihan, a staunch champion of liberal democracy, despairingly wrote:

> Liberal democracy on the American model increasingly tends to the condition of monarchy in the nineteenth century: a holdover form of government, one which persists in isolated or peculiar places here and there, and may even serve well enough for special circumstances, but which has simply no relevance to the future. It is where the world was, not where it is going. (Plattner, 1991, quoting Moynihan, 1975)

Recently, however, there has been a profound change. There has in fact been a dramatic resurgence of liberal democracy. For Huntington (1991), 'the transition of some thirty countries from nondemocratic to democratic political systems' involves – to quote from the cover of his book – a 'global democratic revolution [which] is probably the most important trend in the late twentieth century.'

For many it was, of course, the downfall of communism that was *the* event. And 1989, the two hundredth anniversary of the French Revolution and implementation of the American constitution, was marked as the year of the democratic revolution: this is summed up, for instance, in the title of Timothy Garton Ash's (1990) book about the collapse of the Eastern European regimes – *We the People: The Revolution of '89*. For Marc Plattner (1991), writing about 'the democratic moment', the 'dramatic events of August 1991 in Moscow [the failed *coup* in the former Soviet Union] should convince any remaining skeptics that the democratic revolutions of 1989 indeed marked a watershed in world history.'

The collapse of communism is, in itself, clearly of huge importance for liberal democracy. However, it can also be seen as part of a larger pattern or process. Arguably, the process began with the downfall of the authoritarian regime set up by Salazar in Portugal, which was quickly followed by the downfall of that set up by Franco in Spain. The transitions of Portugal and Spain from authoritarian to liberal democratic regimes were of great importance. They showed not only that it *could* be done; but also *how* it could be done – and this was to be of help in later transitions (politicians from the fledgling democracies of Eastern Europe, for example, were later to come to Spain for advice). Huntington regards the overthrow of the dictatorship in Portugal in 1974 as the 'beginning of a world-wide movement to democracy'. This he sees as the 'third wave of democratization in the modern world' – the previous two waves, which were followed by set backs to liberal democracy in 'reverse waves', having been from 1828 to 1926 and 1943 to 1962. Plattner gives less prominence to Portugal and Spain but he, too, places the democratic revolutions of 1989 in a similar kind of perspective:

> Although the late 1970s witnessed transitions to democracy in Spain and Portugal and its restoration in India, only in the 1980s did it become clear that Moynihan's pessimism was unfounded and that democracy was experiencing a true resurgence. The democratic tide swept through most of Latin America, reached such key Asian countries as the Philippines, Korea, Taiwan, and Pakistan, and by decade's end was beginning to make ripples in sub-Saharan Africa and even the Middle East. Moreover, the 1980s saw such Third World alternatives to democracy as African socialism and bureaucratic authoritarianism in Latin America revealed as political and economic failures. (Plattner, 1991)

The post-1989 transitions of former communist regimes to liberal democracies were, then, the spectacular culmination of what can be seen as a seismic change towards liberal democracy.

It may be objected that this account ignores the massive exception of China (and there are one or two other, less significant, countries which have also retained communist regimes). And it is conceivable – as pointed out below – that China could inspire an anti-democratic reaction in Asia. However, it seems more likely that pressures for democratisation will grow, not least because of the moves towards economic liberalisation. 'Until China's leaders match their commitment to economic modernization with a similar commitment to democracy and political liberalization' China will not achieve the goal its leaders desire '– to make China "rich and powerful"' (Goldman, 1990). Moreover, many of the socio-economic prequisites for democracy exist in China (Nathan, 1990). But above all, of course, there is the hugely important fact, and legacy, of the events of spring 1989, culminating in the massacre in Tiananmen Square. Apart from anything else, they 'revealed a passionate and widespread yearning for democracy' (Nathan, 1990). China, then, has not been immune from the seismic change towards democracy. And it is likely that, in time, the regime will become more democratic (but see below for a possible 'Singapore development'), even though the 'transition to democracy is likely . . . to be hard, prolonged, complex – and inconclusive'. It is also likely that it will end up more like Japanese-style democracy than Western liberal democracy (Nathan, 1990).

There has, then, been a profound change in the world, even including

'A passionate and widespread yearning for democracy' in China: the 'Goddess of Democracy' (modelled on the Statue of Liberty) in Tiananmen Square, May 1989.

China, towards liberal democracy. This has been both a matter of the regime changes themselves – their number and importance – and also of the accompanying ascendency of the ideas and justifications of liberal democracy. Arguably, then, the enemies have been defeated and liberal democracy has now swept the board. On the Right Fascism was defeated in the Second World War and various brands of authoritarianism have been discredited and overthrown since 1974; and now the outcome of the Cold War has been the defeat of Marxism–Leninism on the Left. Today, then, 'we find ourselves living in the new post-Cold War world – a world with one dominant principle of political legitimacy, democracy' (Plattner, 1991).

Can we, then, talk of the 'victory' of liberal democracy? Certainly, the revolutions of 1989 have been widely interpreted in this way. True, they were partly a matter of the economic failure of communist command economies. But, in the words of John Simpson, the BBC Foreign Affairs Editor, who was there as they happened, 'it wasn't just capitalism that had won, it was the Western concept of representative democracy' (Simpson, 1992). And according to Misha Glenny – also from the BBC, and also there as it happened – 'Western Europe and the United States recorded a great ideological victory in 1989. The historical enemy was defeated in a series of stunning revolutions' (Glenny, 1990). Liberal democracy can, then, be said to have won the 'conflict between two fundamentally opposed ideologies – Leninist communism and liberal democracy' (Plattner, 1991) and its 'prestige . . . has never been higher' (Muravchick, 1992). A noted student of Marxism–Leninism sums it up in these words:

> In the last decade of the twentieth century democracy rediscovered its optimism and universality. In the wake of its meteoric reassertion Marxism–Leninism was devastated. It clung on brutally in China only by massacring its own people: otherwise it was only in such backwaters as Cuba, North Korea, and Vietnam that it retained its grip. With its principal ideological opponent effectively defeated, democracy exultantly proclaimed itself the political form of the future. It has now become the preponderant idea of the modern world and has done so by vanquishing its only substantial opponent. Communism is dead! Long live democracy! (Harding, 1992)

But if this was a victory for liberal democracy, how durable will it be?[15]. Some express doubts, including Harding; and Misha Glenny is not optimistic about the future of liberal democracy in Eastern Europe. But others think there has been a final victory that has permanently seen off liberal democracy's enemies.

The notion that there has been this kind of triumph of liberal democracy – dubbed 'triumphalism' by its critics – has become especially associated with the name of Francis Fukuyama. In 1989 he proclaimed this triumph in what has become a famous essay, 'The End of History?', in which he argued that the ideology of liberal democracy was the only viable one remaining:

> what we may be witnessing is not just the end of the Cold War . . . but the end of history as such: that is, the endpoint of mankind's ideological evolution and the universalisation of Western liberal democracy as the final form of human government. (Fukuyama, 1989)

He later expanded his argument in his book *The End of History and The Last Man* (Fukuyama, 1992), which has attracted an enormous amount of critical attention. Here one of his concerns is with the links between liberal democracy and the achievements of modern science and associated military and economic successes. But he gives equal or greater importance to liberal democracy being the only system in which the worth of all individuals is given recognition. The argument is that throughout history there has been a 'struggle for recognition', which culminates in the validation of liberal democracy. The Hegelian analysis in which this is embedded gives weight and depth but it has attracted criticism and might be thought to inhibit readers' understanding. Even so the key thesis remains clear enough. This is not just that liberal democracy is spreading. For it has not, and may not, spread everywhere: even by '1990 approximately two-thirds of the countries in the world did not have democratic regimes' (Huntington, 1991). Rather it is that the spread of liberal democracy reflects the triumph of the liberal democratic *idea*. As Plattner (1992) puts it, liberal democracy is not only 'being adopted in more and more countries, but even its critics are increasingly unable to offer a coherent alternative. It is above all the exhaustion of all serious rival claimants to political legitimacy that lends new credence to the possibility that liberal democracy represents the culmination of human history.'

The idea that liberal democracy has triumphed has been widely accepted and Fukuyama provides intellectual backing for it. However, Fukuyama's thesis has also attracted a lot of criticism. For Plattner, 'perhaps the most compelling counterargument to this view of democracy triumphant has been presented by Ken Jowitt' (Plattner, 1991, referring to Jowitt, 1991). In fact, as Plattner is not alone in pointing out, there is in Jowitt's writing a significant measure of agreement with Fukuyama. For Jowitt, 'Leninism's extinction is an event of world-historical significance. . . . Its collapse is on a par with the Fall of Rome' (Ryan, 1992). This has left the field clear for the dominance of liberal capitalist democracy, and Jowitt has 'no quarrel with Fukuyama's observation that liberal capitalism is now the only politically global civilization' (Jowitt, 1992).

The difference comes in Jowitt's perception of the instability in this present dominance, due to the deficiencies in capitalism and liberal individualism that will provoke reaction against it. There will continue to be opponents who scorn 'liberal capitalist democracy . . . for an inordinate emphasis on individualism, materialism, technical achievement, and rationality. . . . [T]here is a common negative theme: liberal capitalism is indicted for undervaluing the essential collective dimension of human existence' (Jowitt, 1991). This will give rise to ideas and movements which will bring violent disorder and check the spread of liberal democracy. Nationalism – which Misha Glenny also highlights as a danger – is already causing trouble. Now, it is true that Fukuyama does in fact recognise much of this: it has even been argued that the inner thrust of Fukuyama's thesis is in fact – in a way unrecognised by himself – *anti*-liberal democratic (McCarney (1992)). For example, he thinks there may well be 'a high and perhaps rising level of ethnic and nationalist violence.' But for Fukuyama (though McCarney would not agree) the *idea* of liberal democracy will remain predominant and there will be no ideology that offers a serious challenge. This:

> brings us to the heart of the disagreement between these two authors. Fukuyama seems to contend that the liberal democratic idea has definitively triumphed among the advanced nations of the world, and thus there will not again arise a major power animated by an antidemocratic ideology. Jowitt, by contrast, can envisage the emergence of a new ideology capable of generating a new 'way of life' – an ideology whose power to move great nations would be comparable to that of Catholicism, liberal democracy, fascism or Leninism. (Plattner, 1991)

According to some, such ideological challenges already exist. Nationalism has already been mentioned, but also prominent is Islamic fundamentalism. For Fukuyama, however, these are phenomena whose appeal is temporally and geographically limited. Plattner has a similar view: nationalism and Islamic fundamentalism, unlike liberal democracy, do not have *universal* appeal. There is, however, a potentially influential non-liberal-democratic model which just might come to have more than regional influence. This is the economically successful 'Asian market-oriented authoritarian state' (Fukuyama, 1992) that was exemplified in Singapore where Lee Kuan Yew justified his regime 'unapologetically, not just as as a transitional arrangement, but as a system superior to liberal democracy' (Fukuyama , 1992). It is true that current developments in the region are towards liberal democracy, notably in South Korea and Taiwan. But, on the other hand, it seems possible that potentially the most powerful country of all, China, might follow the 'Lee Kuan Yew model'. And there is also the question mark hanging over the future of Russia. As Plattner points out:

> The nature and fate of the successor regimes in the [former] Soviet Union and China will be of decisive importance for the future of democracy – not just because of their size and power but also because of the influence they can exert over Eastern Europe and East Asia respectively. If both these countries were successfully to follow the democratic path, the world might indeed approach Fukuyama's vision of an enduringly triumphant liberal democracy. But if they do not, they offer the most likely seedbeds for the birth of a new antidemocratic ideology. (Plattner, 1991)[16]

Fukuyama, of course, would insist that there must remain a universal tendency for authoritarian regimes – even if economically successful – to lose their legitimacy. This is because liberty and the 'desire for recognition' are even more important than economic success:

> at many ... points in world history, the option of prosperity without liberty existed – from the Tory planters who opposed the Declaration of Independence in the United States, to the nineteenth-century authoritarian modernizers of Germany and Japan, to contemporaries like Deng Xiaoping, who offered his country economic liberalization and modernization under the continued tutelage of a dictatorial Communist party, and Lee Kuan Yew of Singapore, who has argued that democracy would be an obstacle to Singapore's spectacular economic success. And yet, people in all ages have taken the non-economic step of risking their lives and their livelihoods to fight for democratic rights. (Fukuyama, 1992)

Of course, reasons other than economic can be advanced for suggesting that non-liberal-democratic regimes may flourish in some parts of the world. In East Asia – as Fukuyama recognises – Confucianism works against liberal democracy: 'almost no scholarly disagreement exists on the proposition that traditional Confucianism was either undemocratic or antidemocratic. . . . In practice Confucian or Confucian-influenced societies have been inhospitable to demo-cracy' (Huntington, 1991). However, as in the case of Islamic fundamentalism, this is precisely *not* to suggest the basis for an ideology with *universal* appeal that could properly challenge liberal democracy.

We must remember, though, that the question with which we are concerned is whether liberal democracy is the best system overall. The point is, this question cannot be answered simply by showing that no other system is best overall. It may be that no other system is universally better than liberal democracy; but then it may also be that liberal democracy is not universally better than other systems. Indeed, for many this would merely confirm that different systems are best for different conditions. In other words, even if liberal democracy is now subject to no challenge from a universalist ideology, there remains the question of whether it is only appropriate for some societies. Rather than there being a 'best' system it may be that different systems suit different cultures. And here we come back to the ethnocentricism charge.

But, of course, Fukuyama, for instance, does do more than argue that no other system is best overall: he *does* argue that there are reasons for the *universal* adoption – the triumph of – liberal democracy. We have seen this already, but let his words emphasise the point:

> Just as impressive as the growth in the number of democracies is the fact that democratic government has broken out of its original beachhead in Western Europe and North America, and has made significant inroads in other parts of the world that do not share the political, religious, and cultural traditions of those areas. The argument was once made that there was a distinct Iberian tradition . . . To hold Spain, Portugal, or the countries of Latin America to the standards of the liberal democracy of Western Europe or the United States was to be guilty of 'ethnocentrism'. Yet those universal standards of rights were those to which people in the Iberian tradition held *themselves* . . . These same standards have had meaning for peoples in Latin America, Eastern Europe, Asia, and many other parts of the world as well. The success of democracy in a wide variety of places and among many different peoples would suggest that the principles of liberty and equality on which they are based are not accidents or the results of ethnocentric prejudice, but are in fact discoveries about the nature of man as man, whose truth does not diminish but grows more evident as one's point of view becomes more cosmopolitan. (Fukuyama, 1992)

The universality of liberal democracy's hold is also documented by empirical political scientists. 'With the important but still indeterminate exception of the Islamic fundamentalist state . . . democracy is the only model of government with any broad ideological legitimacy and appeal in the world today' (Diamond,1988–91). And, more succinctly and more forcibly: by 'the 1980s the legitimacy of liberal democracy came to be accepted throughout the world' (Huntington, 1991).

These are important arguments. But how convincing are they? We have already indicated that some reject them, or are doubtful. And Huntington himself, goes on to discuss the possibility of a third 'reverse wave' against liberal democracy.

It is, of course, difficult to reach clear conclusions here. But it is of help to focus again on the central point of Fukuyama's thesis, which concerns the *power* of the liberal democratic *idea*. Of course there are critical issues about the extent to which circumstances can frustrate the realization of this idea, but it is too easily forgotten that the idea itself *is* a power working to overcome those circumstances.[17] To a crucial extent the power of the idea can be said to consist in the rational force of the justifications for liberal democracy (discussed earlier in this chapter). To this extent, then, questions about the triumph, or otherwise, of liberal democracy can be read as questions about the validity of the arguments for it. The triumph of liberal democracy is made likely to the extent that these arguments are compelling. At the very least, greater clarity is obtained by recognising the extent to which the issue is that of the justification of liberal democracy.

Evidence for the contention that the rational force of liberal democratic ideas is a reason for liberal democracy's existence is provided by the way in which traditional ideas and arguments figure in *explanations* – as well as justifications – of moves towards democracy. Thus arguments for liberal democracy may be cited as a reason for its advent or consolidation. For example, Huntington (1991) gives as a reason for the consolidation of liberal democracy in Spain, Portugal, Brazil and Peru the fact that the inhabitants 'were learning that democracy rests on the premise that governments will fail and that hence institutionalised ways have to exist for changing them'. But it is the way in which people living under non-democratic systems were fired by liberal democratic ideas that shows most clearly how reasons for liberal democracy being the best system of government are also reasons for it being established. This was obviously demonstrated in the revolutions of 1989. Misha Glenny (1990) sums it up by saying 'human dignity proved more forceful than the arrogance of power'. Anatoly Sharansky dramatises the same point when he says:

Andrei Sakharov was the father of that most dangerous weapon, the hydrogen bomb . . . Later, Sakharov himself activated a still more powerful weapon, which ultimately destroyed the empire – he began openly expressing his beliefs, exercising the moral power of a free man. . . . Sakharov, almost alone, created the moral climate that has undermined the Soviet regime. (Sharansky, 1990)

A striking example of how activists are moved by arguments for liberal democracy is provided by one of the most eloquent participants in China's democracy movement, Fang Lizhi, whose advocacy of democracy is essentially a restatement of traditional justifications of liberal democracy (Lizhi, 1990).

A key point here, of course, is the linkage between people's ideas about having liberal democracy, and actually having it. The existence or non-existence of liberal democracy is not simply a matter of the presence or absence of the 'givens' of certain socio-economic conditions, a point which is sometimes overlooked by those who seek social scientific explanations of political phenomena. It is also a matter of those who subscribe to liberal democratic ideas *choosing* to have it. The strength of the case for liberal democracy therefore becomes a potent force – via the choices of those who are convinced by it. True, a decision, or attempt by some, to establish liberal democracy will not necessarily be successful. But it might well be; or, at the very least, it might well have a crucial effect on what happens. It will also, of course, depend on just who is involved. The importance of 'the people' choosing to have liberal democracy is illustrated by the way in which the people of Spain, Portugal and Latin America overcame the Iberian tradition and themselves chose to have liberal democracy (we have already seen that Fukuyama calls attention to this). And it is illustrated even more clearly in the advent of liberal democracy in the former communist countries of Eastern Europe where circumstances are such that 'the language of prerequisites' is insufficient since 'democracy emerges first as a conscious choice' (Di Palma, 1991). Indeed, the revolutions of 1989 are a dramatic illustration of the importance of choice: *the* central factor was the people choosing to have liberal democracy rather than communism.

It is, perhaps, Fukuyama himself who best illustrates the extent to which liberal democracy is the product of reason and choice:

There are . . . several fallacies about culture and democracy that should be avoided. The first is that cultural factors constitute *sufficient* conditions for the establishment of democracy . . . Democracy can never enter through the back door; at a certain point it must arise out of a deliberate political decision to establish democracy. . . .

The second, and probably more common mistake, is to view cultural factors as *necessary* conditions for the establishment of democracy.... Weber's account of democracy is, as usual, historically rich and insightful. But he portrays democracy as something that could only have arisen in the specific cultural and social milieu of a small corner of Western civilization. The fact that democracy took off because it was the most rational possible political system and 'fit' [*sic*] a broader human personality shared across cultures is not seriously considered.

There are numerous examples of countries which do not meet a number of so-called cultural 'preconditions' for democracy, and which nonetheless have managed to achieve a surprisingly high level of democratic stability. The chief example of this is India ... At other times in the past, entire peoples have been written off as culturally unqualified for stable democracy: the Germans and Japanese ... Spain, Portugal, and any number of Latin American countries ... Greece and Russia. Many of the peoples of Eastern Europe ... (Fukuyama, 1991)

Liberal democracy in the Third World

There are, then, powerful counter-arguments to the thesis that liberal democracy is only suitable for Western societies. The contention that liberal democracy is only appropriate for certain cultures and a limited set of social and economic conditions is belied by the extent to which it has spread through the world in the recent resurgence. And a key reason for the spread of liberal democracy is the force of the arguments for it. Apart from anything else, people convinced by the arguments can, and do, *choose* to have liberal democracy despite the existence of conditions that allegedly render it unsuitable.

Nonetheless, there is no denying that these conditions *may* frustrate such a choice; or, at least make the establishment or maintenance of liberal democracy difficult. It is, then, still arguable that there remains an issue concerning liberal democracy's universality – whether it really is the best, or even a possible, system in all circumstances. As the issue now relates primarily to developing countries, we shall end with a brief discussion of liberal democracy in the Third World.[18]

It is, then, primarily in relation to the Third World that the economic underdevelopment and cultural obstacles objections are raised (although at times there had been such objections with respect to other parts of the world). Economic underdevelopment, in fact, has been the most frequently cited reason for the inapplicability of the liberal democratic model in the Third World. The basic argument is that the overriding priority is the alleviation of grinding poverty, and only the solving of this problem of poverty would make the 'luxury' of liberal democracy affordable. Having sufficient to eat is more important than liberty and self-government. But almost as important has been the cultural objection, the contention that the historical and cultural backgrounds in countries of the Third World are very different from that of Western countries, and are unsuitable for liberal democracy.

In fact it was often argued that the economic, historical and cultural characteristics of Third World countries implied the suitability not of liberal democracy but of a form of 'one-party democracy'.[19] An influential statement of this viewpoint was provided by C. B. Macpherson with his account of the 'underdeveloped variant' of non-liberal democracy, which has already been mentioned (Chapter 3, section 3 above).

This underdeveloped variant can best be understood in terms of its differences from, and similarities to, the communist variant of non-liberal democracy – 'people's democracy' – which was discussed in the last chapter. (We should notice, incidentally, that Marxist–Leninists were prone to argue that the communist variant itself was applicable to the Third World. Indeed, a variety of the conception of people's democracy, known as 'national democracy', was specifically devised to fit the developing countries (Kase, 1968).) The chief difference from the communist variant is that in the underdeveloped variant the idea of class plays no part. There is still some notion of democracy being rule by and for the oppressed people, but the erstwhile oppressors are the former colonial rulers rather than a class. 'The people' are the whole, undivided, nation, so there is the notion of a unified community uncomplicated by a theory of class conflict.

The idea of community, and of community being expressed and sustained by a single unified will, is, indeed, absolutely central. Clearly, there are strong echoes of Rousseau here (Macpherson, 1966; Nursey-Bray, 1983). But there is home-grown inspiration as well. In Africa there is a harking back to pre-colonial days and 'African traditional society [which] is envisaged as an ideal communal society' (Nursey-Bray, 1983).[20] More generally, there was the importance of the independence struggle itself and the subsequent fight to develop economically and to create a cohesive nation. And here we come to an important similarity with people's democracy. The effort to develop and to create a nation involved ideological leadership, disciplined organisation and the rejection of divisive views. All this pointed to the need for a single party with a vanguard role. And in fact, as in the communist variant, there is the central idea of the single, unified will of the community being manifested in the rule of a single party. The underdeveloped variant, like people's democracy, is one-party democracy.

This one-party form was, then, until very recently widely held to be the form of democracy suitable for Third World countries (as we shall see in a moment this argument has all but collapsed since 1989). This was because the stress on community fits with indigenous cultures better than the ideas of liberal individualism; and a vanguard party can implement the severe policies required to deal with the problems of economic underdevelopment. It is argued that such policies, necessary but superficially unpopular, correspond with the real will of the people; but they could not be implemented in a liberal democracy, where governments depend on the present, actual, will of the people as manifested in votes.

It has been widely argued, then, that liberal democracy is unsuitable for the Third World where the only appropriate alternative to explicitly non-democratic regimes is one-party democracy; and that to think otherwise is to be ethnocentric.

This kind of argument was, until recently, powerfully bolstered by the fact of the breakdown of liberal democratic regimes bequeathed by former colonial powers at independence[21] and, in general, by the rarity of liberal democracy in the Third World. It was indeed the case that the unsuitability of liberal democracy seemed to be confirmed by the fact that systems which actually prevailed were one-party democracies and authoritarian regimes of various forms.

However, even at the time of liberal democracy's greatest rarity there was the massive exception of India. The brute fact of its existence in India was in itself an important challenge to the unsuitability-of-liberal-democracy thesis:

> Developing countries are not supposed to offer conducive settings for democratic political systems. . . . Either democracy in India is a misnomer[22] . . . or the theorists of democracy were wrong in writing off the possibility of democracy's compatibility with the most stringent tasks of both economic development and political integration in developing countries. (Das Gupta, 1990)

Moreover, reflection on the reasons for the existence of liberal democracy in India necessarily brings out arguments against the idea of its being unsuitable. And if such arguments exist in respect of the largest of countries in the Third World, then they almost certainly apply elsewhere.

The fact of India being a liberal democracy thus prevented the closure of argument on the issue of whether liberal democracy was the best system in the Third World. And, indeed, some did challenge the arguments of the unsuitability thesis (for a useful and stimulating debate see Nehru and Morris-Jones (1980); see also Niebuhr and Sigmund (1969) and Thakur (1982)). For instance, the superficially plausible idea that poverty and desperate economic conditions require non-liberal-democratic regimes was disputed. Besides Morris-Jones's reply to Nehru (Nehru and Morris-Jones, 1980) see, for example, Frohock and Sylvan (1983), who argue that liberty, instead of being impossible or an unaffordable luxury in such economic conditions, is in fact a first condition for an increase in economic well-being.

And this brings us back to the theme of the the the generality of liberal democracy's suitability being tied up with the universality of the arguments for it. In this case the utilitarian argument for democracy is utilised: arguably, a key reason why liberal democracy is necessary for, rather than an obstacle to, the alleviation of poverty is precisely that popular pressure on rulers prevents them from pursuing policies detrimental to the interests of the mass of the people (Frohock and Sylvan, 1983). This is a clear case of a general argument for the desirability of liberal democracy having an especial relevance for – rather than being inapplicable to – the Third World.

The allegedly ethnocentric idea, then, that liberal democracy *is* suitable for the Third World was not disposed of. And, of course, with the third wave of democratisation and the whole triumph-of-liberal-democracy debate it has made a dramatic comeback. Indeed, as we have seen, it was in fact the resurgence of liberal democracy in Latin America and parts of Asia in the 1980s that actually constituted a major part of the third wave. Besides being generally important as a key part of the overall wave of democracy, this advance of liberal democracy in the Third World had the more particular significance of undermining the argument that it could not normally exist there.

Nonetheless, at the end of the 1980s a form of the unsuitability thesis still had wide support. This was essentially a narrowed-down version according to which liberal democracy was not suitable for *some* parts of the Third World. The spread of liberal democracy had overlapped with economic changes that had taken place, so that parts of the Third World had developed dramatically (indeed, the latter often contributed to the former). The narrowed-down version, then, focused on the parts that had not developed in this way and where liberal democracy was still largely absent – most notably Africa. It continued to be argued that African circumstances were such that if democracy was feasible at all it was only *non*-liberal ('the underdeveloped variant'), one-party, democracy that was suitable (see Wanyande (1988) for a discussion of one-party democracy in Africa).

However, even this narrower thesis is now under very severe attack. A key factor here was the democratic revolution of 1989 in Eastern Europe. This destroyed the communist variant of non-liberal democracy on which the underdeveloped variant was based. The popular rejection and destruction of the original, and powerful, one-party systems destroyed the legitimacy of the one-party model of democracy; and this had a profound effect on the idea and existence of one-party democracy in Africa.

The end of communism also had at least two other important implications. First, the fledgling liberal democracies in the former communist countries had to cope with some of the problems – such as the requirement for severe short-term economic policies for the sake of long-term recovery – the existence of which were used as arguments for the unsuitability of liberal democracy in Africa: to the extent that they did cope, such arguments were undermined. Secondly, the collapse of the Soviet Union meant the end of non-Western material support, which made African regimes more vulnerable to economic pressures from the West. And, indeed, Western governments and international institutions began to make aid dependent on satisfactory human rights records and moves towards liberal democracy.[23]

The delegitimising of the one-party model together with the general, world-wide, raising of the profile of liberal democracy has had a very considerable destabilising effect on one-party regimes in Africa. But it is not just that the general legitimacy of the one-party model has been destroyed. This destruction was the *coup de grâce* in a challenge, which had already been building up, to the underdeveloped variant of liberal democracy; that is to say, a challenge to the specifically Third World – and particularly African – arguments for the superiority of one-party democracy. Central to this is the reversal of the need-for-economic-development argument. In fact we have already mentioned this reverse argument, that lack of development is due to the *lack* of liberal democracy. Insulated from public opinion 'most African leaders have been "underdeveloping" the continent for years' (Ake, 1991). And a major conference in 1990 under the auspices of the United Nations Economic Commission for Africa adopted an 'African Charter for

Popular Participation in Development and Transformation', the major point of which 'is that the absence of democracy is the primary cause of the chronic crisis in Africa' (Ake, 1991). But the challenge goes wider than this:

> Richard Sklar in his presidential address to the twenty-sixth meeting of the American African Studies Association has contended that 'developmental dictatorships' have failed miserably in the economic and political tasks that they had set for themselves. Instead of inducing unity and harmony they generated ethnic favoritism and divisions; instead of ushering in social equality they led to corruption and injustices; instead of promoting economic development they fostered material stagnation and decline; and instead of establishing viable political orders they engendered divisive tendencies, military coups, and civil wars. The dismal performance of developmental dictatorships signals in Sklar's view that the absence of democracy and accountability in African politics can no longer be defended on pragmatic or moral grounds. (Fatton, 1990)

Even in respect of Africa, then, there has been a heavy attack on the unsuitability thesis. And now, even an erstwhile leading African advocate and exponent of the underdeveloped variant, ex-President Julias Nyrere of Tanzania, 'has recanted his earlier advocacy and institutionalisation of "one-party democracy"' (Riley, 1992). It is, indeed, not just commentators and Western governments and institutions that have been pressing for liberal democracy. It has above all been demanded by the inhabitants: 'the question of the role of the West in the democratization of Africa has arisen only because Africans have become more committed to the quest for democracy and are struggling determinedly to attain it' (Ake, 1991). And, of course, the rejection of the one-party model and the struggle for liberal democracy does involve rejection of the unsuitability thesis. In fact:

> complaints about the imposition of external models of democracy on Africa now seem to come mainly from either officials and apologists of the embattled regimes or unswerving ideologues. Most advocates of democracy, on the other hand, are pleased that foreign governments and international agencies are at last supporting the struggle for political pluralism and withdrawing their support from autocrats and dictators. (Joseph, 1991)

There is, then, a rising democratic tide in Africa.[24] Its effect on African political systems has been huge, and it is threatening to engulf the continent.[25] In fact, as Joseph (1991) points out, 'the scale of the African

Africa thirsts for democracy: long queues of voters in Namibia patiently waiting in the heat.

transformations rivals that of the revolutionary upheavals of 1989 in Eastern Europe.'

However, do these dramatic events, which have been referred to as a 'Second Liberation', 'Second Independence' or 'New Wind of Change' (Riley, 1992), mean that liberal democracy is going to prevail in Africa? It is certainly encouraging that under United Nations supervision competitive electoral democracy has been established in the newly independent Namibia (1990). At the time of writing five heads of state had been voted out of office in competitive multi-party elections – the most recent being Sassou-Nguesso of Congo in August, 1992. And there have been various other moves to liberal democracy in many other states (Joseph (1991) identifies seven models of transition to democracy in Africa). However, 'some are quick to point out that the emergence of more democratic forms of government is patchy across the continent. . . . Democratic pressures are having an uneven impact as some political leaders resist or deflect' them (Riley, 1992).[26] Moreover, the fledgling liberal democracies – like those of Eastern Europe – face very severe economic problems and unless they can 'restore economic growth, they will face direct challenges from the very social forces that are currently undermining authoritarianism' (Joseph, 1991). And, again as in Eastern Europe, some of the new democracies are being undermined by ethnic conflicts. On top of all this there is the effect of Africa's 'dependent' position in the world economy: the Secretary General of the Organisation for African Unity has warned that 'while Africa must democratise our efforts will be hamstrung by the nondemocratic international economic system in which we operate' (Joseph, 1991).

Yet, despite these and other reasons for being pessimistic, there is guarded optimism. Despite having few of the 'social and economic conditions that are necessary for the appearance and survival of democratic forms of government . . . it would seem that Africa can nurture some forms of liberal democracy' (Riley, 1992). Indeed, 'Africa's journey towards democracy and sound economic policies has achieved a remarkable momentum' (*The Economist*, 1992).[27] And even though there will probably be difficulties and reverses on that journey, we should remember the contention, central in Fukuyama's argument, that whatever the regimes that may still materialise from time to time there is now no challenge to the *idea* of liberal democracy. This is now becoming recognised as being as applicable to Africa as to anywhere else: 'the democratic ideal – whether imported or not – is taking hold again in Africa' (Riley, 1992). True, if liberal democracy 'is to work in Africa, it must respond innovatively to each country's distinctive cultural traditions, political problems, and social forces' (Diamond, 1988), but it now seems broadly agreed that making it work *is* what ought to be attempted.

4.4
Conclusions

Discussion of the resurgence of liberal democracy in the Third World marks a suitable conclusion for a consideration of the justification of liberal democracy. We have seen in this chapter that it has been doubted whether liberal democracy can be given an objective justification or whether it can be seen as the best system of government for any but a small part of the world. But we have also seen that there *are* compelling arguments for liberal democracy and that it is now coming to be acknowledged as the best system for *all* parts of the world. Indeed, the two are connected. It is because of the rational validity of the arguments for liberal democracy that they are not simply the manifestation of a particular culture; and it is because of their generality that they are applicable to more than a particular set of conditions. The recent dramatic expansion of liberal democracy can be seen, in part at least, as the force of this logic breaking through. And the resurgence in the Third World is especially notable because it was this area that appeared to be so especially unsuitable.

This resurgence is, in fact, a dramatic affirmation of the importance of liberal democracy. And it also raises afresh many of the problems and issues inherent in, or connected with, liberal democracy – both in its ideas and in the attempt to realise those ideas in practice. This, in turn, has led to a renewed interest in analysis, and a renewed desire for proper understanding. It is hoped that *Understanding Liberal Democracy* has been of use here. It also provides a guide to the burgeoning literature on liberal democracy. For there has in fact lately been a revival of academic writing on a subject which is not only of major current interest but is also of very great inherent importance.

Notes

1. Paradoxically, though, some saw this mess as itself providing an answer to the problem of justification: as we shall see below this relativism became *part of* a justification of liberal democracy! On scientific value relativism and the justification of liberal democracy see further Holden (1974, Chapter 8), and Thorson (1962).
2. At the same time developments in the political world – among the most important being the Vietnam War and the traumas of American politics in the 1960s – were destroying the post-war complacency about liberal democracy. Scientific value relativism had been 'tolerated' so long as there had been no perceived need to validate received judgements, but now liberal democracy could no longer be taken for granted and the case for it needed to be made.
3. For a succinct and brilliant analysis of the present position regarding the justification of liberal democracy see Spragens (1990, Chapter 1).
4. But for a contrary view see the work of John Keane (1984, 1988, 1991, 1992). Keane argues that whilst traditionally democracy was justified 'by referring back to a substantive grounding principle ... Belief in these various first principles has today crumbled' (Keane, 1992). However, whilst he decries 'foundationalism' Keane also explicitly eschews relativism and appears to offer a rational defence of (his conception of) democracy. Puzzles remain, however, since, although avowedly condemning relativism Keane apparently accepts a view of human life as 'horizoned and biased' and has an 'awareness of the impossibility of substituting certain knowledge ... for uncertain and tentative theoretical interpretations and revisable practical judgements' (Keane, 1992). In fact Keane's justification of democracy looks very like the 'relativist justification' discussed in the main text.

5. Strictly speaking, to avoid begging a key question, one should say: systems that fail to embody the model, but without prejudging the question of whether the Western systems labelled 'liberal democracies' are ones which fail to embody the model. And we should remember that in the last chapter we were concerned to rebut arguments contending that Western liberal democracies failed in this way.

6. A good example of the relationship between a fuller statement of what from one viewpoint can be regarded as secular principles of liberal democracy, and their Christian foundation, is provided by Maritain's idea of the 'democratic charter'. For an illuminating and comprehensive discussion see Howell (1986).

7. Fukuyama stresses a similar account of the central virtue of liberal democracy – rational recognition of the dignity of persons – and sees Hegel as its source.'Hegelian "liberalism" can be seen as the pursuit of *rational recognition*, that is, recognition on a universal basis in which the dignity of each person as a free and autonomous human being is recognized by all. What is at stake . . . in a liberal democracy is not merely the fact that it allows us the freedom to make money and satisfy the desiring parts of our souls. The more important and ultimately more satisfying thing it provides us is recognition of our dignity' (Fukuyama, 1992). On Fukuyama see section 3 below.

8. It has been said that because the basic idea is one of hypothetical choice by abstract individuals – rather than one of an actual choice by real individuals – Rawls gives us only a 'highly qualified endorsement of democratic governance'. This is because 'the rationale for democratic rule is distinctly derivative. An electorate's various deliverances are always to be constrained by foundational principles that are not themselves the product of democratic choice' (Brennan and Lomasky, 1989, Introduction). But it should be remembered that we are talking about the justification of *liberal* democracy, and this constraint is an aspect of the way in which democracy is qualified in the notion of liberal democracy (see Chapter 1). Rawls's justification of democracy is qualified, then, only in a way that constitutes it as a justification – unqualified – of liberal democracy. It should also be noted, though, that whilst it seemed that *A Theory of Justice* was meant as a true theory and sought an 'Archimedian point', outside of any particular culture, as a base for an objective justification, it appears that Rawls has since moved away from this position – see Rawls (1985,1987, 1989). His theory 'is, now, not regarded as a theory that is true but rather as a theory that can serve as the basis for political agreement' (Lassman, 1992). As such, rather than an objective justification of liberal democracy it does look like a relative justification that is applicable only to a liberal democratic political culture. For an assessment see Neal (1990), and for a contrary view see Larmore (1990).

9. Whether it is a justification of *liberal* democracy is uncertain: as with other participatory theorists, the extent to which Gould is arguing for an

extension of the democratic element within, rather than a replacement for, liberal democracy is open to argument.

10. It should also be remembered that participatory democracy can be justified in terms of its beneficial results (see the previous chapter).

11. It could be argued, though, that rational agreement *is* possible in the absence of a 'theoretical' basis: see the discussion of 'deliberative' conceptions of democracy in Chapter 3 and the reference to Spragens conception of 'rational practice' in the next paragraph in the main text here.

12. In fact, far from entering into a justification it is arguable that relativism is a profound enemy of liberal democracy: 'just as in the case of his follower, Martin Heidegger, Nietzsche's relativism shot out all of the philosophical props holding up Western liberal democracy and replaced it with a doctrine of strength and domination' (Fukuyama, 1992).

13. In these contexts it is usually clear that 'democracy' means 'liberal democracy'. Indeed, the idea that democracy *can* only be liberal democracy – which is implicit in liberal democratic theory – is usually presupposed. And, as discussed, in the main text, since the breakdown of 'people's democracy' this idea has become dominant. However, for a recent restatement of a form of the anti-ethnocentric argument see Parekh (1992). It is, though, a modified form: 'to reject the universalist claims of liberal democracy is not to endorse the crude relativist view that a country's political system is its own business and above criticism, and that western experiences have no relevance outside the west.' In fact Parekh's argument – depending on a questionable separation of the liberal and democratic components of liberal democracy – purports to endorse the universality of a non-liberal form of democracy whilst condemning liberal ideas as ethnocentric; but it is a 'non-liberal' form which nonetheless retains what many would understand as key features of liberal democracy. 'It would appear that the democratic part of liberal democracy, consisting in such things as free elections, free speech and the right to equality, has proved far more attractive outside the west and is more universalizable than the liberal component. Millions in non-western societies demand democracy, albeit in suitably indigenized forms.'

14. The question of the necessary conditions for the existence of liberal democracy is the subject of an extensive literature. Dahl (1971) is still valuable, but see also Dahl (1989, Chapter 18). A comprehensive discussion, from the perspective of developing countries, is contained in Diamond *et al*. (1988–91, vol. 1, *Persistence, Failure and Renewal*); see also Diamond *et al*. (1990, Introduction). Perhaps the best overall analysis is now contained in Huntington (1991). Essentially the same questions arose in analyses of 'democratic breakdown', see, for example, Linz and Stepan (1978). The same is true of analyses of 'democratic transition', see, for example O'Donnell *et al* (1986); these are, of course, taking on a new lease of life with the current dramatic increase of transitions from dictatorships to liberal democracies, which is discussed in the text below; the best source is, again, Huntington (1991).

15. For a sophisticated analysis of the prospects for liberal democracy in Eastern Europe see Przeworski (1991).
16. Both Plattner and Fukuyama also see Japan as significant. 'Another possible source for a future alternative to liberal democracy may be Japan' (Plattner, 1991). But this may be an alternative only to a certain *Anglo-American conception* of liberal democracy, which emphasises alternation in office, rather than to liberal democracy as such. Japan is characterised by a dominant-party system; but though the same party always wins elections, it does *win* – rather than 'fix' – them. Such a system meets 'the formal requisites of democracy, but . . . differ[s] significantly from the democratic systems prevalent in the West' (Huntington, 1991).
17. Of special significance are 'cultural circumstances'. There are complex issues here, but a crucial point is that cultures contain – in a sense they *consist* in – ideas. Hence they are susceptible to factors – including force of argument – that change ideas. A culture alien to liberal democracy is thus vulnerable to the power of the liberal democratic idea and to that extent the degree to which it is an obstacle to the realization of liberal democracy is diminished.
18. The concept of the 'Third World' is fluid, and may cease to be meaningful in the post-Cold War world. Traditionally, there has been a coincidence between the ideas of the Third World and underdevelopment – the Third World consisting of the underdeveloped (or less developed or developing) countries of Asia, Africa and Latin America; and it is with this reference that the term is used here. Although there are theoretical difficulties with the notion of 'development' that is employed (including possible charges of ethnocentrism), there is sufficient clarity about the nature of severe economic hardship to at least make the notion of economic underdevelopment readily understandable. An important point to be borne in mind, however, is that many countries traditionally identified as belonging to the Third World have developed very fast relatively recently, thus blurring the distinction between 'developed' and 'underdeveloped' countries.
19. As before (Chapter 3, section 3) a one-off use of quotation marks is a concise way of indicating a position. Their use here indicates that so-called non-liberal forms of democracy are not to be considered democracies at all (this was argued in Chapter 3, section 3), but to avoid tedium phrases such as 'non-liberal democracy' and 'one-party democracy' will not normally be prefaced by 'so-called' or put in quotes in the main text.
20. The notion that this traditional African society was democratic may be a myth – see Simiyu (1988).
21. For instance, 'by the early 1970s, virtually all of the independent regimes in sub-Saharan Africa were either military or one-party' (Diamond, 1988).
22. Doubts are sometimes expressed about whether India really is a liberal democracy. These mainly centre on the 'interruption' of democracy by Indira Gandhi in 1975. Despite this episode, however, India does remain a liberal democracy. It is true that in 1975 Mrs Gandhi imposed the

Emergency in India and suspended elections. But equally notable were the facts that the Emergency came to an end, and that when it did so Mrs Gandhi was thrown out of power at a free election.

23. In April, 1990 the World Bank President 'listed better governance as the primary requirement for economic recovery in Africa. The World Bank's new African blueprint, *Sub-Saharan Africa: From Crisis to Sustainable Growth*, highlights the need for accountability, participation and consensus building in order to achieve successful development' (Ake, 1991). More generally 'since early 1990, Western governments have indicated that political reform was a necessary condition for further assistance to Africa. Democratisers would be rewarded.' For instance 'the importance of political conditionality in aid disbursement was highlighted at the Harare Commonwealth summit in October 1991 and by the European Community in November 1991 [which] signed a charter which links future aid to greater respect for human rights, less corruption, democratic politics and a free press in recipient states' (Riley, 1992).

24. A factor which should not be overlooked in explaining the growth of the demand for liberal democracy is developments in South Africa. Joseph (1991), for instance, points to 'the antiapartheid struggle's role as a catalyst of the contemporary democratic movement in Africa. . . . As President de Klerk was forced to peel away layers of repressive laws . . . [comparable laws] in black African countries became ever less defensible. As the parallels were drawn, there emerged a continent-wide democratic movement that accorded no immunity to any form of oppression, whatever the race, religion, or ideology of its perpetrators.' And, of course, the movement towards liberal democracy in the most powerful state on the continent is, in itself, a fact of very great importance.

25. It might be more accurate to refer to 'sub-Saharan Africa'. The Arab countries are, to a considerable extent, holding out against the trend. As it was put in an article in *The Economist* in 1990 (February 3): 'the spectre of [Islamic] fundamentalism haunts every Arab regime and discourages experiments in democracy.' The cancellation of the election in Algeria in January 1992 – because the fundamentalists would have won – was a dramatic confirmation of this, and was a set-back to such progress as there had been.

26. By November 1992 there were events that were very discouraging. Angola was to make a fresh start with competitive elections after years of civil war. However, the losing side in the election (Unita) refused to accept the result and there has been a relapse back into civil war. This may be part of a reaction against liberal democracy in Africa. Richard Dowden in an article entitled 'The slide back into darkness' (*The Independent on Sunday*, 1 November, 1992) says: 'Democracy in Africa, a candle of hope which flickered briefly, is guttering.' Nonetheless, on balance there does still seem to be room for optimism: 'the prospects for democracy in Africa are now unquestionably better than they were three decades ago, if for no other

reason that Africans know all too well the cost of the failure of democracy' (Diamond, 1992, quoted in Lemarchand, 1992).

As of January 1993, the latest news – concerning Kenya – has ambivalent implications. That there *was* a contested election (December 1992) in one of the last bastions of one-party democracy is of key importance; but that its fairness was questionable, and that the opposition parties initially rejected the result, is discouraging.

27. As evidence of the remarkable change that has taken place in just a few years (a further demonstration of the existence of a world-wide 'democratic revolution'), contrast the following statement published in 1988: 'the way to democracy in Africa is still a long one and there does not seem to be any indication as to how and when Africa is likely to get to the end' (Oyugi, 1988).

Bibliography

Abrams, M. and Rose, R. (1960) *Must Labour Lose?*, Penguin.

Ake, C. (1991) 'Rethinking African democracy', *Journal of Democracy*, vol. 2 (winter), pp. 32–44.

Albertoni, E. A. (1987), *Mosca and the Theory of Elitism*, Blackwell.

Alderman, G. (1984), *Pressure Groups and Government in Great Britain*, Longman.

Aranson, P. H. (1981), *American Government: Strategy and Choice*, Little, Brown.

Arendt, H. (1959), *The Human Condition*, Anchor Books.

Aristotle (1981), *The Politics* (translated by T. A. Sinclair, revised and represented by J. Saunders), Penguin.

Aron, R. (1988), *Power, Modernity and Sociology*, Gower.

Arrow, K. J. (1963), *Social Choice and Individual Values*, 2nd edn, Wiley.

Arterton, F. C. (1987), *Teledemocracy*, Sage.

Ashcraft, R. (1987), *Locke's Two Treatises of Government*, Allen & Unwin.

Avineri, S. and de-Shalit, A. (eds) (1992), *Communitarianism and Individualism*, Oxford University Press.

Bachrach, P. (1967), *The Theory of Democratic Elitism*, Little, Brown.

Baldwin, T. (1984), 'MacCallum and the two concepts of freedom', *Ratio*, vol. 26 (December), pp. 125–42.

Ball, A. R. (1986), *Pressure Politics in Industrial Societies: A Comparative Introduction*, Macmillan.

Barber, B. R. (1974), *The Death of Communal Liberty*, Princeton University Press.

Barber, B. R. (1984), *Strong Democracy: Participatory Politics for a New Age*, University of California Press.

Barker, E. (1942), *Reflections on Government*, Oxford University Press.

Barry, B. (1965), *Political Argument*, Routledge & Kegan Paul.

Barry, B. (1970), *Sociologists, Economists and Democracy*, Collier-Macmillan.

Bauman, Z. (1992), 'The Lesser Evil', *The Times Literary Supplement*, October 9.

Bealey, F. (1990), 'Footslogging through democracy: reflections of an empiricist', *Scandanavian Political Studies*, vol. 13, pp. 365–73.

Beetham, D. (1985), *Max Weber and the Theory of Modern Politics*, Polity Press.

Beetham, D. (1992), 'Liberal democracy and the limits of democratization', *Political Studies*, vol. 40, special issue, *Prospects for Democracy*, pp. 40–53.

Beitz, C. R. (1989), *Political Equality*, Princeton University Press.

Benditt, T. M. , Oppenheim, F. E. and Flathman, R. E. (1975), contributions to 'A symposium on interest', *Political Theory*, vol. 3 (August), pp. 245–87.

Benewick, R., Berki, R. N., and Parekh, B. (1973), *Knowledge and Belief in Politics*, Allen & Unwin.

Benjamin, R. and Duvall, R. (1985), 'The capitalist state in context', in Benjamin and Elkin (eds) *The Democratic State*.

Benjamin, R. and Elkin, S. L. (eds), (1985), *The Democratic State*, University Press of Kansas.

Berelson, H. , Lazarsfeld, P. F. and McPhee, W. N. (1954), *Voting*, University of Chicago Press.

Berg, E. (1965), *Democracy and the Majority Principle*, Scandinavian University Books.

Berg, E. (1986), 'The proof of capitalism: Usher's celebration of the status quo', *Political Studies*, vol. 34, no. 1 (March), pp. 99–119.

Berlin, I. (1969), *Four Essays on Liberty*, Oxford University Press.

Bernstein, R. J. (1983), *Beyond Objectivism and Relativism*, University of Pennsylvania Press.

Birch, A. H. (1964), *Representative and Responsible Government*, Allen & Unwin.

Birch, A. H. (1972), *Representation*, Macmillan.

Black, D. (1963), *The Theory of Committees and Elections*, 2nd edn, Cambridge University Press.

Blocker, H. G. and Smith, E. H. (eds) (1981), *John Rawls' Theory of Social Justice*, Ohio University Press.

Bobbio, N. (1987), *The Future of Democracy*, Polity Press.

Boreham, P., Clegg, S., and Dow, G. (1989), 'Political organisation and economic policy', in Duncan (ed.), *Democracy and the Capitalist State*.

Bottomore, T. B. (ed.) (1963), *Karl Marx, Early Writings*, C. A. Watts.

Botwinick, A. (1985), *Wittgenstein, Skepticism and Political Participation: An Essay in the Epistemology of Democratic Theory*, University Press of America.

Botwinick, A. (1990), *Skepticism and Political Participation*, Temple University Press.

Bramsted, E. K. and Melhuish, K. J. (eds) (1978), *Western Liberalism*, Longman.

Braybrooke, D. (1985), 'Contemporary Marxism on the autonomy, efficacy and legitimacy of the capitalist state', in Benjamin and Elkin (eds), *The Democratic State*.

Brecht, A. (1967), *Political Theory*, 2nd edn, Princeton University Press.

Brennan, G. and Lomasky, L. E. (eds) (1989), *Politics and Process: New Essays in Democratic Thought*, Cambridge University Press.

Buchanan, J. M. and Tullock, G. (1962), *The Calculus of Consent*, University of Michigan Press.

Burdick, E. and Brodbeck, A. J. (1959), *American Voting Behaviour*, Free Press.

Burke, E. (1861), 'Thoughts on the present discontents', in *The Works of Edmund Burke*, Bohn's British Classics.

Burke, E. (1949), *Burke's Politics* (eds J. S. H. Ross and P. Levack), Knopf.

Burke, E. (1968), *Reflections on the Revolution in France* (ed. Connor Cruise O'Brien), Penguin.

Burnheim, J. (1985), *Is Democracy Possible?*, Polity Press.

Burnheim, J. (1986), 'Democracy, nation states and the world system', in Held and Pollit (eds), *New Forms of Democracy*.

Butler, D. and Ranney, A. (eds) (1980), *Referendums*, American Enterprise Institute.

Calhoun, J. C. (1851), 'A disquisition on government', in Cralle, R. K. (ed.), *The Works of John C. Calhoun*, published under the direction of the General Assembly of the State of South Carolina.

Campbell, A., Converse, P. E., Miller, W. E., and Stokes, D. E. (1960), *The American Voter*, Wiley.

Carver, T. (1992), 'Putting your money where your mouth is: the social construction of individuality in Marx's *Capital*', *Studies in Political Thought*, vol. 1 (winter), pp. 22–41.

Cassirer, E. (1989), *The Question of Jean-Jaques Rousseau*, 2nd edn, Blackwell.

Cawson, A. (1983), 'Functional representation and democratic politics: towards a corporatist democracy?', in Duncan (ed.), *Democratic Theory and Practice*.

Charvet, J. (1981), *A Critique of Freedom and Equality*, Cambridge University Press.

Christophersen, J. A. (1966), *The Meaning of 'Democracy'*, Universitetsforlaget.

Coe, R. D. and Wilber, C. K. (1985), 'Schumpeter revisited: an overview', in Coe and Wilber (eds), *Capitalism and Democracy: Schumpeter Revisited*, University of Notre Dame Press.

Cohen, C. (1971), *Democracy*, University of Georgia Press.

Cohen, C. (ed.) (1972), *Communism, Fascism and Democracy: The Theoretical Foundations*, 2nd edn, Random House.

Connolly, W. E. (1972), 'On "interests" in politics', *Politics and Society*, vol. 2, pp. 459–77.

Connolly, W. E. (1983), *The Terms of Political Discourse*, 2nd edn, Martin Robertson.

Cornford, J. (1972), 'The political theory of scarcity' in Laslett *et al.* (eds), *Philosophy, Politics and Society*.

Crewe, I. *et al.* (1991), *The British Electorate 1963–1987: A Compendium of Data From British Election Studies*, Cambridge University Press.

Crick, B (1982), *In Defence of Politics*, 2nd edn, Penguin.

Cunningham, F. (1987), *Democratic Theory and Socialism*, Cambridge University Press.

Dagger, R. (1982), 'Computers, tables, and citizenship: on the desirability of direct democracy' in Kalleberg *et al.* (eds), *Dissent and Affirmation.*

Dahl, R. A. (1956), *A Preface to Democratic Theory*, University of Chicago Press.

Dahl, R. A. (1961), *Who Governs? Democracy and Power in an American City*, Yale University Press.

Dahl, R. A. (1966), *Political Oppositions in Western Democracies*, Yale University Press.

Dahl, R. A. (1971), *Polyarchy: Participation and Opposition*, Yale University Press.

Dahl, R. A. (1979), 'Procedural democracy', in Laslett and Fishkin (eds), *Philosophy, Politics and Society.*

Dahl, R. A. (1982), *Dilemmas of Pluralist Democracy*, Yale University Press.

Dahl, R. A. (1985), *A Preface to Economic Democracy*, Polity Press.

Dahl, R. A. (1989), *Democracy and Its Critics*, Yale University Press.

Dahl, R. A. (1990), *After the Revolution?*, 2nd edn, Yale University Press.

Dahl, R. A. and Tufte, R. (1973), *Size and Democracy*, Stanford University Press.

Daniels, N. (ed.) (1975), *Reading Rawls: Critical Studies of Rawls' Theory of Justice*, Blackwell.

Darwall, S. (1976), 'A defense of the Kantian interpretation', *Ethics*, vol. 86 (January), pp. 164–70.

Das Gupta, J. (1990), 'India: democratic becoming and combined development', in Diamond *et al.* (eds), *Politics in Developing Countries.*

Daudt, H. (1961), *Floating Voters and the Floating Vote*, H. E. Stenfert Krose, NV.

D'Entèves, A. P. (1967), *Natural Law*, Hutchinson.

Devlin, P. (1965), *The Enforcement of Morals*, Oxford University Press.

Diamond, L. (1988–91), 'Preface' in Diamond *et al.* (eds), *Democracy in Developing Countries*, vol. 2, *Africa.*

Diamond, L. (1988), 'Introduction: roots of failure, seeds of hope' in Diamond *et al.* (eds), *Democracy in Developing Countries*, vol. 2, *Africa.*

Diamond, L. (1992), 'Premoting democracy', *Foreign Policy*, vol. 87 (summer), pp. 25–46.

Diamond, L., Linz, J. J., and Lipset, S. M. (eds), (1988–91), *Democracy in Developing Countries*, 4 vols, Lynne Rienner.

Diamond, L., Linz, J. J., and Lipset, S. M. (eds), (1990), *Politics in Developing Countries: Comparing Experiences with Democracy*, Lynne Rienner.

Di Palma, G. (1991), 'After Leninism: why democracy can work in Eastern Europe', *Journal of Democracy*, vol. 2 (winter), pp. 21–31.

Downs, A. (1957), *An Economic Theory of Democracy*, Harper & Row.

Dryzek, J. S. (1990), *Discursive Democracy*, Cambridge University Press.

Duncan, G. (ed.) (1983), *Democratic Theory and Practice*, Cambridge University Press.

Duncan, G. (ed.) (1989), *Democracy and the Capitalist State*, Cambridge University Press.

Duncan, G. and Lukes, S. (1963), 'The new democracy', *Political Studies*, vol. 11 (June), pp. 156–71, reprinted as 'Democracy restated', in Kariel, (1970).

Dunleavy, P. (1991), *Democracy, Bureaucracy and Public Choice*, Harvester Wheatsheaf.

Dunn, J. (ed.) (1992), *Democracy: The Unfinished Journey, 508 BC to AD 1993*, Oxford University Press.

Duverger, M. (1959), *Political Parties*, 2nd edn, Methuen and Wiley.

Dworkin, R. (1978a), *Taking Rights Seriously*, 2nd edn, Duckworth.

Dworkin, R. (1978b), 'Liberalism', in Hampshire, S. (ed.), *Public and Private Morality*, Cambridge University Press.

The Economist (1992), 'Democracy in Africa', 22 February, pp. 21–3.

Elkin, S. L. (1982), 'Markets and politics in liberal democracy', *Ethics*, vol. 92 (July), pp. 720–32.

Elkin, S. L. (1985), 'Pluralism in its place: state and regime in liberal democracy', in Benjamin and Elkin (eds), *The Democratic State*.

Elster, J. and Hylland, A. (1986), *The Foundations of Social Choice Theory*, Cambridge University Press.

Fatton, R., Jr. (1990), 'Liberal democracy in Africa', *Political Science Quarterly*, vol. 105 (fall), pp. 455–73.

Finley, M. I. (1973), *Democracy Ancient and Modern*, Rutgers University Press.

Finnis, J. M. (1980), *Natural Law and Natural Rights*, Oxford University Press.

Fralin, R. (1978), 'The evolution of Rousseau's view of representative government', *Political Theory*, vol. 6, no. 4 (November), pp. 517–36.

Fralin, R. (1979), *Rousseau and Representation*, Columbia University Press.

Frankel, C. (1962), *The Democratic Prospect*, Harper & Row.

Friedman, M. (1962), *Capitalism and Freedom*, University of Chicago Press.

Frohock, F. M. and Sylvan, D. J. (1983), 'Liberty, economics and evidence', *Political Studies*, vol. 31 (December), pp. 541–55.

Fukuyama, F. (1989), 'The end of history?', *The National Interest*, vol. 16 (summer), pp. 3–18.

Fukuyama, F. (1992), *The End of History and the Last Man*, Hamish Hamilton and The Free Press.

Gallie, W. B. (1955), 'Essentially contested concepts', *Proceedings of the Aristotelian Society*, vol. 56, pp. 167–98.

Garton Ash, T. (1990), *We the People: The Revolution of '89*, Granta Books.

Glass, S. T. (1966), *The Responsible Society*, Longman.

Glenny, M. (1990), *The Rebirth of History: Eastern Europe in the Age of Democracy*, Penguin.

Goldman, M. (1990), 'Tiananmen and Beyond: China's great leap backward', *Journal of Democracy*, vol. 1 (winter), pp. 9–17.

Gooch, G. P. (1954), *English Democratic Ideas in the Seventeenth Century*, Cambridge University Press.

Gould, C. G. (1988), *Rethinking Democracy*, Cambridge University Press.

Graham, K. (ed.) (1982), *Contemporary Political Philosophy: Radical Studies*, Cambridge University Press.

Graham, K. (1986), *The Battle of Democracy*, Harvester Wheatsheaf.

Gray, J. (1983), *Mill on Liberty: A Defence*, Routledge & Kegan Paul.

Gray, J. (1986a), 'Marxian freedom, individual liberty and the end of alienation', in Paul *et al.* (eds), *Marxism and Liberalism*.

Gray, J. (1986b), *Liberalism*, Open University Press.

Green, P. (1985), *Retrieving Democracy*, Methuen.

Grimsley, R. (1983), *Jean-Jacques Rousseau*, Harvester Wheatsheaf.

Gutman, A. (1985), 'Communitarian critics of liberalism', *Philosophy and Public Affairs*, vol. 14, pp. 308–22, reprinted in Avineri and de-Shalit (1992) (eds), *Communitarianism and Individualism*.

Habermas, J. (1976), *Legitimation Crisis*, Heinemann.

Habermas, J. (1989), *The Theory of Communicative Action*, Beacon Press.

Halévy, E. (1954), *The Growth of Philosophical Radicalism*, Faber.

Hall, J. C. (1973), *Rousseau: An Introduction to His Political Philosophy*, Cambridge University Press.

Hallowell, J. H. (1954), *The Moral Foundations of Democracy*, University of Chicago Press.

Hansen, M. H. (1983), 'The Athenian *ecclesia* and the Swiss *Landsgemeinde*', in Hansen, M. H. *The Athenian ecclesia*, Museum Tasculanam Press.

Hansen, M. H. (1991), *The Athenian Democracy in the Age of Demosthenes*, Blackwell.

Hanson, R. L. (1985), *The Democratic Imagination in America: Conversations with Our Past*, Princeton University Press.

Harding, N. (1983), *Lenin's Political Thought*, pbk edn, 1 vol., Macmillan.

Harding, N. (1992), 'The Marxist–Leninist detour', in Dunn (ed), *Democracy*.

Harris, J. (1982), 'The political status of children', in Graham, K. (ed), *Contemporary Political Philosophy*.

Hattersley, R. (1987), *Choose Freedom*, Michael Joseph and Penguin.

Hayek, F. A. (1960), *The Constitution of Liberty*, Routledge & Kegan Paul.

Hayek, F. A. (1976), *The Road to Serfdom*, Routledge & Kegan Paul.

Hayek, F A. (1978), *New Studies in Philosophy, Politics, Economics and the History of Ideas*, Routledge & Kegan Paul.

Hayek, F. A. (1982), *Law, Legislation and Liberty*, vol. 3, Routledge & Kegan Paul.

Heater, D. (1990), *Citizenship: The Civic Ideal in World History, Politics and Education*, Longman.

Heath, A., Jowell, R., Curtice, J., Evans, G., Field, J. and Witherspoon, S. (1991), *Understanding Political Change: The British Voter 1964–1987*, Pergamon.

Heilbroner, R. L. (1986), *The Nature and Logic of Capitalism*, Norton.

Held, D. (1987), *Models of Democracy*, Polity Press.

Held, D. (ed.) (1991a), *Political Theory Today*, Polity Press.

Held, D. (1991b), 'Democracy, the nation-state and the global system', in Held, D. (ed.), *Political Theory Today*.

Held, D. and Pollitt, C. (eds) (1986), *New Forms of Democracy*, Sage.

Himmelweit, H. T., Humphries, P., Jaeger, M. and Katz, M. (1981), *How Voters Decide*, Academic Press.

Hinsley, F. M. (1986), *Sovereignty*, 2nd edn, Cambridge University Press.

Höffe, O. (1984), 'Is Rawls' Theory of Justice really Kantian?', *Ratio*, vol. 26 (December), pp. 103–24.

Hoffman, J. (1988), *State, Power and Democracy*, Harvester Wheatsheaf.

Hofstadter, R. (1967), *The American Political Tradition*, Jonathan Cape.

Holden, B. (1974), *The Nature of Democracy*, Nelson and Barnes & Noble.

Holden, B. (1983), 'Liberal democracy and the social determination of ideas', in Pennock and Chapman (eds), *Liberal Democracy*.

Hornblower, S. (1992), 'Creation and development of democratic institutions in ancient Greece', in Dunn (ed.), *Democracy*.

Howell, C. (1986), *Secular Faith and the Democratic Charter in Jacques Maritain's Political Philosophy*, unpublished Ph. D. thesis, University of Reading.

Humboldt, W. von (1969), *The Limits of State Action*, ed. J. W. Burrow, Cambridge University Press.

Huntington, S. P. (1991), *The Third Wave: Democratization in the Late Twentieth Century*, University of Oklahoma Press.

Jones, P. (1988), 'Intense preferences, strong beliefs and democratic decision-making', *Political Studies*, vol. 36, no. 1 (March), pp. 7–29.

Joseph, R. (1991), 'Africa: the rebirth of political freedom', *Journal of Democracy*, vol. 2 (fall), pp. 11–24.

Joseph, K. and Sumption, J. (1979), *Equality*, John Murray.

Jowittt, K. (1991), 'The new world disorder', *Journal of Democracy*, vol. 2 (winter), pp. 11–20.

Jowitt, K. (1992), *New World Disorder: The Leninist Extinction*, University of California Press.

Kainz, H. P. (1984), *Democracy East and West*, Macmillan.

Kalleberg, A. L., Moon, D. J. and Sabia, D. R. (eds) (1982), *Dissent and Affirmation: Essays in Honor of Mulford Q. Sibley*, Bowling Green State University Press.

Kant, I. (1964), *Groundwork of the Metaphysic of Morals*, trans. H. J. Paton, Harper & Row.

Kariel, H. S. (ed.) (1970), *Frontiers of Democratic Theory*, Random House.

Kase, F. J. (1968), *People's Democracy*, A. W. Sijthoff.

Keane, J. (1984), *Public Life and Later Capitalism*, Cambridge University Press.

Keane, J. (1988), *Democracy and Civil Society*, Verso.

Keane, J. (1991), *The Media and Democracy*, Polity Press.

Keane, J. (1992), 'Democracy and the media – without foundations', *Political Studies*, vol. 40, special issue, *Prospects for Democracy*, pp. 116–29.

Kelso, A. W. (1978), *American Democratic Theory: Pluralism and its Critics*, Greenwood Press.

Kendall, W. (1941), *John Locke and the Doctrine of Majority Rule*, University of Illinois Press.

Kendall, W. and Carey, G. W. (1968), 'The "intensity" problem and democratic theory', *American Political Science Review*, vol. 62, pp. 5–24, reprinted in *Kendall Contra Mundum* (1971), Arlington House.

Key, V. O. (1966), *The Responsible Electorate*, Harvard University Press.

Kimber, R. (1989), 'On democracy', *Scandanavian Political Studies*, vol. 12, pp. 199–219.

Koch, A. (1964), *The Philosophy of Thomas Jefferson*, Quadrangle.

Kolakowski, L. (1978), *Main Currents of Marxism*, vol. 3, Oxford University Press.

Kontos, A. (ed.) (1979), *Powers, Possessions, and Freedom: Essays in Honour of C. B. Macpherson*, University of Toronto Press.

Korpi, W. (1983), *The Democratic Class Struggle*, Routledge & Kegan Paul.

Kymlicka, W. (1989), *Liberalism, Community and Culture*, Oxford University Press.

Kymlicka, W. (1990), *Contemporary Political Philosophy*, Oxford University Press.

Larmore, C. (1990), 'Political liberalism', *Political Theory*, vol. 18 (August), pp. 339–60.

Laslett, P. and Runciman, W. G. (eds) (1962), *Philosophy, Politics and Society*, second series, Blackwell.

Laslett, P., Runciman, W. G. and Skinner, Q. (eds) (1972), *Philosophy, Politics and Society*, fourth series, Blackwell.

Laslett, P. and Fishkin, J. (eds) (1979), *Philosophy, Politics and Society*, fifth series, Blackwell.

Lassman, P. (1992), 'John Rawls, justice and a well-ordered society', in Tivey and Wright (eds), *Political Thought since 1945*.

Lawrence, P. K. (1989), 'The state and legitimation: the work of Jurgen Habermass' in Duncan (ed.), *Democracy and the Capitalist State*.

Lazarsfeld, P. F., Berelson, B. and Gaudet, H. (1968), *The People's Choice*, 3rd edn, Columbia University Press.

Leiserson, A. (1958), *Parties and Politics*, Knopf.

Lemarchand, R. (1992), 'Africa's troubled transitions', *Journal of Democracy*, vol. 3 (October), pp. 98–109.

Lenin, V. I. (1960), 'State and Revolution', in *The Essential Left*, Allen & Unwin. (*State and Revolution* was originally published in 1917.)

Levin, M. (1983), 'Marxism and democratic theory', in Duncan, G. (ed.), *Democratic Theory and Practice*.

Levin, M. (1989), *Marx, Engels and Liberal Democracy*, Macmillan.

Levine, A. (1981), *Liberal Democracy: A Critique of its Theory*, Columbia University Press.

Lijphart, A. (1968), 'Typologies of democratic systems', *Comparative Politics*, vol. 1, pp. 17–35.

Lijphart, A. (1969), 'Consociational democracy', *World Politics*, vol. 21, pp. 207–25, reprinted in McRae, K. (1974), *Consociational Democracy*.

Lindblom, C. E. (1977), *Politics and Markets*, Basic Books.

Lindblom, C. E. (1982), 'The market as prison', *The Journal of Politics*, vol. 14, no. 2 (May), pp. 324–36.

Lindblom, C. E. (1991), *Democracy and Market System*, Oxford University Press.

Lindsay, A. D. (1935), *The Essentials of Democracy*, 2nd edn, Oxford University Press.

Lindsay, A. D. (1943), *The Modern Democratic State*, Oxford University Press.

Linz, J. J. and Stepan, A. (eds) (1978), *The Breakdown of Democratic Regimes*, Johns Hopkins University Press.

Lipset, S. M. (1962), 'Introduction', in Michels, R., *Political Parties: A Sociological Study of the Oligarchical Tendencies of Modern Democracies*, Collier Books.

Lively, J. (1975), *Democracy*, Blackwell.

Lively, J. and Rees, J. (eds) (1978), *Utilitarian Logic and Politics: James Mill's 'Essay on Government', Macaulay's Critique and the Ensuing Debate*, Clarendon Press.

Lizhi, F. (1990), 'Tiananmen and beyond: peering over the great wall', *Journal of Democracy*, vol. 1 (winter), pp. 32–40.

Lucas, J. R. (1976), *Democracy and Participation*, Penguin.

Lukes, S. (1973), *Individualism*, Blackwell.

Lukes, S. (1979), 'The real and ideal worlds of democracy', in Kontos (ed.), *Powers, Possessions, and Freedom*.

Maas, A. (1966), 'Foreword', in Key, *The Responsible Electorate*.

MacCallum, G. C. (1967), 'Negative and positive freedom', *The Philosophical Review*, vol. 76, pp. 312–34, reprinted in Laslett *et al.* (eds) *Philosophy, Politics and Society*, as well as in Miller (ed.), *Liberty*.

McCarney, J. (1992), 'Endgame', *Radical Philosophy*. no. 62 (Autumn), pp. 35–8.

McLean, I. (1982), *Dealing in Votes*, Martin Robertson.

McLean, I. (1986), 'Mechanisms for democracy', in Held and Pollitt (eds), *New Forms of Democracy*.

McLean, I. (1987), *Public Choice*, Blackwell.

McLean, I. (1989), *Democracy and New Technology*, Polity Press.

McLennan, G. (1984), 'Capitalist state or democratic polity? Recent developments in Marxist and pluralist theory', in McLennan, Held and Hall (eds), *The Idea of the Modern State*, Open University Press.

Macpherson, C. B. (1962), *The Political Theory of Possessive Individualism*, Clarendon Press.

Macpherson, C. B. (1966), *The Real World of Democracy*, Clarendon Press.

Macpherson, C. B. (1977a), *The Life and Times of Liberal Democracy*, Oxford University Press.

Macpherson, C. B. (1977b), 'Do we need a theory of the state?', *European Journal of Sociology*, vol. 18, pp. 223–44.

McRae, K. (ed.), (1974), *Consociational Democracy: Political Accommodation in Segmented Societies*, McClelland & Stewart.

Madison, J. (1961), 'Federalist Paper 10', in *The Federalist Papers*, first published 1787–8, Mentor.

Manin, B. (1987), 'On legitimacy and political deliberation', *Political Theory*, vol. 15 (August), pp. 338–68.

Mansbridge, J. J. (1980), *Beyond Adversary Democracy*, Basic Books.

Marcuse, H. (1968), *One-Dimensional Man*, Beacon Press.

Margolis, M. (1979), *Viable Democracy*, Penguin.

Maritain, J. (1945), *Christianity and Democracy*, Geoffrey Bles, The Centenary Press.

Marshall, T. H. (1973), 'Citizenship and social class', in Marshall, T. H. (ed.) (1973), *Class, Citizenship and Social Development*, Greenwood Press.

Marx, K. (1844), 'Contribution to the critique of Hegel's philosophy of Right: introduction', in Bottomore, T. B. (1963), *Karl Marx*.

Marx, K. (1970), *The Civil War in France*, Foreign Languages Press.

May, J. D. (1978), 'Defining democracy: a bid for coherence and consensus', *Political Studies*, vol. 26 (March), pp. 1–14.

Meisel, J. H. (1958), *The Myth of the Ruling Class: Gaetano Mosca and the Elite*, University of Michigan Press.

Meisel, J. H. (ed.) (1965), *Pareto and Mosca*, Prentice Hall.

Mendus, S. (1992), 'Losing the faith: feminism and democracy', in Dunn, J. (ed.), *Democracy*.

Miliband, R. (1969), *The State in Capitalist Society*, Weidenfeld & Nicolson.

Mill, J. (1955), *An Essay on Government*, ed. C. V. Shields, Bobbs-Merrill.

Mill, J. S. (1859), *Dissertations and Discussions*, Longman.

Mill, J. S. (1912), *Considerations on Representative Government, in Three Essays: On Liberty, Representative Government, The Subjection of Women*, Oxford University Press.

Mill, J. S. (1982), *On Liberty*, Penguin.

Miller, D. (1983), 'The competitive model of democracy', in Duncan, G. (ed.), *Democratic Theory and Practice*.

Miller, D. (1989), *Market, State and Community*, Clarendon Press.

Miller, D. (ed.) (1991), *Liberty*, Oxford University Press.

Miller, D. (1992), 'Deliberative democracy and social choice', *Political Studies*, vol. 40, special issue, *Prospects for Democracy*, pp. 54–67.

Miller, J. (1985), *Rousseau: Dreamer of Democracy*, Yale University Press.

Milne, R. S. and Mackenzie, H. C. (1958), *Marginal Seat 1955*, Hansard Society.

Mommsen, W. J. (1974), *The Age of Bureaucracy*, Blackwell.

Mouffe C. (ed.) (1992), *Dimensions of Radical Democracy*, Verso.

Moynihan, D. P. (1975), 'The American experiment', *The Public Interest*, vol. 41 (fall), pp. 4–8.

Mueller, D. C. (1989), 'Democracy: the public choice approach', in Brennan and Lomasky (eds), *Politics and Process*.

Mulhall, S. and Swift, A. (1992), *Liberals and Communitarians*, Blackwell.

Muravchick, J. (1992), 'Eastern Europe's "Terrible Twos"', *Journal of Democracy*, vol. 3 (January), pp. 65–72.

Nathan, A. J. (1990), 'Is China ready for democracy?', *Journal of Democracy*, vol. 1 (spring), pp. 50–61.

Neal, P. (1990), 'Justice as fairness: political or metaphysical?', *Political Theory*, vol. 18 (February), pp. 24–50.

Nehru, B. K. and Morris-Jones, W. H. (1980), *Western Democracy and the Third World*, Third World Foundation.

Nelson, W. N. (1980), *On Justifying Democracy*, Routledge & Kegan Paul.

Nie, N. H., Verba, S. and Petrocik, J. R. (1976), *The Changing American Voter*, Harvard University Press.

Niebuhr, R. and Sigmund, P. E. (1969), *The Democratic Experience: Past and Prospects*, Pall Mall.

Nielsen, K. (1985), *Equality and Liberty*, Rowman & Allenheld.

Norman, R. (1982), 'Does equality destroy liberty?' in Graham (ed.), *Contemporary Political Philosophy*.

Norman, R. (1987), *Free and Equal: A Philosophical Examination of Political Values*, Clarendon Press.

Novak, M. (1991), *The Spirit of Democratic Capitalism*, 2nd edn, Madison Books and IEA Health and Welfare Unit.

Nozick, R. (1974), *Anarchy, State and Utopia*, Blackwell.

Nursey-Bray, P. (1983), 'Consensus and community: the theory of African one-party democracy', in Duncan (ed.), *Democratic Theory and Practice*.

Oakeshott, M. (1975), *On Human Conduct*, Clarendon Press

O'Donnell, G., Schmitter, P. C. and Whitehead, L. (1986), *Transitions form Authoritarian Rule: Prospects for Democracy*, 4 vols. Johns Hopkins University Press.

Oldfield, A. (1990), *Citizenship and Community: Civic Republicanism and the Modern World*, Routledge.

Oppenheim, F. (1981), *Political Concepts: A Reconstruction*, Blackwell.

Oyugi, W. O. (1988), 'Introduction' to Part II of Oyugi *et al.* (eds), *Democratic Theory and Practice in Africa*.

Oyugi, W. O., Atieno Odhiambo, E. S., Gege, M., and Gitonga, A. K. (eds) (1988), *Democratic Theory and Practice in Africa*, Heinemann and James Curry.

Padover, S. K. (ed.) (1946), *Thomas Jefferson on Democracy*, Mentor.

Paine, T. (1969), *Rights of Man*, first published 1791–2, Penguin.

Paine, T. (1976), *Common Sense*, first published 1776, Penguin.

Parekh, B. (1992), 'The cultural particularity of liberal democracy', *Political Studies*, vol. 40, special issue: *Prospects for Democracy*, pp. 160–75.

Parry, G. (1969), *Political Elites*, Allen & Unwin.

Partridge, P. M. (1971), *Consent and Consensus*, Macmillan.

Pateman, C. (1970), *Participation and Democratic Theory*, Cambridge University Press.

Pateman, C. (1985), *The Problem of Political Obligation: A Critique of Liberal Theory*, Polity Press.

Paul, E. F., Paul, J., Miller, F. D. and Ahrens, J. (eds) (1986), *Marxism and Liberalism*, Blackwell.

Paul, J. (ed.) (1982), *Reading Nozick*, Blackwell.

Pennock, J. R. (1979), *Democratic Political Theory*, Princeton University Press.

Pennock, J. R. (1983), 'Introduction', in Pennock and Chapman (eds), *Liberal Democracy*.

Pennock, J. R. and Chapman, J. W. (eds) (1968), *Representation* (Nomos X), Atherton Press.

Pennock, J. R. and Chapman, J. W. (eds) (1983), *Liberal Democracy* (Nomos XXV), New York University Press.

Phillips, A. (1991), *Engendering Democracy*, Polity Press.

Phillips, A. (1992), 'Must feminists give up on liberal democracy?', *Political Studies*, vol. 40, special issue, *Prospects for Democracy*, pp. 68–82.

Pierson, C. (1986), *Marxist Theory and Democratic Politics*, Polity Press.

Pierson, C. (1992), 'Democracy, markets and capital: are there necessary economic limits to democracy?', *Political Studies*, vol. 40, special issue, *Prospects for Democracy*, pp. 83–98.

Pitkin, H. L. (1967), *The Concept of Representation*, University of California Press and Cambridge University Press.

Plamenatz, J. P. (1958), *The English Utilitarians*, 2nd edn, Blackwell.

Plamenatz, J. P. (1973), *Democracy and Illusion*, Longman.

Plant, R. (1991), *Modern Political Thought*, Blackwell.

Plattner, M. F. (1991), 'The democratic moment', *Journal of Democracy*, vol. 2 (fall), pp. 34–46.

Plattner, M. F. (1992), 'Exploring the end of history', *Journal of Democracy*, vol. 3 (April), pp. 118–21.

Pocock, J. G. A. (1975), *The Machiavellian Moment*, Princeton University Press.

Pollitt, C. (1986), 'Democracy and bureaucracy', in Held and Pollitt (eds), *New Forms of Democracy*.

Pomper, G. M. (1975), *Voters Choice*, Dodd, Mead.

Popkin, S. (1991), *The Reasoning Voter*, University of Chicago Press.

Pranger, R. J. (1968), *The Eclipse of Citizenship: Power and Participation in Contemporary Politics*, Holt, Rinehart & Winston.

Presthus, I. R. (1964), *Men at the Top: A Study in Community Power*, Oxford University Press.

Przeworski, A. (1991), *Democracy and the Market*, Cambridge University Press.

Purcell, E. A., Jr. (1973), *The Crisis of Democratic Theory: Scientific Naturalism and the Problem of Value*, University of Kentucky Press.

Rae, D. (1981), *Equalities*, Harvard University Press.

Ranney, A. (1954), *The Doctrine of Responsible Party Government*, University of Illinois Press.

Ranney, A. and Kendall, W. (1956), *Democracy and the American Party System*, Harcourt, Brace & World.

Rawls, J. (1972), *A Theory of Justice*, Oxford University Press.

Rawls, J. (1980), 'Kantian constructivism in moral theory: the Dewey lectures 1980', *The Journal of Philosophy*, vol. 77, pp. 515–72.

Rawls, J. (1985), 'Justice as fairness: political not metaphysical', *Philosophy and Public Affairs*, vol. 14, pp. 223–51.

Rawls, J. (1987), 'The idea of an overlapping consensus', *Oxford Journal of Legal Studies*, vol. 7 (spring), pp. 1–27.

Rawls, J. (1989), 'The domain of the political and overlapping consensus', *New York University Law Review*, vol. 64, pp. 233–55.

Rees, J. (1971), *Equality*, Pall Mall.

Reglar, S. and Young, G. (1983), 'Modern Communist theory: Lenin and Mao Zedong', in Wintrop (ed.), *Liberal Democratic Theory*.

Ricci, D. M. (1971), *Community Power and Democratic Theory*, Random House.

Riker, W. H. (1982), *Liberalism Against Populism*, W. M. Freeman.

Riley, S. (1992), 'Africa's new wind of change', *The World Today*, vol. 48 (July), pp. 116–19.

Rose, R. (1974), *The Problem of Party Government*, Macmillan.

Rose, R. and McAllister, I. (1986), *Voters Begin to Choose*, Sage.

Rosen, F. (1983), *Jeremy Bentham and Representative Democracy*, Clarendon Press.

Rousseau, J-J. (1968), *The Social Contract*, Penguin.

Rowley, C. K. (ed.) (1987), *Democracy and Public Choice*, Blackwell.

Runciman, W. G. (1969), *Social Science and Political Theory*, 2nd edn, Cambridge University Press.

Ryan, A. (1983), 'Mill and Rousseau: utility and rights', in Duncan, G. (ed.), *Democratic Theory and Practice*.

Ryan, A. (1986), review of Heilbroner (1986), *The Nature and Logic of Capitalism*, *Times Literary Supplement*, 16 May.

Ryan, A. (1992), 'After the dinosaurs: filling the political void in Eastern Europe', review of Jowitt (1992), *New World Disorder: The Leninist Extinction*, *The Times Literary Supplement*, August 14.

Sabine, G. M. (1952), 'The two democratic traditions', *Philosophical Review*, vol. 61, pp. 451–74.

Sakwa, R. (1989), 'Commune democracy and Gorbachev's reforms', *Political Studies*, vol. 37 (June), pp. 224–43.

Sandel, M. J. (1982), *Liberalism and the Limits of Justice*, Cambridge University Press.

Sartori, G. (1965), *Democratic Theory*, Praeger.

Sartori, G. (1987), *The Theory of Democracy Revisited*, 2 vols, Chatham House. This is an updating of Sartori (1965).

Schlozman, K. L. (1986), *Organized Interests and American Democracy*, Harper & Row.

Schram, G. N. (1976), 'Reinhold Niebuhr and contemporary political thought: a review article', *Interpretation*, vol. 6 (fall), pp. 65–77.

Schumpeter, J. (1976), *Capitalism, Socialism and Democracy*, Allen & Unwin.

Schwartz, N. L. (1988), *The Blue Guitar: Political Representation and Community*, University of Chicago Press.

Seliger, M. (1968), *The Liberal Politics of John Locke*, Allen & Unwin.

Sharansky, N. (1990), 'The legacy of Andrei Sakharov', *Journal of Democracy*, vol. 1 (spring), pp. 35–40.

Sigmund, P. E. (1971), *Natural Law in Political Thought*, University Press of America.

Simiyu, V. G. (1988), 'The democratic myth in the African traditional societies', in Oyugi *et al.* (eds), *Democratic Theory and Practice in Africa*.

Simpson, J. (1992), *The Darkness Crumbles*, Hutchinson.

Sinclair, R. K. (1988), *Democracy and Participation in Athens*, Cambridge University Press.

Skinner, Q. (1986), 'The paradoxes of political liberty' in McMurrin, S. M. (ed.), *Tanner Lectures on Human Values*, VII, Cambridge University Press and University of Utah Press, reprinted in Miller, D. (ed.) (1991), *Liberty*.

Smart, J. J. C. and Williams, B. (1973), *Utilitarianism: For and Against*, Cambridge University Press.

Spearman, D. (1957), *Democracy in England*, Rockliff.

Spitz, D. (1965), *Patterns of Anti-Democratic Thought*, Free Press.

Spitz, E. (1979), 'Defining democracy: a nonecumenical reply to May', *Political Studies*, vol. 27 (March), pp. 127–8.

Spitz, E. (1984), *Majority Rule*, Chatham House.

Spragens, T. A., Jr. (1973), *The Dilemma of Contemporary Political Theory: Toward a Postbehavioral Science of Politics*, Dunellan.

Spragens, T. A., Jr. (1990), *Reason and Democracy*, Duke University Press.

Stankiewicz, W. J. (ed.) (1969), *In Defence of Sovereignty*, Oxford University Press.

Steintrager, J. (1977), *Bentham*, Cornell University Press.

Svacek, V. (1976), 'The elusive Marxism of C. B. Macpherson', *Canadian Journal of Political Science*, vol. 9 (September), pp. 415–22.

Talmon, J. L. (1952), *The Origins of Totalitarian Democracy*, Secker & Warburg.

Tawney, R. H. (1964), *Equality*, 5th edn, Allen & Unwin.

Ten, C. L. (1980), *Mill on Liberty*, Oxford University Press.

Thakur, T. (1982), 'Liberalism, democracy and development: philosophical dilemmas in Third World politics', *Political Studies*, vol. 30, no. 3 (September), pp. 333–49.

Thomas, D. O. (1959), 'Richard Price and Edmund Burke: the duty to participate in government', *Philosophy*, vol. 30, pp. 308–22.

Thomas, D. O. (ed.) (1992), *Richard Price: Political Writings*, Cambridge University Press.

Thompson, D. F. (1970), *The Democratic Citizen*, Cambridge University Press.

Thompson, D. F. (1976), *John Stuart Mill and Representative Government*, Princeton University Press.

Thorson, T. L. (1962), *The Logic of Democracy*, Holt, Rinehart & Winston.

Tivey, L. and Wright, A. (eds) (1992), *Political Thought since 1945*, Edward Elgar.

Tocqueville, A. de (1968), *Democracy in America*, 2 vols, Fontana.

Tuck, R. (1979), *Natural Rights Theories: Their Origin and Development*, Cambridge University Press.

Tucker, D. F. B. (1980), *Marxism and Individualism*, Blackwell.

Turner, B. S. (1986), *Citizenship and Capitalism: The Debate over Reformism*, Allen & Unwin.

Usher, D. (1981), *The Economic Prerequisite to Democracy*, Blackwell.

Walzer, M. (1990), 'The Communitarian Critique of Liberalism', *Political Theory*, vol. 18 (February), pp. 6–23.

Wanyande, P. (1988), 'Democracy and the one-party state: the African experience', in Oyugi *et al.* (eds), *Democratic Theory and Practice in Africa*.

Ware, A. (1981), *Citizens, Parties and the State*, Polity Press.

Ware, A. (1992), 'Liberal democracy: one form or many?', *Political Studies*, vol. 40, special issue, *Prospects for Democracy*, pp. 130–45.

Whelan, F. G. (1983), 'Prologue: democratic theory and the boundary problem', in Pennock and Chapman (eds), *Liberal Democracy*.

Williams, B. (1962), 'The idea of equality', in Laslett, and Runciman (eds), *Philosophy, Politics and Society*.

Williams, H. L. (1983), *Kant's Political Philosophy*, Blackwell.

Williams, H. and Fearon-Jones, J. (1992), 'Jurgen Habermas and neo-Marxism' in Tivey and Wright (eds), *Political Thought since 1945*.

Wintrop, N. (ed.) (1983), *Liberal Democratic Theory and its Critics*, Croom Helm.

Wolin, S. W. (1960), *Politics and Vision*, Allen & Unwin.

Wolff, R. P. (1970), *In Defense of Anarchism*, Harper & Row.

Wolff, J. (1991), *Robert Nozick: Property, Justice and the Minimal State*, Polity Press.

Wollheim, R. (1958), 'Democracy', *Journal of the History of Ideas*, vol. 19 (April), pp. 225–42.

Wootton, D. (1992), 'The Levellers', in Dunn, (ed.), *Democracy*.

Index